Budget Travel Secrets

S.E. ASIA

Des Gettinby

What Tour Operators Don't Want You to Know

Radge
Publishing

First published 2009 by Radge Publishing

Copyright © Desmond Gettinby 2009

Radge Publishing. PO Box 721 Noosa Heads QLD 4567 Australia

National Library of Australia
Cataloguing-in-Publication data:

Gettinby, James Desmond, 1938-

Budget travel secrets SE Asia : what tour operators don't want you to know / Des Gettinby.

1st edition

ISBN: 9780980637205 (pbk.)

Southeast Asia--Description and travel.
Southeast Asia--Guidebooks.

915.90453

Typeset in Tahoma 9/11/14 pt
Cover Design by Dan Sliwka, Noosa Colour Copy Centre

Table of Contents

There is a tide in the affairs of men,
Which, taken at the flood, leads on to fortune:
Omitted, all the voyage of their life
Is bound in shallows and in miseries

Julius Caesar, IV, iii

SYNOPSIS

This travelogue tells of two people undertaking a low cost four month Asian adventure, of the people they meet and of shared experiences

The story allows the reader to overcome the challenges of budget travel in Asia and to know the ropes before they start travelling.

A daily budget of $50 for two, although self-imposed, proved to be more than achievable and covered all costs for two people. Both the author and his wife took perverse enjoyment in the daily challenge rather than solving matters by throwing money.

Medical concerns and insecurities proved unfounded. Indeed, the trip could well have been government subsidised as both travellers came home leaner, fitter and healthier whilst strengthening an already sound relationship.

Apprehensions about travel bookings and accommodation were easily dispelled and no significant hurdle ever arose. The trip allowed the exploration of Asian culture, its cities, its bargain shopping, its beer and its beaches.

This is the tale of two travellers with some experience of freewheeling travel in Europe, but none of backpacking in Asia.

ABOUT THE AUTHOR

Des Gettinby

Born and schooled in Northern Ireland, the lure of the Antipodes saw Des arrive in Australia in '67, via England, and for the next 25 years base himself in Brisbane where he enjoyed working for a large multinational computer company.

Des and his wife Barb now live at Caloundra on the Sunshine Coast in Queensland. They have three grown up children and six grandchildren.

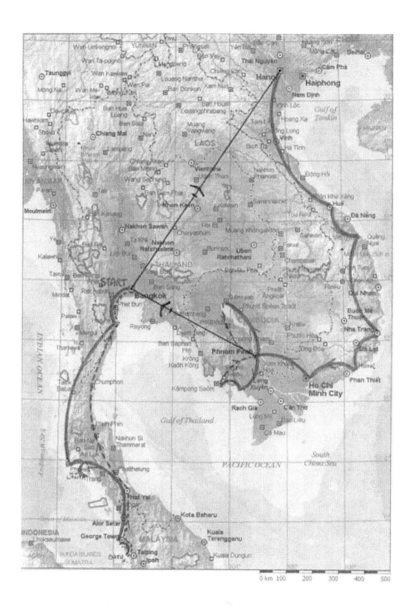

The Gettinby Path.
Map of SE Asia

INTRODUCTION

Firstly be brave and bold.
Secondly savour success.

ASIA - From START to DEPART

A bit like Humpty Dumpty, I wonder if my head is cracked. What, go to Asia and backpack like the kids do? Stay away for months and survive on the smell of an oily rag?

Yes, it's time to do something different. Something new and exciting. It's time for some adventure.

Should a sexagenarian be trying to relive his youth? What about 'the spirit is willing but the flesh is weak'? Clearly a rush of blood to the head.

HAIR BRAINED SCHEME

It was a conversation with a couple of friends over coffee here in Noosa that started me on this harebrained scheme. Both were emphasising how Barb and I had inspired them to go to Asia.

Who, us? Inspire them? 'How?' I asked. 'When?'

Some half dozen years ago Barb and I had freewheeled, each with a heavy backpack, through Turkey and Greece for four months. $67 per day all up, ensuite every night and then home with great suntans. Why wouldn't someone else try the same as us, but this time through Asia?

Come to think of it, why them - why not us too? Suffering from a caffeine hit and with a tendency to be impulsive, on the drive home I decide then and there that Asia is the place for us. An open ended trip, again with backpacks.

'Why shouldn't we do it?' I ask Barb. 'Let's use our time now before you have to pump up the tyres on my wheelchair, or worse still, I have to pump up yours!'

Barb leaps into mental overdrive: 'The house? I'll get house sitters. I'll rent it. I'll abandon it. I'll check the airfares, but you're right, let's go!'

USE IT OR LOSE IT

I shelve my idea of the all-Aussie caravan caper. That's next year's challenge. The kids can use the camper-trailer while we're away. We'll do battle with our backpacks and budget travel now ('while I still can', under my breath). Before I change my mind or before it's too late or I become too set in my ways, staid or sick. Bugger it! We'll go budget backpacking. Shock the kids. Stun the neighbours. We go to bed with the same sense of bravery that Columbus must have felt.

We talk to our friends about our planned trip and they are excited for us, they enthuse with us. They revel in our spontaneity, audacity, courage and pluck. Both of us glow in this reflected support. When we leave they say, 'I always knew they were both mad.'

But our (grown-up) kids are a tower of support and our youngest, Tim, urges 'Mum and Dad, just get off your ass and go'. Not too smart Tim, it's you and Ness who will need to keep an eye on the house whilst we 'get off our ass' and gallivant. Prior to our Turkey trip, our daughter Kelly and husband Don in New Zealand had shown us most of the tricks of backpacking. Our eldest offspring, Kiernan, and his wife Michelle stay well clear of any involvement and apart from dog minding, hide away in Yeppoon.

SECOND THOUGHTS - REALITY BITES

In the cooler light of reason come the first feelings of apprehension, trepidation, perhaps even consternation. Those initial surges of exhilaration, anticipation, titillation and stimulation (along with any other -ation in my lexicon) are somewhat evaporated.

The adventure would be less if we didn't have some concerns and fears. However, I decide not to share my concerns with Barb, she'll think I'm lily livered. I'll wait until she says something first... Fat chance, she's all gung-ho.

So far, so good. Things seem fairly normal. Our friends give valuable encouragement: 'Aren't you afraid of bird flu?' 'Did you read about all the terrorist activity over there?' 'Mad cow disease could get you, even malaria.' However, we know that if we don't go, some migrating chook will land in our garden and we'll be the first in Australia to get bird flu.

PLANNING

Our task is to get some order and direction into our travel plans. With astounding insight I suggest, 'Let's buy the South East Asia guidebook'.

Barb takes the very book out of her shopping bag. 'I ordered it three days ago' says she, with a look that could only be smugness, or self-satisfaction.

Together we peruse the pages. 'This book is absolutely essential' say I.

'We'll need to read it cover to cover.' We are targeting Thailand, Malaysia, Vietnam and Cambodia. The book covers each country in detail, gives maps for each city, and provides lists of accommodation and costs, sights to see and currency details. All we need to know in one book. 'If we have an accident', I instruct Barb, 'save the guidebook first'.

The climate charts clearly indicate that Nov, Dec, Jan and Feb will suit us best. With the speed of a falling share market we decide on return fares Bangkok/Brisbane as being the most economical.

FIRST CHOOSE A GUIDEBOOK

There are several good guidebooks to choose from. You may even buy a couple, but only take one with you as books are heavy to carry. The Lonely Planet 'Southeast Asia on a Shoestring' is probably the most popular book but it comes down to an individual choice. Browse.

Travel pamphlets are good to study. These will give an idea of the most popular destinations and side trips, and suggest start and finish points for these trips. Of course, these tours are often much more expensive if booked before leaving Australia.

Phone your favourite travel agent and enquire about their cheapest airfares, then peruse the internet to see if you can do better there. We found that it was just as cheap and much more convenient to book our return airfare through our agent.

TRAVEL TRAP

We make a nearly disastrous mistake at the time of booking our tickets and certainly learn a good lesson. We now know to only book flights in EXACTLY the same names as are in our passports, in our case, using only the first Christian name and the surname.

I have two Christian names, James Desmond, and it is the second by which I am always known. In a moment of excitement, Barb tells the travel agent that her name is Barbara Gettinby and that her husband's name is James Desmond, with the result that an e-ticket which doesn't show Gettinby as my surname is issued. Luckily, we spot the discrepancy and pay a hefty fee to have the ticket re-issued in the correct format.

And that's not all! The re-issued ticket alters my original seat allocation so this problem also has to be addressed. Barb could find herself sitting beside someone like George Clooney.

BOOKING TICKETS
Make sure that the name on your ticket matches EXACTLY the name on your passport.

PEACE OF MIND

With the tickets finally fixed up for Nov 2, we address the myriad of 'to dos' on our list.

We've allowed three months before we fly out to tick all the boxes and get everything in order. There are two areas; preparing for everything relating to travel, and preparing for everything at home in our absence.

I find I need to slay a few dragons even before I get there. I need to ask myself some questions. Niggling thoughts interrupt my normal placid slumbers. Toilets, money, transport, lodgings, toilets again, language!

Do I have a subconscious fear of the trots? A few tablets here (script from our doctor) and a few corks there put my mind at ease.

Hurdles? 'Hurdles are only there to be jumped' I say. We seek comfort from a globe trotting girl, the daughter of friends, who gives very precise advice and directions to Barb and me. 'Just get to Bangkok and follow your whim' says she. As it happens, this is just how the plan unfolds.

First, I ask her about toilets. 'I had pedestal toilets everywhere I stayed and I only saw the flat "starting block" toilets at comfort stops when I was travelling by bus.'

Money? 'No worries, US dollars are used almost everywhere. Local currency from ATM's is easy to access, and don't worry, everyone speaks some English.'

What about buses and transport? 'Trains, planes, buses and minivans will take you everywhere and are easily booked'.

'And what about a place to sleep?' I ask the expert.

Globe trotting girl replies, 'My best friend and I had a twin room with ensuite every night, at under $15 a night'.

Feeling immensely relieved and suitably comforted I now renew my former sleeping habits without the night jitters. Amazing how we are now of an age to accept advice from the young.

This 'young one' of course doesn't have to deal with a tin hip and heart flutters, never mind Barb's asthmatic tendencies. Nevertheless, we box on.

MONEY MANAGEMENT

How will we manage our money?

Our earlier estimates of day-to-day costs might just as well have been measured by a bit of string. Clearly we want to minimise spending but have little idea of how much we will need. Research indicates that backpackers manage on $20 to $25 a day. With the speed of a bookie's clerk I calculate an arbitrary budget of $50 a day for both of us; we take $50 as our personal daily challenge. Can we average $50 a day and still have our own room with ensuite and visit all the sights? Yes we can! In fact we actually spent only $40 a day for two not including Brisbane/Bangkok/Brisbane airfares.

The question of finances being loosely settled, I address myself like a good quartermaster to attending the trivia of travel. I'm sure Odysseus had a similar task in his day.

OO SHOULD - VEE DO!

When searching about for tips and advice, I'm reminded of some friends in Mission Beach. These friends have a German couple as neighbours who are always offering kindly advice. 'This is what you should do, we do.'

This has now become a catch-cry between Barb and me. 'Oo should - Vee do', with our best German accents. Of course, some would say that those with the best advice usually offer no advice.

Both of us believe ourselves to have been lucky in building our whole journey on a strong platform of positive attitude. On reflection 'attitude' was the glue that stuck everything together. And the good news is that attitude doesn't cost money!

THE TRIVIA OF TRAVEL

Attitude We decide to consider our trip as an adventure, like an extended picnic, and dress to suit a fun outing not a fashion parade. We will travel light, buy as needed, send surplus home and embrace the new experiences.

Footwear One pair of plain leather sandals that we buy for comfort in preference to style, and of course we walk them in before leaving. One pair will be sufficient to take us to any occasion when overseas, and should we wear them out we'll buy more. It'll be too hot for walking boots and we won't need them, or extra shoes.

Luggage The most versatile backpack is the style that comes with strong handles, wheels and shoulder straps. We have a choice between the smallest (around $30 to $40) or one size up ($45 to $60) as either of these will force a weight limit between 7 to 9 kg - we are aiming for 7kg. Both these sized packs are allowable as cabin baggage on international flights. We look for hide-away shoulder straps, widely spaced extendable wheeling handle and, if available, a protection flap to cover the wheels when we are wearing the packs on our backs.

> **AIRLINE CABIN BAGGAGE GUIDELINES**
> Although airlines differ in allowable cabin baggage dimensions the most common rule-of-thumb is: Add the height, the length and the width and aim for 115cm as the total measurement.
>
> For example: 20cm wide, 35cm tall, 60cm long = 115cm
> Approximate maximum weight - 7kg
>
> Current security restrictions severely limit the carrying of bottles and tubes, even bottled water. It is suggested to limit the sizes to 100 ml each.

Clothes Three or four easily washable shirts, two pairs of lightweight shorts and one pair of lightweight slacks.

Four pairs of knickers, swimwear, and a sun hat. Warm clothes can be bought if needed and then sent home. Our choice of shirts is Bisley seersucker. Men's shirts may need a few darts to suit women, but the double pockets are invaluable. Lightweight rain poncho.

Comfort Earplugs, eye mask, small pillow or inflatable one (we only discover this need later). Sewing kit, flat circular sink plugs cut from an inner tube (for when basin plug is missing - essential for washing clothes). Tube of mozzie repellent, some clip-lock bags and a light top sheet (Asia has a great variety of silk sleeping-bag liners) - a sarong will do.

Medical Small bottle of tea tree oil, headache tablets, band aids, sun block, tiny bottle of Dettol, tablets for vomiting and diarrhoea, laxatives, normal prescriptions and a 'moist' tissue pack. Antiseptic gel for cleaning hands when water is not available.

Daypack For security reasons some travellers discard a daypack and choose instead a shoulder bag, to be carried at the front, within hands' reach and big enough for a water bottle. A next-to-skin security belt for money, passport and extra credit cards.

Wash kit We reduce this to a minimum size. Smallest toothpaste tube, one razor, mini-sized deodorant, smallest size shampoo, conditioner and skin care. (All 'mini-sized' toiletries are readily available throughout Asia and can be bought on the go.)

Extras One book each (plus essential guide book), pack of cards each, spare glasses, sunnies, analogue alarm with inbuilt dial light, compact diary, credit-card sized calculator and two small combination locks. (Some guest houses have metal lockers, and the keyed type of lock is too easy to break into.)

So it remains to slay the next dragon, the paper dragon. St George would have been handy, but I've got Barb. She undertakes the task of putting everything in order on the home front.

A comprehensive list of items is compiled, action is taken, problems solved and loose ends tied up (see chapters 30 and 31).

> **WARNING**
> It is too tempting to say 'I'll take this just in case' or 'it's no load to carry'.
> Any forgotten or essential items are inexpensive and easy to buy 'on the run'.
> Leave jewels and gold at home.

LEAP OF FAITH

It is now Nov 2 and our ducks are all in a row. We feel like Bungy jumpers just before they leap. Excited, exhilarated but a bit uncertain.

UP AND RUNNING

From Noosa, our temporary car minder kindly whisks us off to the Nambour railway station for the first leg on our adventure. Farewell hugs and kisses and I watch my four wheel drive disappear down the street. I have visions of the cross-country mountain-climbing and off-road beach frolicking it could be subjected to over the next four months - a fool and his 4 x 4 are easily parted.

We collect our tickets and board the rattler taking us to Brisbane. Our compact backpacks behave themselves and tuck neatly under our legs in the near-empty carriage. Empty, except for another backpack wielding youth. The backpack (black), the size of a water cooler, is forced into the seat beside him. He wrestles free from his front-mounted day pack (also black), careful not to damage the obligatory guitar (black cover). These are difficult maneuvers for our fellow traveller as his two-metre long surf board keeps tripping him up or slipping off the seat.

We smirk. We nudge each other. We smugly pat our well-behaved packs. We contentedly view the passing countryside and listen to the click clack of the railway tracks.

We had originally planned to catch the connecting sky rail from central Brisbane out to the airport. Instead, our friends Jen and Neil meet us and take us to their place for the night and out to the airport next day, and so on to Sydney with a flight into Bangkok. This leg of travel holds no concerns for us.

Our midnight arrival in Bangkok is slightly more daunting. Our security blanket is to be the $70 a night pre-booked 4-star hotel in Chinatown, designed to allow us a few days' acclimatisation, a lull before the storm. Pre-planning had organised the taxi from the airport to our hotel. From then on, it would be seat-of-the-pants stuff.

CHAPTER ONE

I hear and I forget.
I see and I remember.
I do and I understand.

BANGKOK

Excitement city, here we come! We slip easily through baggage collection, customs and immigration. At midnight, we confront our introduction to Thailand.

The arrival gate is wonderfully thronged with a hive of local taxi drivers, mini-van drivers and hotel personnel. Placards wave on high, emblazoned with the names of emerging and expected passengers. We scan enthusiastically for our name, we scan again, not there. Our blank, now anxious faces evoke some sympathy and a Thai man asks, 'What hotel you going to?'

'China Plincess, China Plincess,' he cries loudly and a young man swiftly appears bowing, scraping and apologising. This is repeated - bowing, scraping and apologising, he wrestles the luggage from us and bows and scrapes us to our hotel taxi.

Humid and hot, the taxi air-conditioning is welcome as we are whisked away down the wide roads to a blaze of

1

lights spreading across the horizon - Bangkok. Like the proverbial kids in the lolly shop or clowns in sideshow alley, we swivel our heads right and left with eyes wide and mouths gaping. My remembered impressions of Asia are first and foremost of a busy, bustling continent full of conical straw hats, of peddlers and pedalling, and of noodles and rice and temples of red and gold. Memories of sounds and smiling welcomes.

Through the cab window, sparkling masses of lights and neon colours flank our passage through late-night Chinatown, still bustling with locals and even their children - a glittering fantasyland and a great welcoming sight on our way to the hotel.

'Good eveling, good eveling. Welcome to the Gland China Plincess. You vely welcome.' Registration completes smoothly, although we surrender our passports with reluctance. We don't need to entrust our American dollars and our emergency credit cards to their hotel safe, we have one of our own in the room.

Trundling our obedient backpacks, we head to the elevator. We stumble into our room, swiftly shower and crash into our wonderfully inviting twin beds. Chocolate mints untouched. Hello Bangkok. Goodnight Bangkok.

FAMILIARISATION

A new day

I've never been very sure what the expression 'a stunned mullet' looks like in real life. I now find out. Here we are in our brave new world of Bangkok. I look in the hotel mirror and there it is - the stunned mullet: 'Where do we go and what do we do now? What are all our glamorous plans? What did the pre-trip internet research tell us? What have we marked off in our guidebook?'

The first challenge is to find our way around the flash hotel. My tummy is rumbling and breakfast beckons. In the elevator, in large print and with a coloured photo of an Asian meal, we are directed to the 10th floor. We'll eat and discuss strategy.

Where do we go? How do we get there? What about local money? Where is the ATM, and what sights are top of our list?

It's then we realise that our guidebook is truly 'lonely' and lying on its own on our bedroom table. We can't get very far without it. A quick trip to the room between muesli and Thai omelette rescues the book and a large coloured map of Bangkok (kindly given to us at the reception desk).

During the scurrying back and forth to the breakfast buffet and the tasting of the extensive range of east-meets-west cuisine, we formulate our plans for the next three days. We consult maps, scan the write-ups on significant tourist sights, and establish priorities. I go back, have another slice of bacon and another hash brown. God, it's great to be eating the local food!

Alive and excited, we feel as if we're about to open a Christmas stocking.

Barb and I have, somewhat reluctantly, been shoehorned into a meeting with a long-time Bangkok resident. Today we will meet up with Bill. By phone, we arrange to meet, of all places, in an uptown shopping centre supermarket. (I'll wear the white sports coat and he'll wear the pink carnation.) Bill turns out to be a fantastic help.

Bill's business interests see him travelling widely through South East Asia and he has a wealth of knowledge, which he shares willingly. Bill proves to be a very valuable link in our transition into the Asian lifestyle. Bangkok Bill's first-hand information is passed on here and there throughout this book.

THAILAND AND BANGKOK

King Rama 1 built Bangkok in 1782 and it is now a city of six million people. Thailand was known as Siam until 1939.

Average annual temperature is 29c. Best time to go is November to March.

Electricity is 220 volts using a standard two-pin plug.

Bangkok's International Airport (Suvarnabhumi pronounced **'su-wan-na-poom'**) is thirty kilometres east of the city and opened in September, 2006. A current guidebook will tell you the best options to get to your accommodation.

There are plenty of ATMs at the airport and these will dispense local currency if you have a pin number on your credit card.

You must have an onward ticket before you enter Thailand. Thirty day visas are issued at no charge on arrival. Extensions are available or just cross a border and reenter Thailand to get another thirty day visa.

Most popular areas for budget travellers to stay in Bangkok are either Siam Square (close to the Sky Rail) or the even less expensive Banglamphu (Khao San Road), which is further out of the city centre.

Best way to get around is by the Sky Rail or river ferry. Plenty of information is available at the guest houses or nearby tourist offices.

English is widely spoken so you will have no trouble making yourself understood.

Ninety-three percent of Thais are Buddhists.

ONE SMALL STEP FOR MAN ...

With a similar sense of awe, we springboard ourselves into the Bangkok streetscape. The hotel map leads us down to the river and, like sheep, we follow the crowd to the river express ferry. With great agility, we hopscotch our way over the duckboards and scramble onto a wooden seat. The conductor mechanically clicks out the ticket when we mumble 'Saphan Taskin' and clinks change into my hand. When I ask 'Sky Train?' she casually nods and proceeds to process the next victim. Obviously we have picked the right pier to get us to the train.

The Sky Train station is right there at the pier. Even the three blind mice could have found it. So, up the stairs to what appears to be the ticket booth - not so. We're given change here and directed to a London Tube style map. Unravelling the secret code, we put designated money in the slot and get return tickets to our target; at the turnstile, we swipe and re-collect our tickets and off we go. (It takes us two days and a few trips to work out that it is much cheaper to buy the all-day go-anywhere, jump-off-and-on-again ticket.)

HINT
Most cities produce a colourful fold-out map of the city. Major roads and streets are shown along with all styles of public transport and everything is written in English. The map is usually available at the hotel reception. If not, call into any large hotel and ask for one there.

Finding our way, like Maxwell Smart to a clandestine meeting place, we both skip along feeling clever about deciphering the Sky Train code. I had told Barb that I could easily find the way. (Funny though, it was she who made all the clever decisions.)

Inside the supermarket and pushing my empty trolley with agent 99 beside me, both of us spot Bangkok Bill. He takes us to the shopping centre top floor Food Hall. We purchase tokens for our meals at a central kiosk and are instructed to redeem any unspent coupons as we leave.

Standing in front of the many food counters, I feel like the king in 'The King and I' - it's a 'puzzlement'. So much to choose from and so little knowledge of Thai script – where did my schoolteachers go wrong? I point to the tempting picture of a bowl of noodles and agree to whatever it is they want to put on top.

'Prick! Prick!' the wok chef shouts at me.

I am taken aback at being called a 'prick', only to find that he is asking if I want chilli. I have quickly learned my first Thai word, 'prig', and smartly decide to use sign language to indicate very little use of 'prig'.

Yum, I get lucky - this meal is terrific. So what if I thought he'd called me a prick!

In the evening, we trip down the hotel steps next to a major intersection. The sheer mass of traffic confronts us and we wait to dash across when the traffic stops. We look up at the lights. Side-by-side with the universal and standard issue red, amber and green traffic light is the Asian version. A Cape Canaveral countdown clock. This sizeable black clock, mounted beside the lights, counts down the seconds since the red stoplight. Large, bright green numbered digits count down from ninety seconds. I can only imagine New York traffic backed up behind the line waiting for the 3, 2, 1, GO! Paramedics and recovery vehicles get ready. Hoping that these are close, we dash across.

In the safety of the side streets we enjoy our 'progressive dinner', moving from one barbeque or wok stall to another, eating portions of this and that. Pork, prawn, beef, chicken or vegetarian. It's all here.

RIVER EXPRESS

Ferries travel from pier to pier and passengers jump on and off quickly. A conductor blows a whistle indicating when to board and when to alight and caution needs to be exercised on the sometimes slippery quay. Fares are collected after boarding.

ZEBRA CROSSINGS

Strangers to a Thai city could be put at ease by the sight of strategically placed zebra crossings. Moses could not have done better at providing safe passage, and we westerners are immediately comforted at the sight of this secure path through the traffic chaos to the other side.

Don't be fooled! This black and white broad striped pattern is something Mr Plod used in a Noddy book and someone in the ministry of traffic here thought it looked pretty.

Don't risk adding to the stunning statistic of five road deaths an hour in Thailand.

Zebra crossings are perhaps only used when the circus comes to town.

SHOPPING FLING

We've already familiarised ourselves with the vagaries and variety of Bangkok transport, so we feel comfortable about heading out to the sights on our shortlist. 'Sights' is hardly the right word because our first objective includes researching some retail stores and working through the list of 'must buy' items. Any sightseeing curiosity has been sacrificed on the altar of bargain shopping.

Trawling around multiple markets, I have a clear idea of the watch I need. Expertly I choose an analogue waterproof timepiece - simple and stylishly elegant with a brand name that I'm sure said 'Rolex'. I bargain with the stall owner, I get a twenty-five percent reduction, I pay the huge sum of $15 and I proudly sport my silver selection on my wrist.

For the best part of a day, we shop till we drop. We buy this and buy that. A shirt, a hat. We are very conscious that if we buy it we have to carry it - or find a post office and send it home. We get suckered into paying $4 for about thirty seconds on the internet in a huge shopping centre. We enjoy the local noodle dishes.

When you're having fun, time seems to stand still and I must have had lots of fun that day. The hands on the hazed, fogged up and misted dial of my chosen chronometer lie still and silent. I have just paid $1.36 per hour of elapsed time.

Bangkok has a reputation for providing some very skilled medical and associated services. Popular package deals can provide accommodation and convalescence facilities to access the many surgical, cosmetic or dental services. This doesn't quite fit into our itinerary as adventure tourists. However, although we stick to the backpackers' style of travel, I have brought with me a prescription for spectacles. My Sherlock-style sleuthing proves that I can reduce by approximately sixty percent the cost of new glasses. Cool, modern state-of-the-art indestructible glasses, not like my watch. I'll leave the spectacles until I'm about to fly home.

FLOATING MARKETS

A new day, new horizons, an early breakfast and our first flourish of shopping behind us, we go, breaking in our new trendy sunhats, to visit our sites of interest, our list drawn from the pages of the guidebook.

An early morning visit to the floating markets is easily arranged on the riverside piers. We shop around for the best deal and flashest boat and quickly agree on a trip on the unique long-tail boat.

FLOATING MARKETS
These have become totally touristy but are still great fun. Lots of shouting and yelling from the vendors in boats piled high with all sorts of local produce.

The canal banks are lined with souvenir stalls and boats will come alongside selling bowls of steaming noodles.

You can find your own way to the markets by bus or take a longtail boat ride. Tours are also available of course, but where's the fun in that?

The markets open at 6.30am, and you will need to go early.

Alternatively, you can stay in Damnoen Saduak the night before if you like - check it out in your guidebook and make a reservation at one of the hotels or guesthouses.

The wide river is flanked by topsy-turvy wooden houses, children washing in the river and even courageously cleaning their teeth in the umber brown waters. Ramshackle dwellings line the banks, threatening to collapse and add timber, poles, sticks and tin to the flowing water. The floating markets themselves bustle with the narrow boats and a range of colourful and gaudy trinkets and merchandise. Souvenir stalls line the canals. Farm produce is sold from a few boats and the popular fruit vendors paddle and peddle their wares. Tourists swarm everywhere, capturing the wonders of the waterways with their trusty cameras. Unique, different and hurly-burly of tourist traffic. Scoffing juicy pineapple, we look back at the propeller on the extended steel shaft speeding us back home on this fabulous long-tailed boat. Smoggy petrol fumes waft along.

CITY SCENTS

Here in Bangkok we may well have paid a few Baht entrance fee and donated money at our sights of interest, but the smells come free!

Olfactory awareness is heightened in all aspects of local life. We enjoy pleasant aromas from the myriad food stalls along the streets at night-time. Frying chicken, bowls of steaming noodles, charcoal grilled satay sticks, chestnuts and corncobs. Pungent throat-catching chilli fumes as they hit the hot wok and the tempting smells from rich Indian curries - all of these assault the senses. As do the sweet, cloying and heady aromas of joss sticks diligently placed in front of dwellings, shops, temples or inside at the household shrines. All the aromas of the East.

Now, I will put to one side the gentle non-threatening word 'aroma' and in its place I will introduce 'odour'. Bugger it; let's call a spade a spade - 'smell'. Smells kinda sneak up from behind, I mean behind, not my behind. From time to time the ripest of smells envelop me. I try holding my breath, but as in Ghostbusters, there is no boundary to this miasma. I hope I get through before my breath runs out.

LONG TAIL BOATS
Narrow waisted, slender and elegant, yet with fume-belching car motors in the stern. The propellers are fixed at the end of a long steering pole.

The long-tail boats act as ferries and water taxis on Bankok's Chao Phraya River and on the Khlongs (canals) and nearby coastline.

TEMPLES

In the UK I have always been fascinated with ancient castles and cathedrals. I have spent hours gawking at gothic windows and cathedral spires. Now I can see from our hotel window the Asian equivalent. I stroll off on my own to investigate what's under these shiny tiled roofs.

I wend my way through streets, keeping map in hand and business card of The Grand China Princess in my wallet. Who knows if I may need a cab to get me home? I'm rewarded by finding the temples richly coloured, courtyards and walls allowed to age gracefully, the signs of time evident. Buddha is here, serene as ever, with enigmatic smile and bathed in the eddy of joss-stick smoke. I wander around soaking up the spiritual atmosphere.

I get safely back home, not even needing to follow the breadcrumbs. Barb and I plan the 'big temple' trip. Barb flashes the pictures of her chosen objectives, we finish our noodles, and off we go.

Striding through the streets, we confidently jump on the ferry and head upstream for four piers. A short walk takes us to our target. The gleaming orange and green roof sparkles in the sunshine.

With wide-eyed wonderment, we enter Wat Phra Kaew (Temple of the Emerald Buddha), next to the Grand Palace. The temple is a centre of normal everyday worship with people milling around, albeit with quiet and demure respect. Worshippers are oblivious to the brash camera-clicking tourist. Joss sticks are presented as prayer offerings. Locals are quietly immersed in their own thoughts. Saffron-robed priests move serenely and with unaffected grace through the people.

Barb and I drop some coins into an alms bowl and remark on the complications caused by most of the world's religions. We agree that this place sends signals of peace and of contentment. Arm in arm, we stroll off to our next destination.

At temple number two, nearby Wat Pho, we stand astounded - nay, gobsmacked - at the sleeping Buddha. Half a football field long and as high as a house, and all covered in gold leaf.

My 'Good God!' brings Barb's retort: 'You got that one right. This is what must have happened to the Colossus of Rhodes, they've pinched it and painted it gold.'

Tourists walk slowly, in awe of the majesty of the temples. Colour is used throughout the Wats with unrestricted vitality like a famous TV sports commentary, Gold! Gold! Gold! If you want Buddha's attention, you'll be sure to get it here.

Colour, brightness, murmured mantras, wisps of incense and the tinkle of coins into the offering boxes. Barb mutters, 'Des, your Mum's church in Belfast never had anything like this!' The redolence of musk joss sticks lingers. Holy smoke!

> **RECLINING BUDDHA AT WAT PHO**
> The temple covers 20 acres and the reclining Buddha is housed in one of the oldest temples. The gold-plated sleeping Buddha is so huge that you cannot see it in its entirety, but if you go to the feet you can take in most of it.
>
> There is a massage school here at the temple, so why not relieve some stress and spend $4 or $5 for a bit of luxury. Allow plenty of time to wander around - you'll need it.

CHINATOWN

During dinner we consult our almanac, our guidebook that we've come to look upon as 'The Way, the Truth and the Light'. 'Chinatown' jumps out at us from the map. We switch to our large 'free map' and twenty minutes later, we're revelling in the sights and sounds of Chinatown at night.

A ground-level fireworks show, neon-flashing signs amongst a fairy-lights fantasy world. Trinkets, toys and treasures pack storefronts up to the roof. Wallets to wheelbarrows, perfume to pearls. This is where the rainbow ends, with more gold than Midas ever saw, all in shining red shops.

Barb indulges me at the kerbside food stalls and we eat segments of peeled pomelo citrus dipped in sugar, salt and chilli. We sample food here and there from the night stalls along the streets. Chicken, roasted chestnuts, corn cobs - a pay-as-you-go smorgasbord.

After we've explored the nightlife, our only non-food purchase a wallet for Barb, we retreat to our hotel.

We've discovered a cute low-cost café at the back of our hotel's mezzanine floor. It's here we run the gambit of all of their noodle dishes.

Noodles are an integral, essential part of local life. Everywhere we go, noodles are cooked. Fat ones, thin ones, long or short. Eaten at breakfast, lunch and dinner. We have no trouble accommodating all the local styles and variations freshly emerging from boiling stock or tossed in a sizzling wok - eaten anywhere, anytime. We don't have to strive with chopsticks alone, everyone gets a spoon too.

ROYALTY

Bangkok gives Barb and me a gradual indoctrination into the Thai psyche.

One sees and hears of the sometimes questionable position of European monarchy. To a person, the Danes enthusiastically acclaim the fact that an heir to the throne is ensured. Britain wraps itself in the flag, yet surrounds itself in the ongoing controversy of whether or not the royal family should be allowed to go to pot. Whatever the argument, the Brits seem to rejoice in singing 'God save the Queen' at every sporting event even when they may have Buckley's chance of beating the Aussies.

The Thais, however, demonstrate their fealty with unconcealed testimonials of their affection. Framed photographs of the King and Queen appear on many exterior walls on a variety of buildings and businesses. I gawk out of the window of the Sky Train at the huge regal tributes. Large portraits painted on gable walls and buildings. Princely photographs can be seen in the back of dimly lit shops. Huge billboards depict the full regality of either the King or Queen or both standing decorously side-by-side.

THAI ROYALTY

King Rama IX is worshipped in Thailand and in most Thai homes there are pictures of the King or Queen - sometimes also pictures of Rama V, another much loved King.

Few visitors from the west can comprehend the relationship between the Thai people and their beloved King.

It would be extremely bad form for foreigners not to show respect for royal images, the national anthem and the Thai flag - as Thais do. Remember that the King's image is on the local currency, and the coinage and notes must be treated with suitable respect.

Every day at 8 am and 6 pm the anthem of Thailand is played and everybody stands to show respect. One of the notices regarding this custom says 'Of course, persons in traffic jams are excepted from this rule.'

Folds and swathes of yellow cloth (the colour of Monday, the King's birth day) drape over major monuments. Thai flags fly from every available pole. Boulevards flanked by hedges and walls are festooned with bolts of yellow bunting. My guess is that somewhere a yellow dye manufacturer sits back, counts his sheckles and toasts royalty with a glass or two of rice wine.

We are only half prepared to be assaulted by everything Asian - or rather everything not Western. Both Barb and I have, over the years, tripped off through Hong Kong, Singapore and Bangkok a number of times - but this time we are up close and personal, with our 'grass-roots' go-it-alone travelling.

Light reflecting from golden domes, shining Buddhas and glittering temples - all interspersed amongst the gloomy grey of mouldy walls and ramshackle houses. Frenetic traffic clogging the roads. We ferry-travel on the wide river, which is flowing fast and whisking yesterday's plastic bags out to sea, tangled with dislodged water-lily plants.

My mate and I watch the elegant long-tailed boats conducting their day-to-day business and see them taking fellow tourists on today's trip to the floating markets.

We reminisce on our trip to the Chatuchak Markets. Wow! The sheer size and scope of Bangkok's Chatuchak markets is stunning. Multiple, multiple market stalls, millions of knick-knacks and thousands of people. (Our guidebook reckons 15,000 stalls and 200,000 people every day.) You name it and you can buy it. Push, shove and shoulder your way through.

We squeezed through the jam-packed walkways and passed fifty stalls all selling jeans. We squished past 40 stalls selling shirts and slip past sixty stalls selling sandals.

Think Woolworths, Sears Roebuck and Marks and Spencers and then do mega-multiplication. Colour, sound and action. Lines of stalls all selling similar stuff - multiple choice. Thousands of stalls of baseball caps, watches, DVD's, pots, pans, pork, pets or perfume.

So: we have experienced Bangkok's big glossy superstores, revisited most of the knick-knack and bric-a-brac stalls of night-time Chinatown, survived the floating markets and nibbled on most of the titbits from the street food vendors. We are now masters of the city transport systems. Somewhat acclimatised, it's time to find fresh fields.

Where will we go? Toss the coin! Roll the dice!

Let's steady the ship. Let's make a well-informed decision based on info from Bangkok Bill. After all, he's the local.

Hua Hin, here we come.

CHATUCHAK MARKETS (Weekends only)

Chatuchak (Jatujak) is thought to be the largest market in the world. It covers over thirty acres with 1,500 shops and stalls selling every conceivable item and caters to around 200,000 people a day.

Go as early as possible to avoid the heat of the day and the biggest crowds. Take a water bottle and avoid the market if it is raining.

The market is laid out in a semi-circle and people get lost. Agree a set time and meeting place before entering the market with friends.

Bargaining is the order of the day so try for thirty percent lower than the first price.

If you miss out at the weekend, try the more overpriced Patpong night markets.

CHAPTER TWO

The worn path is the one most followed.
'Tis the rocky one that leads to riches.

BYE BYE, BANGKOK - HELLO, HUA HIN

Our Bangkok time behind us, we collect our bits and pieces, check drawers and bathrooms, scoop up the hotel's free giveaways and get ready to check out. I regain my composure after paying $12 for the two 30-second local phone calls, and we are on our way. Barb's voice echoes through the lobby, 'Hey Des, would it be a good idea to ask for our passports?' Good one!

We've enjoyed our first days on the road, no dramas and no knock-down-drag-outs. We make a good team.

This is the real start of our adventure. Today we leave Bangkok behind for surf and sunbathing at Hua Hin. Happily we wheel and shoulder our packs down to the ferry, get off at the Taskin pier and from there on to the Sky Train. Our destination is Victory Monument where, the day before on our way to Chatuchak Markets, we had checked out the minivan scene for our trip to Hua Hin.

MINIVAN TO HUA HIN

Nestling one street behind the busy terminus for the 'big buses' is the minivan departure area. It's easy to find. Down the flights of stairs from the Sky Train, past the big grown-up buses, squeeze between a few food stalls and into our targeted street.

VICTORY MONUMENT
Victory Monument is a major traffic hub and a well-known landmark, with its tall obelisk making it easily visible. It was built in 1941 to commemorate a Thai victory over French colonialism.

Bus lines employ the traffic centre as a major stop-off point and small private minivans use the nearby street as a terminus.

The expressway exit is nearby, as is the Sky Train station, a large department store and a hospital.

We've decided on Hua Hin as our first go-it-alone backpacking stopover. Bangkok Bill told us that he uses it as his beach hideaway area. It's only a couple of hours south of Bangkok and we don't really want to go north just yet - time first for beaches and sunny off-shore islands.

Various makes of modern 12-seater minivans line the street - along the kerb and behind small tables are the ticket sellers. We ask 'Hua Hin?' We're patiently directed to a table right next door where there is a sign (2m x 2m), 'Hua Hin'. Nine dollars later (for two) we climb aboard and settle into comfortable seats with easy leg room while the driver looks after our bags.

Departure time seems to depend on the van filling up and luckily our destination is in high demand - ten minutes later, we're on our way. Little do we know that this, our first journey by bus, is to be our introduction to the art-form of Asian driving.

HORN HONKING AND DRIVING MADNESS

In Thailand and in Asia generally, careers in bus driving are sought after. Clearly, aspirants who want to be bus or minivan drivers have to start at an early age. How else could they reach the dizzy heights of accomplishment evident in these professions?

We're sure there must be training required to use the vehicle's horn. During our trip, one grand master of the art of horn blowing demonstrated, to our dismay, the ability to roll cigarettes, stack them behind his windscreen sun-visor and toot the horn with his elbow whilst regaining his road position to the correct side of the white line - clearly a postgraduate in the All Asia school of Horn Honking. (Maybe C. S. Forester could write a new novel called Hornblower - Asia style.)

We'll always have memories of Asia's horn honkers. In the city streets, there is rarely a moment of quiet to punctuate the day. Most of the time, the word cacophony doesn't do justice to the constant continuous bleating and blaring of horns. Motorcycle, motorcar or bus - all the drivers have paralysis of the right thumb and it's jammed on the horn button. Only the ruts in the road help the thumb occasionally stutter to a softer vibrato.

Amidst the swathe of seething traffic and the blurting of horns, we still have to admire the skill and confidence of Asian drivers. With the nonchalance of Spanish bullfighters, they sashay and swerve and slip past all obstacles. The noise of their horns is like the overture to a performance spectacular. If 'Driving with the Stars' were here, these street toreadors would score ten out of ten.

21

The capabilities of drivers do not end with the horn; they come with a brand of bravery rarely seen since David took on Goliath. They own the road. Both sides. With flair and daring, they pass petrol tankers on double lines while approaching a blind bend. However, all's well that ends well, and the oncoming drivers seem to have a similar intuition and magically leave space and clearance.

BUS ETIQUETTE
Monks have the right to sit on the rear seat of Thai public buses. You are expected to know this and must give up your rear seat if a monk enters a bus.

SOUND SYSTEMS

Another attribute of the Asian bus driver is one of sound-system management. It seems that they moonlight for Heavy Metal concerts. To keep their hand in, they have multiple speakers in their parcel racks set at a decibel level where the car three spaces behind doesn't need to use its radio. Additionally, Thai buses must get free copies of every DVD produced by B grade musical groups. The sound seems to match Spike Milligan's 'Ying tong, ying tong, iddle I po.' In Vietnam and Cambodia, further luxury is extended to passengers in the form of on-board movies. The captive passengers are subjected to showings of unending Kung Fu fights at high volume. Kaboom! Thwack! Bam! Clump!

The minivan driver (pronounced miniwan) is an acolyte, or apprentice, to the Big Bus driver. Youth brings with it a flair and verve not seen as often in the big bus league. We are to enjoy the trip to Hua Hin in the care of one such youth.

He has developed a system of toots roughly based on the Morse code. One signal warns the cyclist or motorbike driver in front to get back in the box and use the shoulder of the road where they deserve to be. Another signal suggests to the dilly-dallying cars in front to give way to a superior being. Then there is the subtle signal where the minivan driver toots, toot-did-de-toot-toot, for no apparent reason. Maybe just to keep his hand in or perhaps he was tootling along past the abode of a second cousin three steps removed.

HUA HIN

Hua Hin is 230km south of Bangkok and has a population of 60,000.

In the 1920's, King Rama VII brought the royal family here to escape the heat of Bangkok. The royal palace still gets regular use today.

Hua Hin is a relaxing beach town and most of the night life centres on the colourful Chatchai night markets, held in the centre of the town.

HELLO, HUA HIN

Our first feeling of flying solo. The comforts and cosseting of pre-booked and scheduled transport and accommodation is now behind us. It is sink or swim stuff. Bangkok Bill can't help us now.

We fall in love with a guesthouse that looks as if it were built for a Disney movie set (the Pattana at $12 a night for two). All built in dark teak beams and panelling, red roof and cute shuttered windows. Timber stairs to 1st floor, a garden courtyard, timber tables, bright red cushions and trees and plants framed with fairy lights. Beautiful but basic. The in-house, low-cost dining allows us to eat and drink to match our budget. It's an easy choice to book in here for our second night on the backpacking trail.

Hold everything - what about our first night?   Our auspicious arrival ...

Despite all the odds, our youthful minivan driver gets us to Hua Hin safely. We alight in the minivan terminus and, confronted by a bevy of Tuk Tuks, we toss our packs into the back of the most colourful carriage. These little golf-cart sized taxis, built on top of a motorbike, are very manoeuvrable and a handy form of transport.

It's at this stage that we learn an important lesson.

We ask to go to a guesthouse recommended in our guidebook and we get a flat-faced blank look. We name another guesthouse - another blank look. The lesson we learn (in hindsight) is to have a map handy and point to our guesthouse of choice. Better still: check out, from our map, the most major building or big hotel closest to our prospective accommodation before we arrive in a new town. Tuk Tuk drivers really can't read maps that are written in English (just as I can't read the ones written in Thai). Drivers can more easily take us to an address when I tell them of a prominent building close by.

As it is, the lesson is still to be learnt. We know a blank look when we see it and fall back in desperation to tactic number two. We give the name of a hotel we know that Bangkok Bill uses. The face lights up, a flicker of recognition, and he pats the gaudy plastic Tuk Tuk seat for us to jump in. Obviously a longer trip and a bigger fare.

Splutter, splutter, cough and choke and the trusty vehicle warbles into life and phut phuts and farts its way to Jinning beach, quite a distance from our originally selected guesthouse.

Although Bangkok Bill's hotel of choice is quite splendid and moderately priced for what it offers, it is too rich for apprentice budget backpackers like us. We pay off our driver ($2) and ask at a few other more modest guesthouses.

Finally we make a decision - or rather, the ever-sensible Barb makes a decision - 'let's just book in to one of these, then we can get settled and re-group.' So that's how we pay $25 for our first night's adventure accommodation. This proves, subsequently, to be our most expensive accommodation. The room is good, pristine clean, white-tiled bathroom, pedestal toilet and hot shower. Twin double beds, air conditioning, satellite TV, large fridge, table and chairs and a small balcony. All of this situated in a street of small bars and cafes and a 5-minute stroll to the beach.

FINDING A NEW GUESTHOUSE

The next day we walk back into Hua Hin itself and check out a couple of alternative guesthouses. This fairly lengthy use of Shank's pony proves to be the precursor to many walks to come. Check-out time in most of Asia is twelve noon, so we have plenty of time to return to Jinning beach, pay our bill and return to the little teak house of our dreams.

MEETING OTHER TRAVELLERS

Eating and drinking in the Pattana garden setting proves to be a relaxing pleasure and meeting the other guests an illuminating experience. It will turn out that the moments we remember best are of the simple things, the travellers we meet, and the openness of the youth of the world; the adventurous and enquiring spirit of these backpackers in their late teens and early twenties; their single-mindedness in saving up to undertake their world travels. We meet them here.

We admire the capacity of these 'kids' to cope with every hitch and hiccough. There are rare moments when some girl needs a mother's shoulder to cry on and to get a warm hug from Barb. We are fortunate to be allowed to participate, for brief moments, in their world of excitement and adventure. We enjoy the feeling of rejuvenation that comes from our meetings with these young globe-trotters. Their travels are only limited by the number of new places on the map.

We drink beer (for something new and different) at the Pattana with a young Englishman, Nigel, who had cycled down from Alaska through Canada and the US and on down the Americas to the tip of Patagonia. He then flew to New Zealand and cycled from the bottom to the top, and then by air to Melbourne to cycle to Adelaide. His cycling trip then took him through the red heart of OZ to Darwin, up through Indonesia and Malaysia. We meet him while he is resting on the east coast of Thailand before heading north again for China and the sub-continent and somehow back to London. Wow! There's courage. There's real adventure.

After encountering Nigel, we slink down a bit in our seats, sip our beer quietly, and don't say too much about what we had previously been describing to each other as 'our adventure'. Our instant hero is Nigel, the globe-trotting - strike that - globe-cycling Englishman with his trusty bike.

And what about the lady from Alaska who is travelling with her eleven-year-old son? We find out that they travel for about 4 months every second year and are about to head out to Ko Samui and some of the other islands. Two other travellers, a Swedish guy and his Dutch wife, are due to finish their one year's wanderings before heading back to professional lives, as lawyers, in Europe.

We feel rather subdued by the experiences of our companions. No stories of adventure travels to swap, and apart from 'Barbara has recently written and published two successful cryptic crossword books,' we have no notable achievements to inspire awe or induce amazement. Strangely, feigned interest accompanies the news that my paintings are sold on the internet.

Our bedroom in this cutest of cute teak guesthouse proves to be our undoing. There is a ceiling fan which rotates and oscillates above our bed and beats a drum tattoo most of the night. The wonderfully teak panelled room, whilst aesthetically pleasing, turns out to be the Thai equivalent of a Swedish sauna. The screen door proves ineffective in obstructing a family of mosquitoes. This is unfortunate as we don't really experience any more mozzies for the rest of our trip. Suffice to say that the itinerant's life is not an easy one, and we regretfully have to move on.

Mozzies and heat: ten points. Barb and Des: None.

A MOVING EXPERIENCE - AGAIN

Four hundred metres away we select the Bird guesthouse, in the shadow of the Hilton. Our enforced move saves us $3 a night and finds us in an unbelievable location on the ocean front. The guesthouse is built on a heavy timbered pier, stretching out to meet the incoming tide. The sun deck and most of the rooms are built on sturdy timber poles with the waves lapping and splashing up from underneath. We are intrigued with the location and sacrifice a little in the way of sophistication and room décor. Still, we have clean sheets, wall fans, ensuite with pedestal toilet - and this time, we have a TV. Braving cold showers becomes a regular occurrence in a lot of the accommodation in Thailand. Certainly our smallish room could do with a re-paint but being clean is the greatest consideration. An honour system allows us to help ourselves to tea (Liptons), coffee (instant) or even

Ovaltine. The guesthouse serves simple Thai noodle and rice dishes at cheap prices ($1 a meal) and a laundry service is on hand. As with most guesthouses, the cost is only a few baht for each kilogram of washing.

Both of us make use of their clothesline for the washing we had energetically pummelled in our hand basin. (First occasion to use 'everyone's' handy emergency inner tube basin plug.)

HINT
Cut circular beer-coaster sized pieces of inner tube to use as basin plugs, as these are often missing. It is very difficult to wash clothes without a sink plug.

HUA HIN BEACH

Hua Hin has a long stretch of inviting beach and all the variety of beach-side activities that we will come to know well. Sun lounges for rent under the big colourful beach umbrella, tables for our cold beer, and meals served whenever we feel hungry.

Masseurs are on hand to pummel us. Fruit vendors come to our table balancing their wares on their heads and offer pomelos to refresh us. Peddlers invite us to buy from their tray of trinkets.

TROPICAL FRUIT IN THAILAND
Thailand is a real paradise for fruit lovers, with the familiar on sale along with the many quaint species. Thai street vendors hawk 'ready-to-eat' fruit, usually served in a plastic bag with a wooden skewer. Pomelo (large, sweet grapefruit) is often served with a bag of sugar and chilli mixture - delicious.

Hua Hin is a very popular spot with weekenders from Bangkok. Major hotels attract overseas visitors and the streets of Hua Hin see a motley mix of Europeans. The major attraction is the beach.

MARKETS

The town is clean and displays its uniquely Asian flavour through the various styles of markets - morning markets, produce markets, covered markets and more strikingly, the night markets. Large seafood restaurants built on piers out over the ocean are well patronised. It can be quite a novel experience to see a cocktail bar set up in the middle of the street amidst a polyglot of people.

Of an evening, we can stroll up one of the central streets and into the area designated for kerbside stalls. Aromas of curry, of spice, of pungent chilli and of coconut drinks - all to the sound of the latest CD. All the delights of Asian cuisine - all the smells, all the sights and sounds. Food on a stick, food on a plate or food in your fingers. Eat on the go or sit at a table on a plastic stool originally designed for one of Snow White's dwarfs. Eat your Pad Thai or chicken curry and sip on an ice-cold beer. Around $5 sees us both well fed and watered.

DOGS IN THAILAND

In our travels, the dog fraternity was worth bracing ourselves to cope with. Guesthouses may have their own pet. One guesthouse exhibited a fine specimen of a Dalmatian and during this trip we see poodles (pink if you believe), bulldogs, Jack Russels, foxies and spaniels displaying themselves safely inside the portals of hairdressing salons, couturier shops or travel agencies. I confess that I have yet to see an Irish wolfhound or a

Saint Bernard. Still, all the wandering dogs seem to know the road rules. Dogs have their place in Asian society, more conspicuous in Thailand, and are accepted and treated kindly.

Western conventions towards pets are seemingly at complete odds with the Asian attitude. It is true that great pride is exhibited by some Thai families for their own pampered pet pooch, but most obvious is the footloose variety. Thais compassionately tolerate these vagabond drifters. Maybe that's why the Thais are so nice to us.

We notice well-fed mutts drifting through the streets and markets with a superior sense of ownership. Every brand, make and joint-venture dog is here. They are probably best described as itinerant, not homeless, as they are clearly able to take themselves back to some abode. One bitser is seen helping a food-stall holder clean up spilt rice. Good dog!

Indeed, everyone is well disposed towards these Krufts rejects. Obviously there is no such institute as 'The Pound', although I do feel that there must be some unseen control of unwanted offspring. I don't ask about this ...

FOOD, FOOD AND MORE FOOD

We sit and enjoy our Pad Thai in the middle of the night-time street market. Balloon sellers weave through the people and music floats out or blasts from the CD stalls. Battery powered toy cars twist, turn and flip their way through the throng, manipulated remotely by a mischievous salesperson. Silk, soft toys, chopsticks or sarongs, soft drinks or state-of-the-art cocktails. People parade at a benevolent pace, enjoying the evening.

Having dined well, with a glass of Thai tea under our belt and a cling-wrapped plate of pomelo segments in our hand, we amble home through some of the side streets. It's night-time and we see the streetscape come to life. From the dim depths of bars and clubs, sparkling bright troglodytes spring into the glitter and shine of flashing neon. Magically, alluringly, provocatively, the bar girls strut their stuff, inviting us, the streetwalkers, into their dens. What fisherperson wouldn't like to bait the hook as effectively as these girls?

Stockings, suspenders, miniskirt, bustier and cleavage entice the unwary (or is it the needy) to have a seat, buy a drink, enjoy the company and the hospitality of the house. A brilliant colourful scene - colour, music and movement at its best.

Adhering to the maxim, 'Early to bed, etc', we're heading home at about 9.30 pm and the bars already have a fair sprinkling of clientele. It's somewhat saddening to see a predominance of middle-aged men thinking themselves to be modern day Don Juans.

Our day starts with a walk to a corner noodle restaurant - stainless steel table tops, folding chairs and filled with locals. For around $1 each, we have a noodle or rice dish plus a glass of tea. We chat with a friendly local and her daughter. When we are having difficulty ordering, she comes to our rescue and calls out to the cooks. Our breakfast quickly arrives. This delightful lady operates three or four businesses - pedicures, manicures, massage shops and a beach concession. We find out that her husband is an army general. She must be successful - on her finger is a diamond the same size as her noodle bowl.

We buy ourselves the promised sarongs for $4 each and head for the beach and a sun lounge for fifty cents a day. The thirty-five degree temperature makes the swim a lukewarm affair and we soak up our first sunshine for the trip.

Coincidence sees us on sun lounges beside a bar and café that happen to be owned by our diamond lady. We find this out when we pay for our lunch and a complimentary platter of fresh fruit suddenly appears - we see the lady waving and smiling widely from a deck chair at the back of the bar.

We muse about moving to our next destination and decide to toss that one around over dinner.

CHAPTER THREE

Long legs won't help if you don't know the way.

PHUKET AND PATONG

Onward bus travel to Phuket brings with it some surprises.

We're sitting at the rear of our bus, next to a very small cubicle that we had erroneously assumed to be an on-board toilet. Two hours into our trip, the door opens from the inside and a young man in white shirt with blue flashes on his shoulders emerges. Obviously the relief driver. We are mildly surprised as to how he could possibly have rested or slept in such a cramped space. Well, 'abracadabra', next out of the space comes a slim young lady. White shirt, blue shoulder tabs and smoothing down her skirt. The relief driver's relief no doubt. We ask ourselves again, 'What have we learned about buses?' I tell Barb, 'I'm going to train as a relief bus driver!' When we were planning our first big bus experience to Phuket, we hadn't expected this much excitement!

Over dinner in Hua Hin, a cavalier toss of the dice results in a decision to travel over to the west coast first and then take in the east coast islands of Ko Samui and Ko Pha Ngan when we retrace back north. As it happens, this turns out to be a mistake. In a few weeks time, when we are due to retrace our steps (mid December), the monsoon rains have hit these islands.

As we've checked out the bus station ahead of time, we know exactly where it is and what time the bus to Phuket will leave - 7.30 pm. Our accommodation costs at the Bird have been paid and our packs are stored there until we're ready to leave.

We are meandering through the night markets with a fellow Phuket-bound adventurer when I look at my watch - 7.05 - we leave in twenty-five minutes time! 'Shit! Ok Barb, you head to the bus station and secure three seats on the bus. Adrian and I will run back for our gear.'

It's 1 km to the guesthouse. Well, bugger me! Busting a boiler, we get back to the Bird. I heft my pack on my back and trundle Barb's. I congratulate myself on the decision to carry only 7 kg each as Adrian and I bustle our way up the streets - walk, run - walk, run. By this stage 'bugger me' was not an expletive - it was the physical effect. Great, we did it! I collapse into a chair.

WE START TO LEARN PATIENCE

Yes, we've done it, but the bus company hasn't. Our bus to Phuket will not arrive for another hour or so - just sit down and wait. I know that Shylock said 'Sufferance is the badge of all our tribe' - not for this cookie!

Patience and tolerance were never my long suit, and I must admit that Barbara's temperament flies in the face of the familiar saying, 'seldom in a woman, never in a man'. Either way, there is little demonstration of patience or sufferance from either of us during our extended wait.

Our acquaintance, Adrian, sits placidly in a long-suffering sort of way. Add a little fuel to the fire! Two hours later the bus arrives; we grab our gear to board. 'Where's your ticket?' We had been told that we are to get our tickets on the bus. With a fluster and a flare of temper, I flounce back to the ticket office where, with no apology and no smile, Barb, myself and Adrian secure the last three seats on the bus. Phew! Ahead of us is the ten hour trip that, we should have known, turns out to be twelve hours long.

An experience in long-distance buses, our first. This is an air-conditioned forty-five seater bus with forty-five people and three babies. (I'm sure there is a family goat smuggled on board too.) It is a tight fit and very tall people had better get the forward seats otherwise their knees will have splinters from the seat in front. The trip itself goes smoothly enough with comfort stops every two hours.

We ask ourselves again, 'What have we learned about travelling on buses?' The answer? 'Patience'.

ON THE BUSES

Given my healthy respect for our objective to come in under budget, it suits us to travel at night and save one night's hotel costs. Normally it's useful to take a sarong on board for a wrap in case of cold air-conditioning, but in this case we snuggle into the travel blanket supplied and fitful sleep is snatched between stops. We manage a pee and a tea at most stops, although it is at the initial stop that we first come face-to-face, or is that foot-to-foot, with the flat toilet. A bit daunting, but with troughs of water and floating dippers for washing, they present no real problem - anyway, I only needed to pee and what I needed for this was a clothes peg to combat the pee-vailing smell.

BUS TRAVEL IN THAILAND

Thai buses go everywhere and are economical and comfortable. However, the schedules seem to change often.

Ambitious tourists can get around by local buses, but newcomers should start by sticking to the main bus terminals and government buses. There are large government-run buses from the main terminals of larger cities and privately operated buses all over. People usually just go down and get a ticket at the time they want to travel.

FINDING ACCOMMODATION IN PHUKET TOWN

We arrive safely in Phuket after twelve hours and set about following our guidebook maps to the guesthouse of choice. A few questions here and a few there and fifteen minutes of walking sees us directed to our target destination. Not swish, not flash. I fail miserably to negotiate any better than $13 a night for a room with twin beds, ensuite and fan. Big room, clean sheets, but towels that made Kleenex tissues look thick. Still, breakfast is included.

They tell me that you get to accept anything once you get used to it. I'm not so sure. Wet bathrooms became my pet phobia. I never really came to terms with the seemingly universal Asian-style guesthouse bathroom. Showers, toilets, and hand basins are all conventional, but it seems that the outstandingly innovative idea of screened-off shower cubicles is found only in the more upmarket hotels.

Perhaps plumbers toss a coin to decide on which wall to fix the shower: invariably the drain outlet is in the diametric corner and shower water goes everywhere.

Water lies across the bathroom floor for as long as it takes to evaporate or to drain away. Result: I get my feet wet when I go to the loo. I become 'discommoded' - well, in-'convenienced' maybe.

INTREPID TRAVELLER

Phuket, with little to recommend it, is really a staging place for the nearby popular beaches, half an hour away by local bus. Novices that we are, we allow ourselves to be educated by the modern-day Marco Polo of the East, Stewart. We meet him at the breakfast table.

Intrepid is another word we link with Stewart. He is vivid in memory and in hue, colour that is, not location. Stewart is sporting his bright red T-shirt emblazoned with bright yellow stars. We correctly deduce that he had procured it during travels in China.

Stewart is the master of bargaining. He did his postgrad in bargaining in the Peoples' Republic. We also think that they gave him the T-shirt and asked that he leave before he undermined the otherwise booming economy of China. Stewart knows which colour bus is the real economy, long-distance job; he knows where to catch the ramshackle local bus; he knows how to bargain the cost of accommodation, as we were to find out in Krabi, from $12 down to $7. Stewart is travelling the world on $20 a day and though slight of build, he is a giant amongst itinerants.

Stewart would go anywhere in any vehicle except - except he would never again cross the Cambodian/Thai border at Poipet, coming from Siam Reap to Bangkok, by bus. He claims that the bumps and ruts had loosened his fillings. His transport had broken down three times, had three wheels changed, and it took him three days to wash the red dust off. Even when we meet him, he still looks decidedly pink, but then again, he is a Pommie.

LOCAL BUS TO PATONG

We meet Stewart and his friend Helen over breakfast, after which he conducts a few of us to the local bus stop where we pay twenty-five cents each to get to Patong Beach on the cramped and tiny flat-bed truck/bus. Canvas roof with seats along the side and up the middle, and just when we think that no one else can possibly get on board, ladies with baskets of market produce as big as a shopping trolley scramble in and shoehorn onto seats. Who says two into one won't go? When we stop at Patong Beach, passengers kind of explode out of the bus like soda pop.

The invasion of Poland pales into insignificance beside the current invasion of Patong beach. We come to the conclusion that half of Germany must be empty - they are all over here avoiding their winter. German youth is filling up the guesthouses and European families are packing out the organised two-week package tours. The night spots and good-time bars are seemingly swamped with Continental single men, generally over forty and sometimes as old as eighty. We come to the conclusion that we antipodeans have been outclassed in the Asian holidaymaker stakes. No doubt the Kiwis and Aussies are backfilling the space left in Europe.

As well as short term two-week itinerant tourists, we meet quite a few baby boomers from Europe and the UK who spend three months or more a year living in Asia. We often bump into them in the night-time street markets where we sit down with an instant cooked meal and cold beer. They explain how each year they will rent a house or unit for very little cost. They freely admit to running away from the cold winters. What a great place to hibernate in the heat!

TSUNAMI RECOVERY

Tsunami-affected, Patong has recovered remarkably in the intervening period and huge efforts have seen most major damage repaired and rectified. Tourism is alive and well, and making the most of it are the two-week travellers. Everything is pricey and the cheapest, bottom of the range guesthouse any of us can find is $18 a night. The food is expensive, the beer expensive and even the beach sun lounges are $5 per day. It would seem that one pays a premium for the privilege of becoming the target of sarong sellers, shirt sellers, fruit sellers and even carved-elephant effigy sellers.

Patong beach leaves us with a feeling not only of overpricing, but with an underlying uncomfortable image of the ugly tourist. Our sensibilities are disturbed by the sight of many older fat European men walking hand-in-hand with very young local boys or girls and gratuitously indulging them with food and drink. I wouldn't have described myself or Barb as being prudish, but this is just so plainly wrong.

ENJOY THE JOURNEY

At this point on the trip, we realise that it's not about the guidebook sites, it's not about the destinations - it's about the journey. It's about the happenings along the way.

We are not following a script, we improvise and decide as we go along. With four months to travel, we are never pushed to do things, rarely a timeline to meet, so we often just 'hang out'. Often we just sit and sip coffee, water or a beer and watch passing people. We observe that some travellers try to do too much – not us, we learned from the backpackers, take time to smell the roses.

PHUKET ISLAND

Thailand's largest island at fifty kilometres long and twenty-one kilometres wide and connected to the mainland by the Sarasin bridge, which was built in 1967.

The island has seventeen sandy beaches. The most familiar of these is Patong, which is recognised as one of the world's top ten diving sites. Patong is maybe more famous for its nightlife than the beautiful two kilometre stretch of sand.

Neighbouring Karong, Kata and Hat Nai Han are also popular with sun seeking tourists. Phuket suffered dreadfully from the 2004 tsunami, but within a year it was hard to see any traces of the destruction.

Although there is less choice, it is cheaper to stay in Phuket Town than at any of the beaches, all of which are easily reached by local bus.

Both of us are unconsciously avoiding a tightly planned itinerary. We wonder and look with interest and amazement at the uniqueness of each 'must see' sight. However, uppermost in our thoughts and memories are the images of the people we meet and the little incidents and hurdles we cross. I realise that much of our pleasure comes from each other's enjoyment, even each other's predicaments.

TRAVELLING ALONE

One of the things I notice about people travelling alone is simply that - they are travelling alone, not searching for company. They are treasuring their own space and independence. They fit happily amongst other travellers, confident in themselves, yet they walk their own path. I guess life is really a bit like that and each of us is on an individual journey.

Individual travellers will pay more for accommodation. A single room is often the same as a double or only a dollar or so cheaper.

WHERE TO NEXT?

Barb and I plod through the pages of our trusty guidebook. We decide to move on. 'OK Barb, I'll roll the dice.'

'No, it's not your turn, I'll toss a coin.'

Stewart says, 'Put the dice away and think.'

There's a novel experience. Logically, we agree that we need to make the most of our remaining visa time in Thailand, then to visit northern Malaysia before tracking back up to the east coast islands with a new 30-day Thai visa in our hand.

Adopting the sensible approach of thinking logically, we now organise our next leg of the journey - to Krabi. Thank you, Stewart.

'Don't worry, Des, I know the bus station and the low cost bus, so why don't we all take the same bus to Krabi?' says he.

CHAPTER FOUR

It doesn't matter how slowly we go as long as we don't stop.

KRABI

Barb, with eyes as keen as an eagle, spots the Krabi Town store named Svensens. Perhaps, I think, they sell winter beanies or snow skis. No. Beckoning with bright lights is the ice-cream parlour extraordinaire, sparkling tables and tall parfait glasses. Two irresistible chocolate-packed ice-cream and nut extravaganzas, each at least two feet tall, are voraciously scoffed and inhaled by the two of us. So what if we lavish two nights' bed and breakfast costs? We deserve this after our exploits on leaving Phuket and circumnavigating Krabi town.

Barb and I had trundled our lightweight packs to the bus station in Phuket. Walking behind Helen and Stewart, with their bulky packs, we remark on and discuss the friendships forged by young travellers.

BROTHERHOOD OF BACKPACKERS

Backpacker bonding can happen serendipitously. We did notice a few young backpacker couples who clearly had bonded better than most on their trips. More striking, however, is the clear feeling of equality and independence shown by both girls and boys. There is a freedom with their casual acquaintanceships that demonstrates that each is their own person dancing to their own tune. Independence is their long suit. They meet, eat, drink, pay their own way and head off on their own path.

Adrian, who had travelled from Hua Hin with us, headed off on his lone adventure.

We find that we are immediately accepted into the brotherhood of adventure travellers and as such, useful dialogue is exchanged. Information about where travellers have been and where to go next, which guest house is good and which to give a big miss.

And so it is that we travel the same path to Krabi with Helen and Stewart - not a couple, but travelling together. It's not unusual to find platonic partnerships sharing bedroom costs - but not the bed; well, perhaps even the bed, but nothing else.

Less than $3 each covers the bus fare to Krabi. Wonderful local bus, red and cream, and as cheap as chips. Maybe they use 'chips' to fire the bus - it is as old as the hills. Fans oscillate every two metres down the ceiling and it has self-adjusting air-conditioning: you simply move the window back or forward. Music on tap flows from the speakers set into the luggage racks. The driver dodges oncoming traffic despite having to look past the mirror that serves as a dangling haberdashery shop intermingled with Hindu temple flowers and holy pictures.

WRONG DIRECTIONS

Fellow travellers had told Stewart (he cops the blame) at which place to get off to find the central guest house area. Blindly following our fearless leader (since fallen from grace), we circumnavigate the whole metropolitan area of Krabi. Just like Joshua walking around Jericho - except that Joshua found the entrance! Eventually, sweating profusely in the midday sun, we arrive in the Krabi town centre.

KRABI

Just inland from the Andaman Sea, with perhaps the country's oldest history of continued settlement. It is thought that Krabi has been home to Homo Sapiens since the period 25,000 to 35,000 BC.

Krabi is a popular rock-climbing centre and is the port servicing the nearby Andaman Islands. Nearby Ko Phi Phi has attracted the title of most popular island in Thailand.

The four of us head off toward our guest house of choice. We had selected this by pin from the write-ups in our guide book and we pay for two nights. It is here we see bargaining at its best, with Stewart using the leverage of booking two rooms to get a reduction of $5 per night per room. Our room is windowless, somewhat claustrophobic but neat and clean. There is no guest house safe or security locker, which is unusual. Necessity being the mother of invention, I deviously and cleverly wrap passports and money inside waterproof clip-lock plastic bags (carried for just such an emergency) and secrete them under the lid of the toilet cistern. You can't be too careful!

Next day we bid fond farewells to Helen and Stewart as they continue their travels. For us, we spot a colourful brochure in the guest house that shows pictures of idyllic sun-blasted islands standing like plump green pillars in the azure ocean. An all day cruise.

'We have to go!'

ALL DAY CRUISE

Off we head to an all-day four-island tour ($10 each with lunch included) to where James Bond found beautiful women on sandy beaches. Since the time of 007, all these beautiful women have seemingly vanished. We cruise from island to island on the long-tail boat with extended propeller. We snorkel the azure water, don't see any tropical fish and are disappointed with the colourless coral. We lie lazily on sandy beaches and stroll across the sand bar to the next-door island - mystical, magically towering tall and craggy - we suck up the sun, eat the hygienically pre-packed lunch and talk with our fellow travellers - sixteen of them - English, Australian, Kiwi, German and a multilingual Spanish clown. It is here that we met Maria and her mother Ann; Maria is from England and Ann from Spain.

MARIA

Happy memories and pleasant times leave both of us thinking of Maria, the beautiful buxom bird from Bury. Bury St Edmonds, England that is. Fair to say she was a bouncer in every sense of the word. She had worked two jobs to finance her travels and one of these jobs was as a bouncer at the local pub. One of her working sayings was; 'You - outside and 'ave a word 'iv yourself.'

ADOPT A DAUGHTER

Well, over the next few weeks we travelled with Maria - or was it vice-versa? Whatever, it suited all of us to travel to some places as a convivial team. Ko Lanta Island in Thailand, where we enjoyed her young happy-go-lucky and jovial approach to life plus the odd beer. After a couple of different guest houses, we again kept company into Malaysia, Penang and Georgetown. We revelled in Maria's 'joie de vive'. Au revoir, Maria (sticking with the French).

Maria has continued to keep us well informed of her subsequent travels to Singapore, Australia, New Zealand and Fiji - internet is a wonderful thing. Somehow, I feel that we haven't seen the last of Maria. Au revoir was correct.

The email at the end of this chapter, doing the rounds and forwarded by Maria, might say it all about shared dorms.

I'm well ahead of myself in this narrative and must retrace my steps to the finish of the all-day cruise. Maria and Ann have invited us to visit their Krabi guest house on the hill. Cute cottages scattered here and there, simple structures, usual basic fit-out. We drink a few ales and, voila! - we notice hamburger and chips on the menu! We break the noodle voodoo and comfortably revert to western indulgence.

Perusing the noticeboard, Maria spots the island resort of our dreams. The nearby island of Ko Lanta, bamboo and thatch beach cabins on the almost deserted beach. $10 a night twin room! We'll be in that!

All too easy - we've forward booked our island adventure through Maria's guest house. Pick-up is organised from our own guest house for a few days' time, with an early start to catch the island ferry.

CHANGING OUR GUEST HOUSE ONCE MORE

With that accomplished, we enjoy Krabi. We meet up again with some other travelling acquaintances who tell of a lower cost hotel to ours but with bigger airy rooms. We check out and switch to Harry's B & B guest house, trundling the 100 m round the corner to the new abode.

SHARED BATHROOMS

This is our first experience of sharing toilet and bathroom facilities - but for our own curiosity, we wanted to check these out, and this was it. Our inspection satisfies us: twin double beds similar in quality to many of the usual Aussie airport motels. For $6 a double per night, we have a big first floor airy room adjacent to one of the bathrooms. Clean white tiles, pedestal toilet, hand basin and hot shower. Five similar style bathrooms served 9 rooms. We are pleasantly surprised and this prepares us to consider shared bathrooms in the future. As it transpired and as our trip unfolded, it was never necessary to use shared bathrooms again

MONEY-LAUNDERING CATASTROPHE

Moving to Harry's place exposes one of our trip's catastrophes. Packed up and halfway out of the door of our original Green Tea guest house, I hear Barb's soft voice. 'Don't you want to take our money, passports and credit cards?'

Had I heard this one time before? Really - I am just testing her. Sheepishly and suitably chastened, I take the lid off the cistern and remove the secreted package. Good God! Honestly, I had seen it done in the movies and I had read it in the detective novels. Guatemalan crack dealers never have this happen!

A fat, water-filled plastic bag dollops onto the floor. My mouth drops open like the lid of a kitchen tidy bin. Barb stands, legs apart and arms akimbo. 'I told you that was a silly idea.' I tease open the first of the sodden packages. 'How on earth are you going to get them dry?' echoes in my ears.

My passport and visa stamp are a pale wet shadow of their former selves. I think a voice cries for a second time, 'I told you that was a silly idea.'

Distraught, I open the second package and a crisp, crackling passport emerges. Bloody typical, Barb's paperwork is safe and dry. Delaying our departure to Harry's, we towel dry as best we can the passport and spread out our 'laundered' dollar bills. Luckily the currency (our emergency reserve) is mostly the Aussie plastic version. Barb separates passport pages and inserts absorbing toilet paper. Regrouping, we move to Harry's B & B Guesthouse. I breathe a sigh of relief - things really could have gone down the toilet.

Krabi acts as a staging station for beach destinations and west coast islands such as Ko Phi Phi and Ko Lanta. Our decision not to visit Phi Phi because of high costs was, in hindsight, wrong. Catching up later with our adventurer friends who had been there, we found that their greatest increase in spending was, not the guest house factor, but at the bars where they consumed more 'buckets' of grog than they can remember.

RIVER FESTIVAL

We enjoy Krabi, in particular the River Festival held in November each year, where floats of flowers are placed in the river to be carried out to sea for good fortune. Cross-sections of banana tree act as a plate-size base for flowers and candles. Hundreds of floating flowers each with a lighted candle. Truly, a river of light. We wonder how many banana trees bit the dust to cater for this floating armada of light and good luck. Add to this our visit to the night carnival where every kid in Krabi appears, fresh from getting good luck at the river festival. Bright lights, loud music and all the fun of the fair. Fairy floss, peanuts, pork crackling, balloons and a myriad of market stalls. Ferris wheels spin and games of skill elicit screams of delight.

CUTE KIDS

Asian children can take out any 'cute' award. Smiling faces, big eyes, white teeth and welcoming cries of 'Hello, hello.'

They play hand-in-hand with little brother or big sister - all the innocence of childhood. The gentle nature can suddenly or seemingly do an about-turn. Tiny five year olds, girls and boys, start practising their kick-boxing on each other with what I thought to be quite devastating results - yet they play on happily. The kid who has just been cleaned up with an overhead reverse kick jumps up with a laugh, feints with a fearsome foot and hugs the 'foe'. Kids will be kids. Together they share the sticks of candyfloss or sip on a straw stuck into a clear plastic bag of juice.

In Krabi, the placid nature of the Thai people is demonstrated on their streets. Although the speed limit could be 50 or 60, they seem to drive at approximately half this speed or less. Cars and motorbikes cruise the streets with benevolent bonhomie, although all pavements seem fair game. Riders park their current-model motorbikes on the footpaths and pedestrians weave their way amongst them.

We wouldn't finance our children into a panel-beating shop here. There are few dents, scrapes or scratches to be seen. Of course, another reason not to sponsor a panel beater could be that the existing repair shops are so good that any dingle gets the super fast, overnight, back on the road at dawn treatment. This would fly in the face of the western work ethic where 'super-fast' means a three-week turnaround.

Our farewells to Krabi are softened by the promise ahead: Ko Lanta Island. The lure of the offshore island hideaway is beckoning - a true tropical paradise. Sand, sunshine, palm trees, monkeys and gentle waves. My boyhood dreams and fantasies about to come true.

To all backpackers & ex-backpackers

Having trouble readjusting to life back home? Use these handy hints to help settle back in.

1 Replace your bed with two or more bunk beds and every night invite random people to sleep in your room with you. Ensure at least once a week a couple gets drunk and shags on one of the top bunks.

2 Set your radio alarm to go off randomly during the night. Have several mobiles ringing, without being answered. Ask a friend to bring plastic bags into your room at 6 am and proceed to rustle them for ½ hr.

3 Keep all your clothes in a rucksack. Remember to smell them before putting them on and reintroduce the use of the iron SLOWLY.

4 Buy your favourite food and write your name on all bags. This should mainly include pasta, 2-minute noodles, carrots and beer.

5 Ask a family member to randomly steal an item of food, preferably the one you have most been looking forward to or the most expensive.

6 Always vacate the house by 10 am, then stand on the street corner looking lost. Ask the first passer-by of similar ethnic background if they have found anywhere good to go.

7 When sitting on public transport, introduce yourself to the person sitting next to you, say where you got on, where you are going and how long you have been travelling. If they tell you they are going to "A", say you met a guy who said it was terrible and that you've heard "B" is better and cheaper.

8 Finally, stick paper in your shower so the water just drizzles. Adjust the hot/cold taps at regular intervals so that you are never fully satisfied with the temperature. As a result, shower infrequently.

These simple instructions should help you fall back into normal society with the minimum effort. Good luck, Maria XXX

CHAPTER FIVE

Firelight will not let you read fine stories, but it is warm and you won't see the dust on the floor.

KO LANTA ISLAND

Last Beach Resort - A castaway island setting. Bamboo and thatch cabins nestling above a white crescent-shaped sun drenched beach. Tropical palms and coconut trees shading the shimmering blue waters of the Andaman Sea. Timber and thatch recreation area. Bar and restaurant all decorated with shells, woven lanterns and driftwood. Our little personal hideaway huts nestling in the palm sheltered hillside. We're raring to go.

PICK-UP PANIC

Normally prompt and punctual to the point of being painful, we wake up at four minutes to 8 am in Krabi with our pick-up for the Ko Lanta ferry 240 seconds away. Frenetic activity at its worst. Stuffing books, wash kits, damp shirts and knickers into our packs, we scramble into our clothes and tumble down the stairs.

Our driver is with Harry drinking coffee. One glance at our dishevelled distress and he smiles widely. 'Why don't you have coffee? I've sent the van to pick up the other people first.' We don't know whether to be miffed or mollified. However, despite the kerfuffle, I remember, without the voice from 'she who never forgets anything,' to get the passports and money belt.

In the bus is Maria, smiling and cheerful (her wonderful Mum, Ann, has gone back to the Costa del Sol leaving her free to frolic).

Our transport drops us off at the splendid and imposing harbour complex. From one extreme to the other. We leave the spectacular glass and glitter wharf in Krabi and after an hour's enjoyable ferry ride in a boat created in the image of the Manly Ferry, we are handed down to the rickety dilapidated wooden plank wharf in Sala Dan on the island of Ko Lanta.

KO LANTA ISLAND
30 km long and 6 km wide, with nine white sandy beaches along the sunset coast on the Andaman Sea.

The coastline has more that seventy small islands with forests, coral reefs and abundant under-water life. A glorious tropical island not overdeveloped - yet.

TSUNAMI RECOVERY

The island had suffered in the tsunami and has now completed the first stages of reconstruction. It seems that all the original timbers and planks have been saved for the re-built wharf. Same again for many of the houses built out on piers with the sea lapping underneath them.

We had pre-booked what looked like, on the brochure, a great location. Somewhere special where one could think up selections for the BBC's 'Desert Island Discs'. Our hotel ute meets us at the wharf to take us 15 km to the Last Beach Resort - somewhat logically, at the very bottom of the island. Ten people pile into the back of the ute and I sit in the cab (courtesy of my tin hip and nothing to do with being older that anyone else). Four kilometres from our destination, we leave the tarmac and take to the 'as yet to be re-constructed' road. After bumps, bounces, shudders and shakes, the resort comes into view. A panorama of paradise.

HEAVENLY HIDEAWAY

Guests all have their own separate bungalows - floor plan and design courtesy of Robinson Crusoe. Timber, bamboo and thatch with 2 m square block-walled ensuite. Rooms with two single beds plus small veranda in front, complete with hammock. Rickety pole steps up to the front door - home for the next week. 'Swiss Family Robinson,' eat your hearts out.

The setting is idyllic. Nearly 1 km of beautiful beach fringed with jungle palms. Barb and I need nothing other than our swimmers and sarongs. I didn't mind at all that some of the young guests seemed to have mislaid half of their bikinis. Swimming is leisurely and lukewarm. Everything is laid back - so much so that sunbathing is almost classed as energetic. Read a little, drink a little and read a little more. I interrupt Barb's dedicated efforts at 'patience' to tell her how fortunate she is to have a travel guide such as me.

The restaurant has a happy mix of Asian and western meals. Cold beer when we want it, and my bottle of rum gets the odd nudge. The bar is jutting out on poles over the beach and strewn with cushions, along with reclining sun-bronzed bodies. We are happy to stretch out with them.

The tsunami had hit this resort and caused major damage - almost a total wipe out - and great efforts have been made to pull it back into shape. The bar, restaurant, internet room and kitchen have all been re-built. Residents' bungalows are not as high on the list and still require work.

Taking off my rose coloured glasses and putting on my $5 Paco Raban sunnies, I take a more critical look at the Last Beach Resort. Paradise? Paradise Lost? Yes! And not quite reclaimed yet.

HOTEL BILLS
More than one traveller reports finding fault with the running tab at some resorts and can't reconcile the bill. It is best to insist on paying as you go to avoid trouble.

Because of the tsunami, we have excused, or overlooked, some of the resort's temporary shortfalls. With little extra effort, the gardens could be better nurtured and the high-tide flotsam easily picked up. There were certainly enough 'idle hands'.

Am I being overly critical? Don't sweat the small stuff. I simply lie back in the hammock and enjoy the bliss of the beach resort.

When I first use the bathroom and remove the hand basin plug, a gush of soapy water hits my feet. Perhaps the tsunami had blown away the pipe joining the basin to the floor outlet. Gales of laughter emerge from the bedroom - at least one of us is happy. Look at it this way, my feet are nice and clean.

LINGERIE LIZARD

Maria's consternation was a sight to behold the morning her bikini top was missing - eventually found in the farthest corner under her bed. She certainly hadn't put it there.

With deduction usually only attributed to Hercule Poirot, Maria excitedly told the dining room patrons that 'A lizard must have dragged it there.' She had seen a large gecko in her room the night before when she had gone to bed. 'Must have been a mighty big lizard,' comes the chorus from the dining room. We look each morning for cross-dressing geckos.

Our stay proves to be very relaxing. There are heaps of stunning memories. Beach walks, sunbathing, swimming in the blue blue sea, superb location with trees right down to the beach. Monkeys in the palms, waterfalls in the forest and elephant rides a short walk away; cute little geckos. However, despite the beach bliss, we are ready for the road again. We feel that we need plastered walls, cornicing and tiled floors. Barb has no trouble dragging me on to the next adventure on Ko Lanta - the Blue Andaman.

RESORT-STYLE LIVING

The Blue Andaman awaits and we change our back-to-nature treasure island setting for a tidy and tiled bungalow resort a few kilometres from the port.

Neat gardens, neat paths and neat hedges. Tiled floors, tiled patios, tiled bathroom walls and even terra cotta tiled roofs. We have swapped 'rustic' for 'carefully-cared-for' comforts. To we castaways, this looks like the Promised Land flowing with hot water, fluffy towels, laundry and swimming pool. Milk and honey is readily procured in the all day café. Earlier in the week, I had called in and booked and prepaid $7.50 for a splendid fan room but with cold water.

When we arrive they haven't got our room available so we are upgraded at no extra cost to the hot water, air-conditioned, and cable TV bungalow - usually $10. We score the upgrade for two nights.

When I did my recce, the beach was narrow with the sea gently lapping the golden sand. The latter proved to have been high tide and in reality, for most of the day, rocky outcrops dotted through the waves - hence the need for the sparkling pool. We enjoy the pool, the restaurant, the happy service and the free book swap. A cold beer is still enjoyed on the occasions we catch up with Maria.

On most days, Maria was off doing her own thing. Maria's excursion, on this particular day, sees her off emulating Annie Oakley on an all-day horse-trekking adventure through the jungle. The promised mare changes to a spirited stallion. The experienced groom is a fourteen year-old boy. The adventure bit is true when a feral dog harries the horses and the stallion takes off for its life through the trees. Needless to say, while we sit and listen to the story, Maria stands and gently pushes and prods her backside.

MASSAGE

Yet again, the comforting services of masseuses are on hand (a blessing to Maria). They appear everywhere there is a beach. The ladies seem to have mastered two arts - when not calling out 'Hello, you want a massage?' they peacefully sleep on their mats. They must have eyes in the backs of their heads (like my mother had) - between closed eyelids, they still instantly spot any muscle-tired tourist. We agree to a half-hour ($3) and a one-hour session ($7) and it's our turn to drift into a relaxed limbo while the magical fingers push, prod and sooth away those tight tensions brought about by lazing on the beach.

We revel in the three-star comforts around us; we sit on the veranda, play cards and soak up the sun. We haven't ever experienced so many clean tiles and tastefully selected patterns. I become convinced that at some time this resort had benefited from a visit by an Italian tile salesperson. No doubt a contra had been organised. A lifetime of free holidays for as many end-of-run tiles as they needed. I'm delighted that Asia and Italy have managed an 'entente cordiale'.

BIRDS

We are a bit confused at this stage of our trip about the absence of birds. Maybe the tsunami wiped out a few nests. Certainly the Thais haven't enough wild birds in evidence to film even one take of an Alfred Hitchcock movie. Very few sparrows or anything else is visible and little birdsong is to be heard in the wild - when it is, we lift our heads at this novel sound.

This of course 'flies' in the face of the Asian pastime and hobby of breeding songbirds. At one rest stop, we see what we take to be a Bird Fancier's Convention and notice a preference for square bamboo cages rather than round ones. This obviously allows more cages to be hung in a row when attending the local Bird Meet. Our Bird Meet is somewhat like a car-boot sale for birds, where fanciers assemble on a spare block and hang their 'star' bird and cage side by side. One can only imagine the dedication of the bird fanciers who travel miles to know that their bird can out-whistle the one next door. Sometimes our lodging houses have birds in gilded cages, beautifully trilling their tuneful evensong.

MONEY MISHAP

One young 19-year-old Scottish girl travelling with two girlfriends found money had been stolen. Stolen might not be the right word - perhaps if I'm being kind - misappropriated.

She shared a room with her friends and, as always, she kept her wallet under her pillow at night. Rising early to connect with a ferry to one of the islands and after a half-hour trip to the ferry terminal, this girl found her wallet missing. She, in her rush, had left her wallet under the pillow.

A speedy trip back to the resort found the beds re-made, sheets changed and no money! Missing - not to be found - or returned. There was no chance of laying hard evidence against any of the three house staff - there was, however, a distinct lack of care from the resort.

Barb comforted the distraught girl and we were assured that she had the financial support of her travelling friends. More than one offer by fellow travellers came out of the blue, with one chap offering cash in hand with the understanding that the girl could pay it back when her travels had been completed and she got back to Scotland. What a gesture.

THONGS

Whilst strolling along the narrow beach at the Blue Andaman, it strikes home to me that not every Asian beach has crowds of people - most are simply 'thonged'.

That is THONG'D. This proves to be the same for nearly all of the Asian beaches we walk on.

For my purpose, I refer to thong as in the one worn on the bottom of your foot, not on the bottom. Somewhere there is located a thong, flip-flop, jandal manufacturing plant churning out left-foot-only or right-foot-only multi-coloured rubber thongs. There is no other way to account for the plethora of non-matching orphaned footwear found at the high tide mark on all beaches - even a single lost sole or two abandoned along a road or outside the local corner store.

I see a great opportunity. I can visualise it. A new TV lifestyle programme with swimsuit-clad contestants required to find a matched pair of thongs along the shores of some sun-drenched sandy Asian beach. Perhaps 'Celebrity Thongs'.

On a 'lighter' note - same theme - there could be a follow-up show where the object of the search could be abandoned disposable cigarette lighters. 'Light up with the stars.' It appears that there are just as many coloured lighters as coloured shells.

MOTORBIKES

To bike or not to bike - that is the question. Motorbike, that is. There is a strong appeal to taking a carefree, wind-blowing bike-riding day trip around Ko Lanta.

We reluctantly refuse the motorbike operators' tempting offers. Either drive yourself or pillion ride. Both Barb and I are wary of travelling on motorbikes. We decide, early in our trip, that we won't take the risk of an accident and its attendant costs of overseas hospitalisation or medical treatment. Bangkok Bill had warned us.

If we had been regular motorbike riders in Oz, perhaps our thoughts would have been different. Barb has pretty well forgotten all the bike skills she had when mustering on the family cattle property west of Emerald in Queensland. (She had also disclaimed any ability at horse riding when Maria proposed the horse-riding excursion.)

MOTORBIKE INSURANCE

Unless you have a current international car or motorbike licence, you will not be covered medically should you hire or ride a motorbike and have an accident in Asia.

We were advised that for medical insurance purposes, never to admit that you have been on a motorbike - perhaps just a pushbike?

With all this advice and info, we become entrenched in our cowardy-custard viewpoint. That's not to say we don't review and re-think our firmly held position. The relatively, and I do say relatively, calm traffic conditions experienced in some locations lull us into a sense of security. As they say, 'Never say never.' Eventually, in Vietnam, we board the backs of motorbike taxis (Motos) and relive our youth. 150 cc and 250 cc bikes are to weave us and waltz us through the many cities, even with packs strapped to our backs.

Once outside the older and centralised sections of some cities, the roads are nearly normal in terms of terrifying traffic. Our initial fears of injury or of hospitalisation evaporate in the exhaust fumes of a motorbike.

Apart from being a pillion passenger on a motorbike, there is always the alternative of the $1 a day hire of push-bikes, a great way to get exercise and take ourselves to the nearby tourist sites or beaches. There you can relax on the deck chairs and recover your breath and rest your legs - even get a back, foot and leg massage to enable muscles to get you home again.

During this trip, we don't ride motorbikes ourselves but promise to get some practice when back in Australia and get our motorbike licenses before travelling again. However, in recounting these bits of avuncular advice, I have deviated from my chronological sequence of travel.

MOTORBIKE MAYHEM
A young athletic 20-year-old Swedish lad who we had first met with his girlfriend in Krabi. As is often the case, our paths crossed a few times on our travels and one month later in Saigon, we meet him swinging along on crutches with his left leg bandaged. He too had come a cropper, injuring himself (leg, knee and thigh), and his girlfriend (arm skinned and bruised) and also injuring a young local boy on a push-bike (not too badly hurt). On our second meeting, he was due for another visit to the Saigon hospital for more treatment. He told us that he didn't think there would be any repercussions from the local boy or the police. Hmm! Maybe, maybe not.

ON, ON - EVER ONWARD

Our batteries recharged, we are ready to mix it again. Both of our Ko Lanta resorts are removed from the cut and thrust of the cities and the markets and the street food vendors. Maria has kept us company - she did her thing and we did ours, and we were lucky if we met up at the end of the day for a drink and perhaps a meal. We talk together about our next leg of the trip. We will use Hat Yai as a stopover to get to Malaysia.

Visas need renewing and we want to see Penang in Malaysia. Maria is heading to the Cameron Highlands, so the three of us book onward tickets. We will cross the Thai/Malaysian border and when we come back to Thailand, Barb and I will get new 30-day visas. We are heading to Georgetown in Penang, a melting pot of cultures. A mixture of race and religions, a polyglot of people. The lure of different food sensations, Malaysian, Chinese or Indian has us licking our lips in anticipation.

NOT ANOTHER MOTORBIKE STORY?

A young German girl we meet whilst still on Ko Lanta had come a cropper from her motorbike. The rough roads had become quite rutted, her bike had hit a gutter and she had a bad crash. No traffic on the road - just inexperience. Nothing broken, but with her left leg very badly bruised and extensively skinned, she was hospitalised for 3 days. She was unable to travel and when we met her, she had been resting up for 10 days with some time to go before she could resume her trip. Still, she had found for herself a wonderful sunny stretch of beach and an idyllic island on which to recuperate.

CHAPTER SIX

A short visit is best and that not too often.

TO HAT YAI - A one-night stand, then Penang

It's wet; our choice of guest house is at best marginal and proves to have the worst mattress we experienced on our whole trip. The double-bed mattress is made of rubber and is as tough as old boots, in fact, I think it was made of old boots or compressed car tyres. If I hadn't had a bad back before, I have now! Where is our chiropractor's recommended latex mattress when we need it? We have very limited sleep. Consoling news is that Maria is in the same boat - bad bed, no sleep. Still, our trip from Ko Lanta had been uneventful.

ONWARD, EVER ONWARD.

Getting from Ko Lanta to Penang and Georgetown necessitates this stopover - one night in Hat Yai. Our pre-booked minivan collects us from the Blue Andaman and winds its way for two hours through the red lanes, red roads and rubber plantations of Ko Lanta, onto the river ferry and into Trang and to our connecting red bus. Ahead of us is the three hour trip to Hat Yai ($2.25 each), where we will look for a suitable place to sleep.

The red bus takes us to the Hat Yai bus station. Lack of effective planning sees us taken right through the central city area past where we want to be. Not having done my homework, we have to take a ten minute Tuk Tuk ride back into the centre of action at the huge cost of twenty cents each. Once again, our lesson learned is to know the location we want and ask the bus driver to drop us as close to the spot as possible.

The old maxim is that 'it takes two to make an argument'. Well, we go one better and the three of us argue about who was the bloody fool who didn't read the map. The refrain of a long ago song plays in my mind: 'When will they ever learn? When will they ever learn?'

In frustrated mood, we book into the nearest guest house.

Our initial impressions of Hat Yai are of a dark forbidding city without soul, although the night-time streets are somewhat brightened by the usual street food vendors. A Paddy's Market style emporium provides us with some light relief. 'Light relief' is correct as Barb finds here one of her treasured possessions - a perpetual flashlight for $3. Shake it half a dozen times and a halogen light beams out. Her other purchase, stylish in brushed aluminium, is her digital alarm clock - also $3.

Hat Yai brings out the worst in me. The weather is bad, and prompted by a dirty looking local, I complain to Barb of my pet 'hates'. Top of my Asian negative list is the common habit of spitting. Not just spitting, but the very audible process of clearing the throat, nose and antrums before expectorating. This seems to be restricted mostly to the male of the species. (Thank God for small mercies.) It's worthy of note that this Asian habit has been eradicated in Singapore. I guess that Lee

Kuan Yew's directives some 40 years ago had good effect, something to do with the $1,000 fines or the chopping off of heads.

Whilst walking back to our lodgings, I trip over a low-lying plastic bag, which brings to mind the second in my list of Asian negatives: litter. People seem to clean, fastidiously sweeping their own doorsteps, but beyond that it seems to be someone else's problem. Litter is everywhere, despite the nightly collection of garbage. What a shame that the image of a country can be so adversely affected by this plague of plastic bags discarded at whim.

The foreboding darkness of Hat Yai had prompted us to book our forward transport the night before. We booked our 9 am escape passage on to Penang - good decision.

HAT YAI

Hat Yai's major claim to fame, and perhaps reason for existence, is the railway yard where the east and west lines from Malaysia join to form a single track to Bangkok. Commercial interests have developed because of this.

Large numbers of Malaysian tourists invade and stay overnight in town at weekends. It is whispered that these are mostly young couples exploring new boundaries. Rules of society are somewhat more lax here in Thailand. The weekend influx brings with it an excitement and enthusiasm for shopping that brightens this town.

Hat Yai did, however, provide a great service that made the balance of the trip more restful. In Ko Lanta, Barb had 'liberated' a pillow whose seams had accidentally burst open and the overflowing crumbled-rubber stuffing was responsibly put into two of our carry bags to keep the room tidy. In Hat Yai, hiding away in a dungeon under the railway bridge, we find Rumpelstiltskin on a sewing machine and he magically makes us each a soft pillow. The size of a loaf of bread, the pillows prove their worth on quite a few occasions.

EXIT THAILAND

We are picked up promptly from our guest house by the ubiquitous minivan and, bleary from lack of sleep, we set out on our five hour trip to Penang, doorstep to doorstep for $7 each. When we reach the border from Thailand into Malaysia, we are processed through both border posts and immigration checks with no hitches and spend about 10 minutes at each stop.

This proves to be a huge relief for me as my previously water-soaked passport has survived its aquatic adventures - but only just. Whilst the front-page photo is fine, the typed details are decidedly dimmed and dulled. What is an even greater concern is my visa docket. White flimsy paper with blotted and blotchy ink stamps. Forget about being inscrutable - the scrutinisation at the Thai border by the immigration officer is intense. It's true that I can gauge little from his face but I somehow evoke some sympathy. We show him Barb's clean and crisp visa and there are sufficient matching marks on mine to get him to re-stamp and push us through.

PHEW!

So, we've jumped the first hurdle - not just the first hurdle, but both border posts.

VISAS
Australian visitors to Thailand are issued a 30-day visitor's visa on arrival in the country - free of charge.

If you wish to stay longer, a visa extension can be organised for a fee that varies depending on where you ask - shop around the various tour operators and make enquiries at your hotel reception.

Most visitors choose to border hop rather than pay for a visa extension - trips where you can leave the country for a few hours are readily available and an automatic 30-day visa is issued again on re-entering Thailand.

Recently changed rules allow for only three 30-day visas in a 6-month period - so a maximum of 90 days in Thailand every 6 months. This new ruling is an attempt to stop people living and working in the country without the necessary permits.

CHAPTER SEVEN

Better to wear out shoes than sheets.

PENANG

Majestically bearded Sikhs, wonderful turbans, colourful saris and the rich aromas of Indian cooking. Little India, in Georgetown. Meals served directly onto individual sections of fresh banana leaf - rice, dhal, dhosa, chicken korma, beef vindaloo, roti and chapatti - all finger food. No need for a dishwasher here.

With all this to look forward to but still moderately apprehensive, we move through the Malaysian customs checkpoint. Successfully processed, it's into the minivan and off to Penang. Phew! Again!

Does the countryside immediately change? Yes - the roads are two lanes and broader, the central divide is gardened and sculptured. The road shoulders are wide and tidy, with no evidence of the usual litter. A cleaner, neater, tidier first impression of Malaysia.

Let's see how Penang, Georgetown and Chinatown match up. New country, new towns, new experiences.

Our trip from Hat Yai is great value at $7, a bargain with five hours of comfortable travel, numerous toll gates and a trip on the big, every-day, commercial vehicle ferry across to Penang Island and Georgetown. This is where east meets west at its best. Old British colonial buildings cohabit with historic Malay and Chinese meeting houses and temples. A sooty veil, the patina of age, seems to rest on all the Chinatown buildings. Bright jewels of Chinese Kongsi meeting houses sparkle amidst this greyness.

PENANG ISLAND

European settlement was established here in 1768 by the British East India Company and the harbour was used to serve ships on their way to China.

History tells us that to clear the island forests, Captain Francis Light loaded the ship's cannon with silver coins and fired into the trees. No shortage of willing workers.

Penang became a duty free port to encourage settlers.

GUEST HOUSE HUNTING

Our drop-off point is the traditional centre of action, Chinatown, wonderful door to door service. Guest house hunting takes longer than usual, 30 to 40 minutes. All the buildings are somewhat shabby, hiding under the umbrella of age.

Caffeine-deprived, we sag into chairs and order cups of coffee in 'Jim's Place'. Lean, lanky and laconic, wide smile in shiny mahogany face and crowned by a black fedora, Jim serves us coffee. Affable, amiable and hospitable (perhaps having the buxom Maria with us helped?) Jim gives us a veritable verbal Cooks Tour of possible Chinatown guest houses.

We end up in a big Chinese-built teak establishment, $13 room, fans, ensuite, but no satellite TV - indeed, no TV at all. This is no great loss as we rarely turn a TV on. Still, the beds are comfortable and the sheets clean, but towels are once again tissue thin. Thoughtfully, management organises the night-club entertainment and music to seep through the room walls, which pulse like giant woofers. The walls can't remember when they were last painted. In the early morning, our patio chairs and table look over the aged courtyard to the walls of the next door Mosque - Allah be praised - and he is, starting at daylight.

In planning our budget trip, we had bravely promised ourselves that we would experience backpacking at the grass-roots level. The kind of thing our kids would have done - the kind of accommodation they would have used. This was it: our promise came to pass - basic but clean. This is certainly the grass-roots level of grass-roots guest houses. At the end of our trip, we were well under budget and could easily have afforded 2- or 3-star accommodation any time we hit a 'Georgetown Chinatown'. For example, the flash up-market 2-star hotel along Chulia Street offered rooms at $25 for a double.

CHINATOWN

Penang, in particular Georgetown and Chinatown, is for me a delightful blending of old and new. Wonderfully stylish and elegant colonial residences set back in their spacious gardens. Some tainted with age, others restored with freshly painted shutters and bright white walls. The redolence of the East India Company and the rule of the Raj lingers. Clean-cut school gardens and evidence of past glories are to be seen dotted throughout the modern and emerging city.

The old town buildings contrast beautifully with the new city high rise. Remarkable - side by side with the Chinese history are the large docks, new buildings and a super dooper very long low-line modern bridge connecting the island to the mainland.

PENANG BRIDGE

At 13.5 km long and 6 lanes, Penang Bridge is the one of the longest bridges in the world and links the island to the mainland. The bridge carries huge amounts of traffic and plans for Penang Bridge 2 are underway.

This is a toll bridge but only for the trip from the mainland; coming back is free. Could this be why the minivan took us to Georgetown by ferry and back by bridge?

I have vivid flashbacks of Hong Kong tenements with long bamboo poles sticking out from the balconies and festooned with drying washing - not so in these handsome new Penang high-rises. No pegging out of undies here for all to see.

Amongst all this, sparkles the clean white and gold minarets of the mosques, the flamboyant orange/red tiles of the Buddhist shrines, Hindu temples and richly ornamented Chinese Kongsi. Hanna-Barbera Productions could well have taken their colour schemes from these revered buildings.

KONGSI

During the eighteen hundreds, the Chinese flocked to Penang and the resultant Kongsi (clan meeting houses) sprang up. Today, a particularly impressive example

(Khoo Kongsi) with its glorious hall, ornamental beams richly and intricately carved can be visited.

Ask permission to enter between 9 am to 5 pm weekdays, and 9 am to 1 pm on Saturdays.

OFF TO CHURCH

On Sunday, we take ourselves off to the nearest 'Sunday Service', where tall Samson resistant pillars form the portals of the Anglican Church. Usual kind of pew arrangement and order of service, in English. The local equivalent of Ian Paisley blasts out his 30-minute hellfire and damnation sermon and our escape route is blocked. However, we are entertained to a somewhat logical but emotional tirade against any belief that isn't Christian. Did I say a strong sense of the ecumenical exists here? Well, I don't know. I think I'll go to the mosque next week.

PENANG TRANSPORT

Welcome to the world of Chinatown and its various layers of transport. The bicycle is commonly used by the locals, and the vintage of the bikes seems to predate the Boer War - as do the riders. Old and young alike use late model 125 cc motorbikes and these throatily phut phut their path through impossibly large groups of people and market stalls, miraculously avoiding everything in their way.

Asserting their dominance, these motorbike owners feel it's compulsory to park their bikes up on the footpath (haven't I whinged about this before?), hence we poor pedestrians are compelled to filter off the footpaths, between parked cars and on to the road, sidestepping the traffic.

Twenty or thirty year old cars can still be seen beside the latest Lexus or Mercedes. Not so with the local buses. It seems that when Noah finished the ark, he started building these charabancs. Still, cheap and effective and they get you to Penang Hill, Batu Ferringhi or even around the island.

Despite the variety of vehicles, all seem well mannered and tolerant - tranquil traffic. Road rage; road rage; what road rage? Clearly a Western indulgence.

MOTORCYCLES IN MALAYSIA

More than half of the vehicles in Malaysia are motorcycles (over 7 million) and nearly 60% of the road fatalities are due to motorcycle accidents.

Helmets became compulsory in 1973 and this law immediately reduced the number of deaths by 30%, but, amazingly, some riders and passengers still travel without helmets.

PENANG HILL

Here in Georgetown we are surrounded by the colour and richness of the many temple structures. At the back of my mind during the entire trip through Asia is my fixation with rooflines. I have a childhood love of the image of pagodas with their steep inclines and sweeping turned-up corners. Even when building our own homes in Australia, I can now see my unconscious design flirtation with steep angles and fancy finials.

Naturally, the shining tiled roof of the Kep Lok Si temple, near Penang Hill beckons us. Like the Grand old Duke of York, Maria, Barb and I march up to the top of the hill where we lie exhausted at Buddha's feet amidst the very large hill-top temple complex and look into the pond enclosure with what seems like one thousand and one turtles. We had climbed up more steps than they speak about in Russia. Twisting and winding, large granite steps zigzag up to the temple. Market stalls and souvenir shops of every style flank the upward path on both sides. When our lungs are bursting, we stop and peruse some useless knickknack. Convenient to do our browsing whilst climbing the stairway to heaven.

PENANG HILL
As the funicular railway proceeds upwards on its half-hour climb, a spectacular scene of Georgetown slowly unfolds.The view from the top of the line is a lovely way to watch night descend over the island.

The fare is $1.50 each and trains leave every thirty minutes from 6.30 am.

Golly, this must be what heaven's like. I'm struck by the colour and splendour of the richly decorated figures and images and the sheer magnitude of the temple. Still further up the hill, under construction and towering above us, is a nearly complete huge concrete Buddha. The shape and form obviously waiting for the artists and gold leaf experts to work their magic - or for the collection boxes to fill up and pay for all that gold.

At what stage does a child stop believing in Santa? When do kids lose interest in the Easter Bunny? Does familiarity really breed contempt? It's about this stage of our trip that I reach overkill with temples. I'm almost 'templed' out. 'Not another bloody temple' becomes the catch-cry.

A scenic ride to the top of Penang Hill beckons. I remember as a child my father taking me on a fun-filled funicular train ride and I relive my excitement, somewhat dulled by the thought of another temple at the top. In my childhood memory, the trip was clickety clack and fast, but not this train - it lumbers up the steep hillside railway track, allowing a wonderful, redeeming panoramic view of the island.

JACKIE

Here, our meeting with Jackie is a high spot - at a high spot. Jackie, the effervescent English, 'English' teacher. Jackie, a little slip of a girl, but a giant among backpackers.

We literally meet in the top carriage of the near vertical train travelling to the top of Penang Hill, with its white mosque and the spectacular and profusely decorated Hindu temple. At this stage, the elegance is lost on us. A bit like watching five consecutive nights of holiday slides - they lose impact.

We do the right thing; we struggle our way up from the station; in the temple surrounds are the 'Money Changers', the ever-present souvenir shops and accompanying food hall. A wildly exciting choice of about ten different eating places, each selling the same-same meals. We are a captive audience and we all order the obligatory noodles and slowly munch lunch. The hill top breezes cool the sweat on our brows and the fabulous views reward us for our patience.

On the downward trip, squeezing into the cramped train compartment along with our 'new best friend' Jackie, we (Maria, Barb and Des) are confronted by the Black Uhlans - no, no - I'm mistaken. It's a group from the mosque's women's auxiliary. Black from head to toe; I'm guessing they have toes because the only parts visible are the eyes. The eyes are also black but we did hear them laughing behind their Zorro masks. The Chador hides most everything that is in any way feminine. I guess one gets to be really turned on by eyes.

Jackie helps Barb, Maria and me survive that night's drinking and dining in Chinatown. (Jackie introduces the term 'beer o'clock' and this becomes, for us, a regular meeting time.) The oldies eventually leave the two girls to terrorise the tourists. It is our understanding (which we think is a lot better than the girls') that Maria and Jackie get up to some serious shenanigans with some poor unsuspecting members of the Australian armed forces casually and peacefully doing reconnaissance work in the bars of Chinatown.

We haven't been troubled at all by mozzies but in the morning, one of the girls has been afflicted. 'Isn't that bad luck getting bitten?'

I get a nudge from she who sees all. 'That looks more like an Aussie bite than a mozzie bite.'

So, braving their wounds, post hangover, the girls join us for a day's recce to our proposed next guest house location at the seaside town of Batu Ferringhi. It's at this stage that we are each about to go our separate ways (No - not Barb and I; we're having a fine time.) However, Jackie and Maria are going to travel together to the Cameron Highlands, the mountain home of the tea plantations.

BATU FERRINGHI RECCE

We are wowed by the Batu Ferringhi beach location and book ourselves into a comfortable guest house. Barb and I will check-in next day.

The girls insist that we have a couple of early farewell drinks with them at the tables on the beach (it was beer o'clock.) Too busy watching the snake charmer entice his giant reptile from the basket and with my chair legs in the soft sand, I give everyone the benefit of an accidental swan-song demonstration of sitting down, falling over backwards with multiple somersaults - thereby entertaining all the beachside drinkers and bar staff. Without any thought as to my sensitive nature, or indeed well-being, all three female companions fall about in hysterical gales of laughter.

However, he who laughs last laughs longest, or some such cliché. God gets her! As soon as sanity is restored and the beach bar clientele settle back, Barbara returns to the table with her packet of chips, promptly sits back and does a back flip with a degree of difficulty in the high nines. She shows her knickers to the world and a clean pair of heels to the air. Well - the girls collapse, I collapse, the combined forces of the bar staff and drinkers collapse. Surely this is imported entertainment from 'Cirque de Soliel'. The snake charmer packs up his basket and flute, knowing when he's beaten.

MEETING OTHER TRAVELLERS

We do seem to sit at café tables quite a bit, but it's here that we strike up conversations with backpackers. The invariable questions are asked, 'Where do you come from?' and 'What prompted you to backpack?' etc, etc.

Earlier in Georgetown, at Jim's Place Cafe, we met Bill and Beth from New Zealand. They had travelled Europe some three years previously for four months and were inspired, this time round, to do Asia. Bill was sixty-four years old and Beth was sixty-five. Talking about all things backpacking, we found that they were already contemplating India for their next safari.

Drinking coffee at Jim's Place has its benefits. Beth and Bill told us how they'd rented out their house to fund their walkabout. Why didn't my super-clever wife think of that before we left home? Next time around, we'll do the same. The rental income from their house covered their daily costs in Asia. They had travelled down from Laos, Vietnam, Cambodia and Thailand and were heading south to the Cameron Highlands, Kuala Lumpur and then home.

They infected us with their enthusiasm for the travelling lifestyle. We swapped stories along with the usual backpacker banter and, to our advantage, got information on quite a number of good clean low-cost places to stay. Each had their own backpack, OK slightly bigger than ours, but they had braved some colder regions and still carried their cold-weather gear (needed for the Cameron Highlands). Still, they envied us our light packs and thought that they could do the same through India.

They had a better-planned route than us, starting in the cooler areas in the north and finishing at Kuala Lumpur in the south. At the same time their schedule, like ours, was decided on the run and by whim. They had included Laos, whilst we didn't. When planning their trip, Bill had renewed his motorbike licence and had made a point of pre-trip practicing, and on the trip, found it to be invaluable - all this whilst admitting that he was not about to challenge the local riders in most of the major cities. It did, however, allow them to see a greater amount of local countryside than we had experienced. Therewith, I took it under notice to do the same for our next trip and, with caution, review my prejudices and fears relating to motorbikes.

They met their daily budget through eating at the local small cafes and street vendors and trying anything once, same as us. (As long as it is cooked in front of you, there's not much to worry about.) They also told us that in all their travelling, neither of them was affected by the attacks of diarrhoea - same-same for us. Beth admitted to going up-market a few times on their trip. By this she meant for accommodation. To prove her point, she showed us their $25 room in a Georgetown hotel and compared it to our $13, less than commodious, cold-water lodgings. We took this on board and swore to each other to abandon the $50 a day budget when push came to shove, and catch up later in a less expensive area.

Up to this stage, Barb and I had congratulated each other on the smooth and logical approach to our trip, but after meeting Bill and Beth, we weren't so sure. Unlike my scribbled, corrected and dog-eared exercise book, Bill's very neat and precise book of accounts showed an average daily outlay neatly converted to NZ dollars. Using my rapier-like fingers I converted this to real Aussie money - $56 per day.

LITTLE INDIA

Chinatown affords us the chance to indulge in all types of differing foods and given that we are ready to move on the next day, we make the most of Little India, just a block or so away from our guest house. We stroll through the sitar-sounding streets past the Hindu shrines, mingle with the turbaned Sikhs and end up (as we have most nights) at the Sri Ananda restaurant. Bill and Beth join us for the evening feast.

PENANG STATE
The second smallest state in Malaysia but the eighth most populous.

Penang State encompasses the island itself plus part of the mainland.

Butterworth (the military centre) is the major port on the mainland, across from Georgetown. Georgetown has Chinatown as its traditional 'Old Quarter' and Little India squeezes itself amongst the streets of Chinatown and offers Indian cuisine at its best.

BATU FERRINGHI, HERE WE COME

The next morning in Chinatown we have a farewell breakfast with Maria and Jackie. It is during this, our final breakfast with the girls, that our bus to Batu Ferringhi arrives and we hurriedly 'kiss the girls and make them cry' and scramble onto the bus. So what if we leave them with the bill for our breakfast! Oops!

Parting is such sweet sorrow. We parted from Maria and Jackie with fond farewells and fond memories - in the words of the old song, 'We'll meet again, don't know where ...'

And indeed, we did meet Jackie again! Her trip had taken her up and down Malaysia and back into Thailand. We kept in touch by sporadic emails. She went out of her way to arrive in Sihanoukville, Cambodia, the night before we were to leave and we had a few laughs together - and at beer o'clock, also a few drinks. After we all left Serendipity beach Jackie stayed on in Cambodia for a month or so doing volunteer work teaching English in a local village. Something of a busman's holiday, seeing as Jackie teaches English in England.

But, once again, I digress. Let's talk about Batu Ferringhi.

CHAPTER EIGHT

Riches can buy pleasures but they can't buy peace.

BATU FERRINGHI

Remember when your mother cried, 'You little monkey!'?

Now I know why. Her pretended exasperation was clearly as a result of some mischievous antic. Here in Batu Ferringhi we see 'little monkeys' at their best. During our beachside idyll on Ko Lanta we had, at a distance, seen its resident tree-swinging Simians amusing us with their aerial acrobatics one moment and pilfering any unattended shirt, towel or thongs the next. We heard tales of the odd wallet and camera last seen disappearing into the treetops. Here the cute monkeys are up close and personal, gangly and precocious.

Only a 25c local bus ride away, but what a splendid contrast to choc-a-block Chinatown and Georgetown. Batu Ferringhi is a seaside beach village clearly designed for the international two-week tourists and well-to-do Malaysians.

Well tended and tailored gardens ease down from the marbled entrances, foyers and lobbies of the 5-star hotels. The lawns are bedecked with comfortable sun lounges, with ready access to the pristine pools and shaded cabanas.

BATU FERRINGHI – FOREIGNER'S ROCK
The word Ferringhi is said to be the original Malay term for foreigner. There is a strong probability that the word is derived from Arabic as it is used as far afield as Ethiopia. Even the Thai word Farang, for foreigner, is obviously a derivation. In the town itself, there are several different spellings of Ferringhi: Ferenghi, Feringgi, etc. Confusing.

The beach itself provides a range of activities: paragliding, surf skiing, jet boating - all the water sports.

Go for a swim and then have your ears cleared with the ancient hot candle treatment. Reflexologists peddle their services to the perambulating pedestrians and the ever-present masseuses pound those weary holiday makers, reassuring them that they haven't a care in the world except that maybe the icemaker in their room doesn't work. Looking down from their lofty luxury, the '5 starers' can spot us a little way along the beach - the bed and breakfast mob. Same beach, same sea, same sports activity - less luxury, less cost.

Guest houses offer rooms at a range of prices, from single room with shared bathrooms for $8 to twin with air-conditioning, fan and bathroom with hot water for $12 to $15. In Batu Ferringhi, the guest houses share the rustic end of town with the colourful beach bars and bistros offering a range of food and drinks. Indian almond trees, casuarinas and coconut trees fringe the beach, giving dappled shade to those sun worshippers who want it.

I confess that most of the young travellers seem determined to toast themselves to match the colour of the bamboo thatch. It's mandatory, obligatory and imperative for every young European traveller to wear a bronzed suntan as a badge of honour when returning home. Their whole globetrotting trip would 'pale' into insignificance if they were not able to sport the golden glow of an exotic suntan. We are not beyond this conceitedness ourselves - hence our plan to spend the last few days of our adventure on the beach at Sihanoukville in Cambodia.

BATU FERRINGHI HOTELS

Batu Ferringhi - Renowned for its status as a resort town with the Hotel Rasa Sayang being voted, in 1985, 'Best hotel in the world' by the British Tourism Organisation.

The beach location sports hotels such as Holiday Inn, Golden Sands, Park Royal, etc., and some of the package prices seem quite reasonable at $150 for a double room.

MEETING OTHERS ON OUR SHADY VERANDAH

Batu Ferringhi is the perfect foil for the busy hurly burly of Chinatown. Romantically ensconced in a small family run guest house, we walk the beach, swim in the sea and fraternise with our fellow travellers on the front veranda overlooking the beach. It's on the veranda that David, an English accountant, patiently introduces Barb to Sudoku and debates with her the key strategies needed to win at Patience. Another guest, Kerry, our vivacious veterinary nurse, enthrals us with stories of her last few months of voluntary work with the gorillas in the Borneo rainforest, while her travelling mate Allison is planning her return to South Africa. Back to volunteer veterinary work with cheetahs, and maybe even to visit a South African wildlife officer? We are destined to catch up again by chance with David and Kerry.

During our stay, we meet the American gentleman in his eighties who has been on his lone trip for over two months. His pack is easily slung over his shoulders, the size of a shopping bag. That wipes the smug smile off our faces.

THE MONKEYS ARRIVE

We often have a light breakfast on the front veranda of our guest house, overlooking the thatched beach bar and café. We watch the sea through the big green leaves of Indian almond and banana trees. One morning, to our delight, our mates arrive. Primates that is.

Tripping and skipping and gallivanting along the telephone wires in front of us, long legs, arms and tails all used to balance their tightrope walking adventures. Then, mid-pendulum-like swing, they flop into a banana tree. They bite, chew and masticate the stems and soft centre of the banana tree and leaves. We are enthralled. The tree owner isn't. He shoos off these amusing acrobats, whose bodies are the size of kittens, their skinny arms and legs carrying the little monkeys off to some other tasty tree.

INDIAN COOKING LESSON

Food-wise, we luck in again with a small Indian restaurant 200 metres away. It is here that we undertake a hands-on, one-on-one Indian cooking class. The friendly owner Mihir, with whom we often exchange friendly banter, offers to show us how to prepare the style of meals that we regularly eat there. No charge!

His sister and his chef both help teach and we are shown the art of Roti-, Chapatti- and Dhosa-making.

MIHIR'S ROTI RECIPE

3 cups whole wheat flour, 1 tablespoon melted butter, 1/2 cup warm milk, 1 cup warm water, 1 tablespoon sugar and 1 teaspoon salt. (Our Indian cook actually used condensed milk instead of the milk and sugar.)

Combine flour, butter, salt and sugar.

Knead mixture until soft dough is formed, cover and rest for 2 hours.

Roll out into big circles and cook on lightly greased pan pressing down on roti with a damp towel to make air pockets form.

MIHIR'S CHAPATTI RECIPE

2 cups plain flour (whole wheat is traditional), cold water and salt to taste. 1 tablespoon of oil for the mixture, and oil for frying.

Put the flour in a bowl and add salt and oil and mix well. Slowly add the cold water and knead thoroughly to make soft dough.

Cover with a damp cloth and leave for 2 hours.

Divide mixture into 10 pieces and roll out very thinly, dusting with flour as you go.

Cook in a pan with a little oil until bubbles appear then turn and cook the other side.

'What wonderful meals we'll cook at home'. I mention that we are shown, but I didn't say that we learn. Subsequent attempts back in the comfort of our own home somehow just don't quite compare. However, the two-hour session indulged our taste buds and we made sure to pay the roti makers for their trouble. We did, however, enjoy the 'learning' process.

NIGHT PERAMBULATIONS

Every night we meander the 1 km into the town itself. Magically, from about 5 pm onwards, the footpaths become lined with mobile or demountable stalls.

Have Bazaar, will travel.

Sunglasses, shirts, watches, DVD's, handbags, toys and sarongs - every imaginable piece of merchandise is for sale. Shoulder to shoulder, these vendors line the way and it makes for a delightfully distracting walk to the central food hall in the main part of town.

Set up under one roof, the food hall offers about 25 different styles of cuisine. It usually takes us half an hour to make up our minds and choose from one or other of the meals. The tables cover at least half a football field and when we sit at a table after ordering our food, the vendor mysteriously finds us amongst the 100 other tables. Dinners so far have cost us, on average, $6 for both of us, with breakfast or lunch about $3 or $5 for two.

Surprise! Surprise! Isn't it wonderful when you absolutely and unexpectedly bump into an old friend you knew in Australia? Here Barb and I are, climbing up this set of tiled stairs in a town building. First we see black shoes, then white trousers, then black string tie and white bearded face. Colonel! How good to see you! We have hit on our first western food outlet. KFC. With no thought of weight control or waistline, we barge in and give ourselves a quick fix. Braving an unknown menu item, we order the potato basket and wedges topped with a cheese mayo. I'm now hoping that this delicacy finds its way to Oz!

RELIGION

Islam is more visible here. The day-to-day signs of predominant Moslem beliefs are in the head gear. Men have white cotton skullcaps whilst the women are more noticeable and eye-catching in their traditional dress and headscarves. Colours range from foreboding and boring black to delicate shades of pastel, some edged with embroidery, tasteful in their simplicity. The effect of the girls' faces framed and swathed in gentle colours is, to say the least, enchanting.

It is here in Malaysia that the mosques are more numerous. Elegant, simple white buildings sporting onion-shaped cupolas trimmed in blue and gold. A contrast to the Hindu and Buddhist temples and pagodas.

RELIGION IN MALAYSIA

The official religion in Malaysia is Islam, but freedom of religion is guaranteed by the constitution.

The Chinese population in Malaysia is basically Buddhist or Taoist and the Indian residents usually Hindu, with a few being Sikh.

The vast majority of ethnic Malays are Muslims, with some Christianity being practised, particularly by the indigenous people of Sabah and Sarawak.

ACCOMMODATION

Once again, the contradiction of the Asian lifestyle confronts us. Whilst Thailand is very untidy with litter and a noticeable difference obvious in Malaysia, I am disillusioned by the debris left on Ferringhi Beach after a weekend of Georgetown visitors. Beer bottles in the sand at the very front of a beach bistro and left for a few days. This flies in the face of the fastidious efforts of the cafe owners to keep their work areas wiped down, clean and dust free. Our current guest house, Shalinis, at $13 a night, demonstrates this fussiness in the presentation of their rooms and bathroom areas and with their attention to changes of pristine towels and bed linen.

Batu Ferringhi is the only place where I don't check out the $20/$25 a night accommodation - perhaps we are too content at Shalinis guest house. Perhaps I just didn't walk past a mini hotel. Only the big flash numbers.

Guest houses have different levels of appeal, as we see for ourselves when we first reconnoitre potential accommodation. However, if the standard is too basic, for a few dollars extra one can usually book into a handy 2-star hotel. Whilst we find ourselves confronting and even enjoying the daily challenge of a $50 budget, our final result of $40 a day shows that we could have enjoyed 2-star accommodation whenever we wanted by paying $10 more.

In hindsight, would we upgrade? Not very often. Yes, sometimes. Yes, in Georgetown. $25 a night will secure all the comforts of home, fancy rooms, fluffy towels and every feature we desire; for Barb this really means a big deep bath.

WHERE TO NEXT?

Winding up our time in Batu Ferringhi, we prepare to backtrack to Georgetown and wend our way to the east coast islands of Thailand - Ko Samui, Ko Pha Ngan and Ko Tao.

Versatility and flexibility have to be the bywords for every adventure traveller. Hanging loose and not sweating the small stuff are admirable attributes. It is now our turn to practise what we preach.

By chance, we catch a weather forecast that clearly shows that yes, there is weather in the South China Sea and no, it's not good and that yes, it's going to blow wind and rain for the next 3 weeks.

Our plans to fraternise with the full-moon party-goers blows up, like the wind, in our faces. We do not intend to view Ko Pha Ngan and Ko Samui through rain-speckled glasses.

Flexibility comes to the fore and we adopt plan B: from Batu Ferringhi we'll go back to Georgetown, on to Hat Yai again, then re-visit Hua Hin for a few days at the beach, albeit without the rave parties and buckets of margaritas. From Hua Hin back to Bangkok. This time to Khao San Road.

Batu Ferringhi's internet cafes are dotted along the main road, and in one of these we plan for two weeks hence and book our flight out of Bangkok and into Hanoi. It would then be Dec 22nd, so we think that the flights might become booked out.

SOME INTROSPECTION

It's our wedding anniversary - Ha! I remembered first! All those years of connubial bliss! I don't think so.

The trials and torments and frustrations of raising three self-minded kids. The temperament of an Irishman and the wilfulness of an independent woman. Never peaceful - but never dull. We are well met. Both allow each other the mental space needed to be our own person, even while backpacking.

I am reminded of one line from a work on marriage by Kahil Gilbran: 'Let there be spaces in your togetherness and let the winds of the heavens dance between you.' Some of these winds are tornados, but in our case, there is always calm after the storm. Gee, I'm a really forgiving person - isn't Barb lucky.

It's on our last morning before retracing our steps that we get a farewell performance from the local monkeys. We are saying some goodbyes on the veranda when three or four of them troop along the telephone lines in front of us. A great note to leave on.

FULL MOON PARTIES
The Ko Pha Ngan Island Full Moon Party draws a crowd in excess of 10,000 on the night of every full moon.

The party carries on until the sun rises on Haad Rin town beach, with all the bars staying open and ear splitting music blaring forth.

Buckets of grog sell for about $3 and usually consist of a bottle of alcohol (often local rum) poured over a small plastic pail of ice with Coke and Red Bull syrup thrown in for good measure. An infinite variety of grog is available but illegal drug use has lessened in recent years, due in part to the attendance of people from a wider range of backgrounds.

BACK IN CHINATOWN

Our one-night stand back in Chinatown is most fortuitous. By some unaccountable bad luck, Barb's 'Gucci' watch purchased here seven days ago for $6 has buggered up. Two watches in one month - first mine and now Barb's! What extraordinary ill fortune! And both of us have gone to such lengths to buy name brands.

We amble back to the watchmaker/hawker's place of business under the pedestrian walkover and against the diamond-mesh fence. Expecting to be told to 'go-root-your-boot', we are pleasantly surprised at his accommodating attitude and skip on our way, with a new watch, to Little India and one of our last authentic Indian meals for the rest of our holiday.

LITTLE INDIA
One of the most imposing landmarks in the Chinatown area is the Sri Mahamariamman Temple in Queen Street, probably better known for the scores of fluttering pigeons at its entrance than for the fact that it is Penang Island's first Hindu temple.

This charming inner city area boasts rows of pre-war terrace shophouses teeming with seemingly everything Indian, from pottery to spices, jewellery to flower garlands and silk saris. There are barbers and astrologers, money changers, fruit sellers and music stores blaring movie songs in Hindi and Tamil.

The sheer energy and colour makes this community a must-see in Georgetown. Restaurants abound and the whole enclave of activity is 'in your face'. Fabulous

---

CHAPTER NINE

A wise man knows his mind.
A wiser man knows when to change it.

BACKTRACK TO BANGKOK

Is it a scene from Pickwick Papers? An Aladdin's cave of books? Perhaps a scene from Harry Potter? Back in Chinatown, Georgetown, we find ourselves in a quaint shop. Book shelves top to bottom, right to left. A little bit of dust here, a cobweb or two there.

We chance upon the narrow entranced bookshop with a turban-topped, silver-bearded ancient Indian proprietor perched on his stool reading the paper. What a happy stroke of luck. Both of us have finished our books, we can swap or buy here.

All these books are second-hand, many bundled in fours or sixes and tied with string, circa 1970's. The latest pre-loved popular publications, sold as one offs for $3 to $4. We blow cobwebs from shelves and flick through the most likely looking of the paperbacks.

French, German, Swedish and English language books all segregated ready for eager foreign backpackers.

The ancient barter system works well for books and we make our selections (one book each, of questionable age - Wilbur Smith and Ayn Rand). We proffer our own four newish books for his two well-used volumes and he graciously bows, thanks us and as a special gesture gives us each a one litre bottle of water. We feel good. Clutching our 'new' books, we pop into the friendly Chinatown tour office and collect our bus tickets for the trip back north.

Next morning, it's an early pick-up at the tour office and we settle into the minivan to re-trace our steps, via Hat Yai, to Bangkok and the lure of Khao San Road's bright lights. Eight people in the twelve-seater means that we can spread out. Swishing over the 13.5 km long Penang Bridge, we are on our comfortable way to the Malaysian/Thailand border. Previous border experience leaves us with no jitters and, true to form, we slip effortlessly through both border posts with no fuss and no cost.

Hat Yai holds memories of our worst night's sleep … ever! Why am I doing this to myself? Why risk the pain again? Why not 'throw a six' and go straight to Bangkok? However, we need to overnight here to catch the northbound sleeper train.

Our driver kindly drops us at the central railway station. Dodging a few light spots of rain, we scurry a hundred metres around the corner looking for accommodation. Voila! The Ladda Hotel. We inspect, push, pull and prod and pay our $8. A clean spacious two-star room, light, airy and with hot water.

Soft spots of rain change to heavy drops so we fish out, for the first time, our lightweight raincoats. We're off to try to book our train trip, first time on a train since leaving Noosa.

We jump and skip across the puddles on our way back to the railway booking office. Twenty minutes later, we have checked out our options and booked a bottom sleeper each on tomorrow night's train that will take us north to Hua Hin.

Rain is still falling, but heavier now, with the drops turning into bigger blobs. We check the weather forecast again, which confirms bad weather all up the east coast. Good decision not to head off to the monsoon rain-swept islands. Overnight we hear the heavy rain pouring down outside our window. For something new and different, we breakfast on noodles and lunch on noodles at $3 each time for both of us. I can't remember what we had for dinner, but I do know that it must have been good as my notes tell me we spent $4 each! Barb will have to stop spoiling and indulging me this way.

We are to book out of our hotel room by noon and board the train at 6 pm. Our plan is to eat at around 5 pm and take with us a dilly-bag with water, some apples and two small packets of biscuits. We had doubts regarding the quality of food on the train, having heard varying reports. As it turned out, the on-board food received good raps from other passengers. The time between noon and 6 pm, we fritter away mindlessly cruising around the shops and getting our provisions whilst leaving our packs at the hotel. The balance of waiting time will be spent reading or playing cards in the hotel reception area.

TRAIN TO HUA HIN

We arrive in the station half an hour before scheduled boarding time because of my inherent nervousness regarding all modes of pre-paid transport - so naturally, we have the dubious pleasure of waiting three hours before departure. This tumult in their timetables causes no concerns to railway staff or the patient Thai passengers. Everyone, except me, is ambivalent.

Six o'clock comes with a trumpet call and crescendo of music. The train guards jump up, the security people, the luggage men, the ticket collectors and even the fruit vendors jump to their feet. Dumb old me - I sit until heartily kicked by Barb. 'Stand up, stand up!' says she. Momentarily, I think that I'm back singing in Sunday school. No, it's the evening tribute to the King. We dutifully stand rigid, emulating every other being in the place. I think even the dogs stand still.

THE KING OF THAILAND

Born in Cambridge, Massachusetts, USA, RAMA IX is the only Thai monarch ever to have been born abroad.

In 1996, Bhumibol Adulyade (Rama IX is only used in English) celebrated his 50th anniversary as king and in 2000 became the longest reigning monarch in the world (Queen Elizabeth II is the second).

Educated abroad, Rama IX came to power following the death of his brother from a gunshot wound to the head while he was in his bedroom in the Grand Palace. The circumstances of his brother's death remain a mystery to this day.

Rama IX is one of the wealthiest men in the world, with estimates of his fortune ranging from 2 to 8 billion US dollars. He is an accomplished jazz musician and composer, painter, photographer, author, translator, sailor and sailboat designer.

May 5th is a public holiday in Thailand in honour of the king's coronation. Yellow is the King's colour, being the colour of Monday, the day of his birth.

It seems that our 'good manners' and respect for the national anthem are noticed and appreciated by station functionaries because thereafter our tickets are solicitously inspected and we are smiled at and repeatedly assured that the train is indeed due at any moment. It is explained that the delay is because extra carriages are being added. Our yellow-painted boarding position on the platform is indicated and we are suitably reassured that we are headed in the right direction when they point up the tracks in the direction of Bangkok.

ALL ABOARD

With bells and whistles and electronic wheezing, the train arrives. We hustle and bustle our impatient bodies and backpacks onto the train. The door is exactly opposite the yellow platform mark.

Clutching our bag of biscuits and goodies, we flop onto the two bench-style seats of the sleeper carriage. The 'top bunk' seats are unclaimed. We settle down one on each side of the train with a double-bench seat and demountable table each. We watch as the steward folds down other people's top and bottom bunks, quickly placing a sleeping mattress and trim sheets with crisp white pillows and a light white blanket on each.

The speaker system solicits orders for the on-train meals and we politely decline the steward's offer. We choose to sit up, eat apples and biscuits, discuss the inclement weather, play cards and read until bedtime. The steward quickly makes up our beds when requested.

Having more English than the steward, the purser tells us to expect an altered destination arrival time of 9 am. In our estimation, this will be about right when the delays are factored in. Glad of an excuse to use her new matchbox-size analogue light-up-at-night alarm clock, Barbara set the alarm for 8.30 am. We had ditched our digital alarm. (No need to mention that none of the button-pressing combinations we tried would allow us to re-set it ...) I wrestle with a conundrum in my mind: Why does Barb insist on a light in her clock if she can't find it in the dark to start with? Why did we buy the super-dooper halogen torch?

Now that Barb is comforted by an infallible analogue alarm system, we both curl up in our respective comfortably-curtained beds to sleep the sleep of the just - or just exhausted. 'Goodnight, Hon', I slip into the crisp sheets, pull the gangway curtain closed, switch off the reading light. And so to sleep.

Overnight Barb's voice has changed. 'Wake up, wake up, Hua Hin in ten minutes.' It is 6.45 am and the steward is gently shaking my shoulder. We don't know if the train has picked up the travel time or whether there is a built-in tolerance in Thai timetables - or maybe the arrival time of 9 am is for Bangkok, not Hua Hin. Nevertheless, we scramble about and ready ourselves in quick smart time. Both of us have slept well in the comfy beds and closed-in cubby houses.

HUA HIN

We had got out of Hat Yai just in the nick of time. The rain had been the one constant during our time there and as we found out when we arrived in Hua Hin, the city behind us had become inundated with rain and was now flooded everywhere, with no trains or buses able to leave the city for days. The water was above people's knees in the town centre. We really do get lucky sometimes.

De-trained and bleary-eyed, we trundle our trusty packs along the Hua Hin platform. We are vaguely reminded of the turn-of-the-century Queensland railway stations, except that the wonderful timber Thai buildings are a trifle more ornate. These remarkable fascinating buildings could have come straight out of a Hans Christian Andersen story, something Dreamworld could emulate. Next to the station is another authentic Thai pagoda building, resplendent with curved finials on every roof, coloured beautifully and well preserved. This proves to have been built to receive visiting royalty to Hua Hin.

'Let's be lazy and take the easy way out.' We barter for a taxi. First rule of navigation is to know where you are and the second rule is to know where you want to go. We learn fast. In this case, the driver knows both, so for $2 we front up at some few minutes past seven to our previous sea-front accommodation, The Bird. A near neighbour is the Hua Hin Hilton. Just a smidge more opulent, but a near neighbour just the same!

The extendable concertina-type iron gates are closed but the door panel is unlocked, so we slip in with our packs, step over the dog, make ourselves coffee at the self-serve honour bar and wait for the rest of the world to come awake.

We know from our last stay here, quite a few weeks before, that the long sandy beach is the nerve centre for budding sun-bronzed bodies, but not this week. Grey sea is washing against the sea wall, covering the usual strips of sand. A cool breeze from threatened monsoons sees most in sweaters and warmer clothes - except, that is, for those with Teutonic blood in their veins. Ice man would have been proud of the few young ones who recline, in the midday murk, at the end of the guesthouse jetty. Towels spread out and books in hand, they prepare to attract any wayward sunbeam. I guess they may get some through the grey skies via osmosis.

A COOL CHANGE

'Be prepared' should be the motto for travellers, and with only 7 kg of luggage each, neither of us was! We had told ourselves that we would buy what we needed when we got to cooler Hanoi, then discard or post home surplus apparel when leaving.

Our plan alters because even before getting back to Bangkok we need something warmer. For Barb, a warmer long-sleeved knit sweater and for me, trendy sports slacks and a long-sleeved top. Necessary for our trip, these costs are added to our expenses for the day.

Sweaters and slacks pad out our packs. Until now, we've been able to pack with relative ease but I guess this is the great trade-off, size of pack versus tight squeeze packing. So, with astounding generosity, I reduce my pack a bit and donate a book to The Bird's scratchy library.

We'd spent time in Hua Hin on our southward journey, so we know our way about town. Finding our way to the minivan terminus again is no great fuss. $4.50 each buys us the tickets and after overnighting, we are up and off back to Bangkok and the minivan terminus in the street close to the Victory monument.

KHAO SAN ROAD

Exciting, invigorating and illuminating. Colour is everywhere - down the footpaths, across the roads and up the alleys, with Neon claiming the taller buildings. Amongst this melee, motorbikes, Tuk Tuks and taxis sashay through the midst. We expect bikes to arrive from any direction, down one-way streets, up the alleys and on the footpaths, even into hotel lobbies. We wouldn't have been surprised if a bike zoomed past the bedroom door, but with all the recommendations from backpackers up and down the track, how could we not spend some time here?

To get from Victory Monument to Khao San Road, we lavish $2.50 on a taxi to deliver us to the Four Sons Inn.

The fact that there are several Four Sons Hotels or Inns in the Banglamphu area adds about 5 minutes to our trip, but booking ahead sees to it that we have a good welcome and a small twin room for $19 on the second floor. The elevator nullifies any threatened heart seizure.

What a different feeling arriving in Bangkok this time. Full of confidence, knowing the ropes, and a good hotel at less than a third of our original China Princess hotel cost. Tuk Tuks, Sky trains, underground, buses, river ferries - all familiar. We even bump into friends of long standing (well - six weeks long standing). We love Khao San Road already.

BANGKOK TRANSPORT

SKY TRAIN The Bangkok sky train has revolutionised travel within the congested city. Opened on the King's birthday in 1999, the system is spotlessly clean, fast, efficient and cheap. Fly over the Bangkok rooftops and see the city from a different perspective.

BANGKOK RIVER FERRIES A fun way to travel is to use the river ferries. They run from piers along the river. You can use the larger Chao Phraya Express boats, which have white hulls with red stripes, private long-tailed boats or the flat shuttle boats with just a few seats. Boats don't stay long at the pier so be quick - and take great care as they move off suddenly.

BANGKOK'S SUBWAY Also known as the Metro or MRT (Mass Rapid Transport). There are currently 18 stations linking with two Sky Rail stations, forty-five kilometres of track and plans to achieve 290 miles of track by 2010.

KHAO SAN COMMUNITY

What colour and activity. What a celebration of youth, no doubt enhanced by the visual comparison of a couple of intermingling oldies.

An eighty-five percent content of the youth of the world, along with a small complement of fifty-plus itinerant hippies waiting for flower power to have its second coming. Then there is the ten percent from the golden age. The solid representatives of the community, like us!

This is the Petticoat Lane, the Portobello Road of Asia, only more so.

KHAO SAN ROAD

A short road in the Banglamphu neighbourhood about one kilometre from the Grand Palace. A backpackers' 'ghetto', with a swirl of lights and sound and teeming with young people from all parts of the globe.

One Thai writer says that Khao San Road is 'a short street that has the longest dream in the world' and this street certainly attracts some bizarre characters. Some say that 'people-watching' in Khao San Road can only be compared to a visit to the zoo. True!

It's packed with cheap lodgings, exotic foods, footpath vendors, Indian tailors, tattoo parlours, traditional massage, hair extensions, tour offices and all types of bars and cafes. Be prepared for Khao San Road - it's full on.

A positive plethora of street vendors and stallholders, with goods tumbling from inside the shop to the edge of the pavement, each owner displaying their merchandise, and tables of wares. An erratic zigzag space is left on the footpath, meandering through each vendor's bunch of goodies. Obviously the narrow path down the pavement is designed to slow up the shoppers at each curiosity shop.

A kind of confluence of happy activity exists, but we find it a trifle tedious passing yet another Indian tailoring shop. 'Hello sir, good suits inside, you come and see.' I think I'd prefer it if they said 'God, you look like a dag, we can help you with your image!' Anyway, they should know that at my age I don't need any more than one suit, and that for funerals.

THAI MASSAGE
The effect is uniquely relaxing as well as energising. Sessions typically last one or two hours and are performed on a floor mat, with gentle pressure from both hands and feet.

Thai massage has been used for countless generations to treat degenerative conditions and promote wellness. It is designed to adjust the skeletal structure, increase flexibility, relieve muscular and joint tension, stimulate internal organs and balance the body's energy system.

The modest cost is absolutely justified under nimble fingers.

MASSAGE

The other perpetual plea emanates from groups of young girls. They each wear a sparkling-clean pastel-knit sports shirt with embroidered logo. They lie, sprawl or sit outside sparkling-clean brass and glass doors and interrupt their girlish giggles with 'You want massage?'

In my case they say 'Papa' - clearly a mark of great respect for my age, my grey hair and perhaps my 'happy Buddha' belly.

They joke, smile and flirt with me. (Why wasn't my youth more misspent?) Barb stands back; she smiles quietly and enigmatically . 'You wish,' says she.

Whatever the product, the locals all politely accept any congenial refusal. They are a pleasant, friendly people who make us feel welcome in their city.

Everywhere there is a veritable rainbow spectrum. Balloon sellers with wares floating on high with their amusing, twisted inflated animal creatures. Flashing signs on hotels, guest houses, cafés and pubs. At the time of our visit, the Christmas lights add to the already flamboyantly illuminated shops and stalls. In and out of all of this creep the very vigilant and helpful cab drivers. Taxis come in multifarious hues, red and blue, yellow and green and even Lady Penelope pink. This suburb creates its own sunshine. Later in the evening, even more colour and movement is exotically displayed by the ladies of the night who are stunningly, provocatively advertising their wares. Perhaps men on their own are approached with more insistence but at no stage did we feel pressured by the sex-industry practitioners. It was all part of the local scene and at times quite hilarious to see old geezers flirting with these delightful temptresses.

Street walking takes on a new meaning here. We become the streetwalker, not selling but buying. We can't help but succumb to one temptation. Our old friend 'Svensons' appears on the corner and with great glee, we scramble in and repeat the 'death-by-chocolate' trick.

FAKE DIPLOMAS
This is the place to procure the paperwork for a new life. You can have any type of driver's licence, ID card, Tertiary Diploma, etc. You name it - they'll print it.

TRESSES AND TATS

Perhaps Barb should get her hair done? The street hairdressers, three or four at a time, are busy plaiting long tresses. They twist it, they bead it, they frizz it and extend it. That boy's hair will be a big hit with his mother. Yes, coiffured sculptures are created, along with daggy dreadlocks. These street locksmiths can certainly bring things to a head.

INDIAN TAILORING
Suits, dresses, skirts, jackets. You name it, you can have it. A fraction of the price of tailoring back home.

Ask to see examples of the work. Inspect seams, linings, stitching strength and finish.

Good tailoring takes time and a few different fittings. If you really want the 24-hour tailoring, you may have to compromise on some aspects of fit and finish. Discuss this with the tailor.

Don't make the final payment until you are completely satisfied.

Tattoos are much in evidence - the blue-ink variety, not the military. Half the young backpackers seem to sport some chosen masterpiece to enhance breast, biceps, back or buttock. I wonder if these mementos of Khao San Road will eventually be regretted. I can't even think about hanging the same painting for ten years, never mind fifty years of looking at the same butterfly. Still, the boys strut around with Celtic symbols or loops of barbwire etched on biceps. The girls adorn bare midriffs with their chosen icons, even with tantalising etchings trailing beneath blue jeans down to their tail bones.

BIG NIGHTS OUT

Whilst the cabs snake through the crowds, our fellow travellers (the young variety) make savage attacks on sobriety. The Temperance League of Thailand must surely have given up any attempt at success here! Despite the obvious dedication to drinking, there are few demonstrably disorderly drunks. We, however, are rarely to be found mooching around at one o'clock in the morning, so no doubt we miss seeing any of the really drunk and disorderly. To our knowledge, there are few upsetting incidents despite the high alcohol content of the local beverages. The local police are always quietly vigilant.

However, having said all that, there is one evening when a somewhat disoriented duo swerve and stumble their way home, the local brew being a shade or two stronger than the Aussie stuff. Damn it! We had run into David and Kerry again (from Batu Ferringhi) and those backpacking kids should have known better than to let us drink and walk.

ON …ON!

What a great return trip to Bangkok. With pleasant memories, we collect our visas for Vietnam, easily organised through the tour office. We head off at day break to the Bangkok airport and Hanoi. The pre-booked and pre-paid ($4) minivan collects us for the battle with Bangkok traffic and sets us down at the correct part of the international departures terminal. Amazing really, when we had paid $58 to get a taxi into Bangkok on our original arrival.

Barb notes, 'We will go-it-alone on our next visit and arrange our own transport.' Perhaps this bravado will founder on a 2 am airport arrival.

Let's go! Vietnam beckons. We excitedly check in our small backpacks (although small enough for carry-on luggage, there is the restriction regarding scissors, etc.) Clinging enthusiastically to boarding passes and each other, we bounce around the glittering terminal stores - cameras, perfume, cigarettes, grog and bookstores. Our finely tuned 'budget' consciousness serves us well, no purchases.

Anticipation of Hanoi and our first visit to Vietnam is uppermost in our minds. The infection of airport excitement strikes again. Tales of best bargains in bed linen, vivacious people, the wonders of Ha Long Bay and shopping in Hoi An all tumble through our minds.

CHAPTER TEN

Autumn days come quickly like the running of a hound on the moor.

HANOI

'Hang about' - a good throw away expression, one would say. Not here - 'Hang about' could mean exactly that.

Hanoi provides the easiest street directory of any Asian city. 'Hang' means 'the street of', and so you get Hang shoes, Hang sweaters or Hang handbags. All we do is ask the Vietnamese word for each product and we get the hang of it pretty quickly. The Old Quarter, central city bargain basement, is crisscrossed with Hangs. After we've found one item, we simply walk down the street from shoe shop to shoe shop making price comparisons. Hang around and hang on to your hat because this is where all the good deals hang out.

We've landed safely, but hanging out is exactly what we do for the first half hour of our time in Hanoi airport. Pent up with anticipation at the Hanoi airport luggage collection, we jostle foot to foot in order to catch a glimpse of our luggage.

HANOI

The hustling, bustling capital of Vietnam since 1010, with a short break (1802 to 1945) during the Nguyen Dynasty, when it was eclipsed by the city of Hue.

Home to more than three million people, located on the Red River and speckled with soothing lakes. Vietnamese dong and American dollars are accepted everywhere.

The area around Hanoi has been inhabited for at least 3,000 years and the people are overwhelmingly honest and good-natured. Hanoians tend to be forward-looking, down-to-earth and very hard-working, particularly the women.

Hanoi was occupied by the French in 1873 and became the capital of French Indochina from 1902 until 1953. Although the last French troops left Vietnam on April 28th 1956, a strong French influence remains.

The Old Quarter, with its original 36 bustling streets (now more than 50), is the centre of the action and within walking distance to the Ho Chi Min Mausoleum and Hoan Kiem Lake.

Note that all museums throughout Hanoi and Vietnam are closed on Mondays and some on Fridays.

Like Gold Lotto balls, cases pop down onto the carousel. Hello, they both appear. We've got a winner!

We walk out of the airport into gorgeous weather where a delightful girl greets us in perfect English. 'Taxi right here, Sir and Madam,' and directs us to a waiting cab. 'Set price of $10 to the city.' This is a wonderfully smooth welcome to Hanoi. No immigration dramas, no customs hiccups - streamlined through! Transport on tap.

Our welcome to Vietnam is simple, uncomplicated, trouble-free travelling. Our bonus is sharing a cab with two chaps Barb was chatting with whilst waiting at the luggage collection. This is a cost saving ploy we use whenever the opportunity arises.

Given the hotel name, sourced from our guidebook, the cab drives straight as a die to the very place. 'Sorry, no room at the inn.' (After all, it is now 22nd December.)

'Oh, could you direct us to some other manger?' Yes, the Vinh Quang Hotel at 24 Hang Quat. Hang Quat Street (literally meaning 'fans') specialises in funerals and festivals and is choc-a-bloc with lacquer work and bright red banners. This street seems to be a suitable place to spend a week or two.

'Welcome, welcome! Sorry, some guy named Joseph has already booked the stable, but yes we have rooms usually $18 to $25 a night, only for you, $15!'

We inspect the room and I mention the spirit of Xmas and all that. I point to the star in the east and he agrees to $13 a night. What a wise man. Wonderful beds, ensuite, room the size of half a volleyball court, cable TV, fridge and a desk at which to pen this masterpiece - oops, I nearly forgot the reverse cycle air-con, which we immediately put at a Sunshine Coast settings of 25 degrees. Home was never like this. And to boot, the accommodation cost provides free internet plus breakfast and coffee whenever we want. Sheraton beware!

Our fears regarding language and communication are laid to rest. The staff speak excellent English, better than in Bangkok.

Best of all is Thu - 'Autumn' in English. (Thu could have taken the lead in 'Miss Saigon'.) She welcomes us with coffee, completes the sign-in procedures and persuasively talks about helping us get the best price for any tours we may choose to take. Personally, I'm not interested in her charm and looks at all - I really do want to go on all those touristy trips. Once again Barb smiles enigmatically.

HANOI
Hanoi is a shopping paradise for inexpensive silk, lacquerware, wood, custom tailoring and beautiful embroidered bed linen.

There are **two major shopping malls** in Hanoi - Trang tien Plaza and Vincom City Towers. Both are in the Hoan Kiem District. More fun though to trawl through the streets of the Old Quarter where Hang Gai is the main shopping street.

On the streets, it is difficult to find any women's shoes bigger than a size 40.

Sapa, a French hill station 380 km from Hanoi. Trekking enthusiasts can organise two-day trips for $50. Spectacular scenery and home to the hill-tribe people in their colourful costumes.

Ha Long Bay. Two-day trips from Hanoi for under $50. Sleep on the boat overnight.

GETTING LOCAL CURRENCY

Our pockets and purses are empty so off to the nearest ATM, 500 metres away. Greeted by an array of four machines, we are rejected by three of them. The early birds have snaffled all the Dong and it is only the 4th ATM that has reserves of Dong bills. (Other ATM's prove to be easy to find.) We push the plastic and get thousands of Vietnamese Dong for our Australian $200. Rich as Croesus, we stroll around the neighbourhood and select an inviting restaurant filled with locals.

We order veal, pork and a green garlic spinach dish with steamed rice. What a taste sensation. Superb food, great service, and all for $5. Gosh, this is a pleasant improvement from basic Thai dishes of rice or noodles.

First impressions of Vietnam? Open and welcoming - plus 'Autumn', of course. Tomorrow we'll extend our visa!

LIFE IN THE FAST LANE

Hanoi brings new meaning to life in the fast lane. We literally take our life in our hands trying to cross the road. Firstly, we have to forget everything we've been taught since primary school about road safety. Now we must train ourselves to look to the LEFT, then to the right and so to the left again. Why couldn't the Pommies have added Vietnam to their list of colonial conquests? The French influence has them supposedly driving on the right - supposedly. In truth, they come from any side they like - left side, right side, backside, down the middle or up the middle. Bus, car, motorbike, Vespa and pushbike operators all took their driving tests at the same school as Brown's cows. I think that they imagine the red and green lights are all part of the Christmas decorations.

In Hanoi, we develop a special kind of courage once only found in Evil Knievel. We step off the footpath, defined only by a kerb, because motorbikes drive on footpaths and park there too. We boldly walk slowly, I might even say blindly, across the hiving band of tarmac. Miraculously, the bikes swerve apart and around us; just like Moses and the Red Sea. It seems that no one gets hurt and no one crashes their vehicle. We can't even call out any warnings as our hearts are solidly in our mouths. But hey, that's the life of travel adventurers! The adrenalin flows.

STREET FOOD IN HANOI
Northern Vietnamese cuisine has a strong Chinese influence with stir-fried dishes and less spicy food. A specialty of Hanoi is the ubiquitous noodle and meat soup known as 'Pho' (pronounced Fur), which used to be eaten at pavement food stalls for breakfast but now is eaten at any time of the day or night. It is served at street-side cafes all over town, at low plastic tables with even lower plastic chairs. Sitting down is possible but getting up sometimes requires assistance!

Pho soup. Pho Bo is beef soup and Pho Ga is chicken. The Pho chef dunks a strainer full of pre-cooked noodles into boiling water and slides them into your bowl. Shaved ginger, spring onions and coriander go on next, followed by the raw meat, which is then cooked by the addition of a few ladles of boiling stock. On the table are various accompaniments - spring onions, red chilli sauce, sugar, vinegar and often a plate heaped high with herbs. All this for a dollar or two. You can live on noodle soups and not get bored, such is the infinite variety.

Leaving chopsticks upright in a bowl is reminiscent of incense sticks that are burned for the dead and is not considered polite anywhere in Asia.

My collective research, guidebook, internet and travel brochures had somewhat prepared me for this introduction to Hanoi traffic. A bit like someone telling me the 'Wall of Death' is easily done if I go fast enough.

Here I may survive better if emulating a tortoise, not a hare.

Mesmerised, from the safety of the footpath, we watch an aged octogenarian cross the road. Festooned with woven wicker baskets of every conceivable size and shape, she quietly insinuates herself into the traffic. Baskets hang from a bamboo pole, balance on her head, garland her neck and hang from her arms. Mid-road she drops one, which rocks and spins at her feet. With a suppleness that we lost two decades ago, she scoops up the errant item, oblivious to the swirl and sound of vehicles. Like a rock in the middle of a raging river of traffic, she eyes the eddies around her and continues peacefully to the safety of the kerb.

Traffic becomes enshrined as one of our enduring memories. Barb braces herself and I quietly call on my reserves of courage and tell myself not to be faint-hearted. Just fearlessly step into the traffic and walk with some care and dignity through any oncoming vehicles. The intrepid walkers. Mind you, this exercise is still a terrifying experience for any such timid antipodeans, so be prepared.

HANOI TRAFFIC

There are an estimated 2 million motorcycles in Hanoi owned by city dwellers and a further 500,000 motorcycles from outside of the city. Put these on the streets with all the other types of traffic, from trucks and buses to ox carts, handcarts and pedestrians and you will be getting the picture that is 'Hanoi Traffic'. The city's old, narrow streets were not designed for today's population and the meandering alleys are choked with vendors' stalls.

HANOI TOURIST ATTRACTIONS
The Turtle Pagoda, standing on an islet in Hoan Kiem Lake. Walk there via the bright red footbridge from the shore. View the 1.5 m glass-enclosed turtle, a tribute to the taxidermists' trade. Open dawn to dusk daily.

Ho Chi Min Mausoleum. Closed from September to early December each year while the body goes to Russia for yearly maintenance. No cameras, talking, short pants or other signs of disrespect while viewing Uncle Ho's body. Closed Monday and Friday and open other days from 8 am to 11 am. The One Pillar Pagoda, Ho's simple house on stilts and the Ho Chi Min Museum are located in the mausoleum's area.

The Temple of Literature. Two kilometres west of Hoan Kiem Lake on Van Mieu Street. Open 8 am to 5 pm. This well-preserved gem of traditional architecture is well worth a visit. KOTO's restaurant is opposite and serves good coffee.

The Museum of Ethnology. On Nguyen Van Thuyen Street and covering 3.3 hectares with cultural displays, including folk art performances, both inside and outside the building. Open (except Mondays) 8.30am to 4.30pm with a lunch break between 12.30 and 1.30.

VIETNAMESE PEOPLE

The longer we stay in Asia, the more enamoured we become of the winsome smiles. Flashing white teeth from the boys, delightfully unselfconscious laughter from the young girls. I never really knew what 'fey' meant but I guess it is epitomised in these elfin, smiling, happy girls. Both Barb and I are enchanted.

There is a happy serenity about the Vietnamese people. They exude, for the most part, a pleasing demeanour along with grace and charm. Their command of English surprises us as we thought that the French influence would still be very much in evidence. But no, the only remaining frogs are the carved wooden ones created with notches along their backs. They 'croak' when stroked with a stick. We talk easily with the shopkeepers and vendors, who have adequate English and are most helpful in giving directions and answering our strange questions. We eat at the ordinary street-side kitchens and here we usually resort to sign language or finger pointing.

Enchantment continues at our hotel with the four young housemaids who greet us each morning with widening smiles and hugs for Barb. Each day starts fresher and brighter because of these effervescent, smiling and laughing girls. The quick-witted and helpful boys around the hotel are equally infectiously charming.

Jauntily we set off on each day's adventures, only to be topped-up with smiles at the various places previously visited. Returning to shops where we had stoically resisted yesterday's buying temptations; we are welcomed like the prodigal son and daughter. Wide smiles, words of welcome. 'Glad to see you again, we give you the very best price.' All the while nudging each other and calling to a girl in the back storeroom: 'They come back! They come back!' They smile, giggle and touch our hands. What warm and wonderful people. We walk down the street with our purchases, bouncing and buoyant, inwardly richer from this simple encounter with these Vietnamese people. Infectious.

CHRISTMAS DE LIGHTS

Surprise! Surprise! Santa is coming. The spirit of Christmas is alive and well. Jingle bells, fairy lights and reindeers with large red flashing noses. Everywhere we are reminded that 'it's only two days till Christmas.' Our familiar western symbols of Christmas surround us, every Hang has its bandoliers of tinsel and Xmas lights. Locals in Santa suits ring their bells and prance around. 'Happy Christmas.' 'Happy Christmas.'

We hadn't imagined that the twelve days of Christmas would be so widely celebrated. Somewhat homesick and missing family, we resolve to phone home for some warm fuzzy feelings.

The toy shops are busy. Filled with bright lights and coloured decorations and with the newest kids' games piled up to the shop ceilings. Kerbside deals are done when Mum, Dad and two offspring zoom up to the shop, all sandwiched onto one Honda motorbike. Somehow, the chosen presents are loaded and the family foursome, plus parcels, take off like a modern day Dancer or Prancer.

CATHOLICS IN VIETNAM
Vietnam's population is estimated at 83 million (65% under the age of 30) and of these, about 7 million are Catholics. Most Vietnamese, including Catholics, worship their ancestors. When Vietnam was united in 1975, many of the Christians were treated with suspicion by the new government. Slowly since then, the Communist-led government has been working out a rapprochement.

On Christmas Day, the Catholic Cathedral is resplendent with many strands of fairy lights tracing down from the high spire. Outside, chairs are set out like bleachers surrounding a 4 m by 8 m candle with flickering light. Overflow worshippers fill the seats.

Inside, we are jostled by the congregation. The believers are Vietnamese, with not another white sinner in sight. The church is packed and familiar rituals are observed. Not that we can understand anything that is said (I always thought that sticking to Latin would be best.) We understand nothing until the collection 'sock' is flashed in front of us and I break the backpackers' golden rule of economy and stuff in some dollars.

Happily invested with the feeling of goodwill towards men, we 'trudge through the snow' (I only add that bit to get the Xmas card feeling of the moment). We walk briskly 3 km through the city to our target, KOTO restaurant. Eventually finding it, we try to get in, but it's Christmas Day and the place is chocka. We're pretty naïve to think that we can possibly find a table at this late hour and we should have booked.

Turning back, we hear: 'No stay, stay. We have one table left and two meals.' Flanked by two Santa-capped local boys, our Caucasian hostess smiles and beckons us into the warm hallway. 'Happy Christmas, welcome.'

The friendly waiters escort us to a small square table in the room off the hallway. Already the ambience of warmth and hospitality pervades. Simple décor, basic furniture and a traditional bar add to the friendliness. Christmas decorations grace the room and our table, even a miniature 'cracker' each. The other tables hum with goodwill and friendly nods. The patrons are mostly Western.

Our traditional Xmas dinner is served. A variety of roast meats, stuffing, gravy, potatoes and vegetables. Plum pudding rounds off the meal.

Now for the entertainment! All the staff, all in Santa hats, chefs, cooks, kitchen hands, waiters, boys and girls crowd the doorway and serenade the customers with

'Jingle Bells' - except no one has told them how to finish, so we 'Jingle Bell' for the fifth time until someone flags a halt. Two traditionally suited Santas present every guest with lollies and a wrapped gift. Opening our small gifts, we find a message, 'Have a Silent Night' and a pair of ear plugs each in a little case. Sweet.

If we imagine that we are missing a family Xmas at home, all such thoughts melt away. We toast each other with a glass of red. 'Happy Christmas, Darling, love you.'

Our meal costs us $50, duly recorded in my records, the other $50 donation put down to extra-curricular spending.

KOTO RESTAURANT.
61 Van Mieu St, Dong Da District.
6.30 am to 4 pm; 6 pm to 9.30 pm Fri, Sat and Sun.
Overlooks The Temple of Literature - worth a visit.

This is a 120-seat restaurant and internationally accredited hospitality programme that gives some very special young people a start in life. (KOTO is a registered charity.)

KOTO is one of the charities helping to break the poverty cycle amongst street and disadvantaged youth of Vietnam and graduates are highly valued. Several ministries are responsible for protection of street children in Vietnam, with the aim being to reunite them with their families - if they have families. Statistics say that there are 23,000 children living on the streets in Vietnam and 1,500 in Hanoi.

The food is fabulous. There is a relaxed restaurant upstairs and a café downstairs, and many young people now have the skills to work in top hotels and restaurants throughout the world.

MASKED AVENGERS

Is it possible that the one and only Daring Duo, Batman and Robin, had some years back visited the East along with the Lone Ranger? Daughters of the masked men ride around everywhere on cycles, motorbikes or Shanks' pony. From ear to ear and nose to throat, the girls proceed through their day-to-day activities wearing masks. Sardine-packed motorbikes sidle through the cities with Mum, Grandma and sandwiched offspring all wearing the trademark mask.

'Sensible,' I say to myself, 'how else does one avoid pollution from Hanoi to Bangkok?'

> **HANOI POLLUTION**
> At present, the air quality in Hanoi may not seem as serious as in other Asian countries. With the rapidly increasing number of vehicles - one motorbike for every two people in Hanoi – the situation is likely to get worse if no corrective measures are taken. Prevention, rather than cleaning up, is the answer for the future and a Swiss-Vietnamese Clean Air Programme is already in place.

However, my enquiries allow me an insight into this secret masked society. Not just smog and smuts but sun and suntan have to be avoided. Later in our travels, we notice beach vendors plying their trade throughout the day along the beach with slacks and long sleeved shirts under their wide brimmed hats. This also explains why we had seen long-sleeved ladies' gloves in department stores. It isn't that they are preparing for the debutantes' ball. They are worn to protect their skin whilst riding their motorbikes.

Whatever their function, the said masks are widely available in every market. Seen dangling by long ties, multi-coloured masks are everywhere. It is the flesh-coloured jobbies that initially flummox me; these dangle on their straps looking for all the world like one half of a lady's bra. I'm glad that my curiosity is eventually answered by a giggling teenager in a coffee shop. This stops me looking for lopsided girls.

HANOI ARCHITECTURE

Vietnam's colonial buildings are more than a replica of French architecture. Adapting to a different climate led to a genre in its own right.

Good examples of colonial buildings can be found all over the country and especially in Hanoi, and the General Post Office is a good example.

Few buildings in Vietnam are more than a hundred years old and unlike Europeans, the Vietnamese people don't venerate old buildings. When a Vietnamese person says that a building is 'old' they often mean that its original purpose has been preserved on that site - not the building itself.

VIVE LA FRANCE

The French colonials may have left in 1956, yet the memory lingers on.

Like a Parisian model, Hanoi houses are tall and svelte and presented beautifully, retaining a touch of the 'je ne sais quoi', of colonial French splendour. Allotments are very narrow, adding to the sylph-like effect, with road frontages as little as 3 m. The houses are therefore built up and back, up higher and back further than any cottage found in Sydney's Paddington.

In the Old Quarter of Hanoi, the hurly-burly of day-to-day life continues. Not every building is faithfully restored and painted, usually only those such as our hotel or the major business houses. Nevertheless, side by side, the hotels and the hustlers co-exist. Footpaths seem to be common property - the goods and wares of chopstick and china sellers rub shoulders with families cooking meals amidst the myriad of motorcycles.

COBBLERS

Shoe shiners are found here and there, for the most part ignoring my sandaled feet. The high-tech street-side shoe man has his powered buffer next door to the small-time repairman who only uses elbow grease. Shoe repairs of any sort are handled on the street corners. Equipped with the three-pronged shoe last like our grandfathers had, they set up business trimming new soles, stitching new uppers and tacking on heels.

WHEELER DEALERS

Bicycling is for the young or old. School kids doubling up on a bike; old people with tied-up loads of stuff. Regardless of age, these cyclists negotiate the everyday confluence of cars and motorbikes. Once again, bikes appear to range in vintage from Stone Age to maybe 50 years ago. These are bikes with stand-up-and-beg handlebars and metal handbrakes, and all vividly coloured black. They have chain guards that I thought went out with the war - WW1, that is.

The bikes creep up on us, quietly, stealthily, and even surprise us into making life-threatening side steps amongst the other traffic. Grandmas are to be seen riding with loads on their bikes the size of a fridge. Granddads have masculine accoutrements on their bikes such as lengths of plank or PVC piping, one even pedalling along with several 1 m square panes of glass, another with a large cage the size of a washing machine and stuffed with feathers. The frenetic feather ruffling clearly indicates that the chooks are still wearing them.

The millions of miles travelled on two wheels bring the blow-outs, the flat tyres and the punctures. But, ready to hand, are the kerbside Samaritans. Young or old, these servants to the deflated sit amidst their pavement paraphernalia and ply their trade. Spare inner tubes, long-stemmed hand pumps and patches all on hand, along with a basin of water ready to betray the tell-tale bubble. These mechanics of the motorways are ready to apply the perfect patch, fix broken chains and replace missing pedals - or anything else that needs repairing.

Then there is the super 'wheeler dealer', the Dunlop or the Bridgestone of kerbside entrepreneurs. He has the ultimate in high-tech equipment - not a wheel balancer, but his own compressor. Yes, a compressor on the kerb! Beside all of this is the roadside vulcanising service, carried out over a blackened, smoking flame on the pavement. Fixed up, patched up and even blown up.

WATER PUPPET THEATRE.

Hanoi is famous for its Water Puppet shows. My imagination tells me this will be the Oriental version of Punch and Judy on Ice. Yes! Melt the ice and we have a rough parallel. Traditionally dressed, metre-high wonderful carved wooden puppets depict Vietnamese folklore stories. The battles of good and evil, of local lives and loves, of poor people and princes.

This is on our 'must see' list and we're advised to book ahead to get the good front-row seats. Ensconced in our best view seats, we're ready for action. We duck and dive under the splashes and dodge the deliberate squirts of water. If it's not fishermen, it's fire-breathing dragons and lion dogs competing in feats of derring-do. It helps to take along your best child-like view of the world 'cos this is imagination at its optimum. Fun and frolics in the best pantomime tradition. Barb sits squeezing my hand.

The many stories and sagas are narrated by a boy puppet, ably and noisily supported by voices and musicians in the wings. The puppeteers, hidden by a background screen, stand in nearly waist-high water, manoeuvring submerged four metre long bamboo poles attached to the floating puppets; action is created by means of pulleys and strings.

After nearly an hour of fantasy and even fireworks, we emerge into real-life hectic Hanoi. Across the street is the fabled Hoan Kiem Lake with not a puppet in sight. Barb is still somewhat enchanted and enthralled. I tell her, 'Maybe for my taste, they should use the music from HMS Pinafore.' Let's have a beer.

WATER PUPPET THEATRE
In the Old Quarter, Roi Nuoc, Thang Long, Hanoi
Shows 6.30 pm and 8 pm daily and 9.30 am on Sundays. Admission $3 to $5. Duration 1 hour

Many tourists feel that this is a unique and entertaining show. Water puppetry is a Vietnamese art that dates back to the tenth century.

Puppeteers control the puppets from behind a screen, using long bamboo rods and string mechanisms hidden beneath the water. The skits are humorous and the show is a lot of fun.

STREET SCENES

Reds and golds and daubs of the brightest colours relieve the dreariness and monotony of side streets. Throughout the Old Quarter, we are confronted by the traditional image of the Vietnamese woman. Every 50 metres or so, a local pyjama-clad lady in pointed woven bamboo hat, balancing baskets at each end of a bamboo pole, asks us to buy pineapple, doughnuts or barbecued corn cobs. The inviting aroma of freshly grilled corn is too much for us. For a few cents, we gnaw on sweet corn and slurp pineapple on a stick.

Women and girls, men and boys canvass their territory toting various wares. Entrepreneurial youths carry boards sporting sunglasses or cigarette lighters or tote boxes of rip-off books locally copied and printed, all the popular best-sellers for a few dollars. The ever-present aged lottery sellers service the inveterate gamblers, only directing their attention to the locals. Losing tickets confetti the footpath. Leave the litter to the street cleaners.

In Hanoi, the streets, roadways and pavements have less litter than our previously visited locations. Maybe I am becoming inured to the sights of paper and plastic. Still, Hanoi has less obvious detritus and a notable absence of the more pungent street odours.

In the evenings the clang, clang of a bell can be heard. 'Unclean!' 'Unclean!' Not so. This bell means 'Clean, Clean.'

The din heralds the arrival of a hand-pushed galvanised skip about the size of four wheelie bins. The buggy is pushed by a cleaner in green smock with headscarf and face mask, who collects the plastic-wrapped kerbside rubbish from outside every house or store in the street. Every dumpster has a silver lining. Theirs is the most secure job in town. They know that every day will bring with it more paper, more plastic and more street debris.

WEIGHT WATCHERS

Weight, weight - there's more - trundling along streets and pavements, here she comes pulling a 2 m-tall slender machine balanced on small rear wheels. Digital numbers flash on the eye-level panel. Height and weight dispensed on the go and at our whim.

A deal on wheels! 'Youse pays yer money and gets yer weight and height' publicly announced. Spruiked out in a tinny loud mechanical voice for the entire world to hear and snigger at. Luckily it is in Vietnamese, but the printed ticket tells me the real truth - absolutely just what I need. I imagine that I'm bound to have lost heaps of kilos on the travelling trail and this is happily confirmed for 15 cents.

BEER DRINKING – BIA HOI

Here we are, strolling up one of the many Old Quarter streets, when we hear 'G'day mate, 'ave a beer, mate.' Three T-shirt-clad backpackers sit on impossibly small plastic chairs in a somewhat dingy street-side café. Mugs of beer are raised in a gesture of welcome. We pull up chairs and squeeze around the small table, watched by a motley group of drinkers. 'Good stuff, mate. Cheap as chips. Better than Fosters.'

Barb and I order our own 2-litre jug (less than $1). The ancient owner/barmaid grins with missing teeth and plonks two ice-cold mugs plus an overflowing jug on the rickety table. She doesn't ask for money. Still, we fish out our supply of Dong and pass the correct money via a helping granddaughter to the dingy back of the shop. Grandma stands beside a 1.5-metre-tall multi-litre drum, refilling jugs by means of a clear plastic tube. We watch as a local patron tries to get on his motorbike to go home. He stumbles, fumbles and tips himself and bike onto the road. We keep on drinking.

This is our first and fortuitous introduction to Bia Hoi. We sip our beers. The Aussie guys are right. It's good stuff, light in colour, light in taste and supposedly 4 to 4.5 percent alcohol. Not too fizzy, just brewed for easy quaffing. Like the Irish poteen makers say, 'Give the first drops to the fairies and take as much as you can for yourself.'

Bia Hoi is made daily, has no preservatives, and should be drunk the same day. It is sold in a variety of dingy cafes and we now look for the homemade sign scrawled in paint on cardboard. The easiest to find was in Ngoc Ha Street, right behind Ho's mausoleum. For the rest of our trip, we were able to spot the 'Bia Hoi' boozer shops.

They say that 'there are none so blind as those who will not see,' and that could be us. For some days, we have walked past and not seen these beer cafes, as is the case with linen shops when we are shopping madly for sheets. Clearly, our travels will have to be repeated to catch up with the rest of the things we missed - any excuse will do.

SHOP TILL YOU DROP

Bed linen, bed linen, bed linen. Our pre-trip preparations had placed this as Barb's top priority purchase. There are many items claiming the tourist's attention. Lacquerware, embroidery, art work, silk - but Barb's mission was seemingly to get enough bed linen to equip the Holiday Inn.

We trudge the streets looking for bedding shops. Looking, looking, looking. It takes us until late in the second day to find out that there are no specialist bed-linen stores but just about every other small shop sells a variety of popular style embroidered sheets. We feel a little dumb.

Barb selects from a few styles, plain and embroidered, white or coloured, king or queen, off the shelf or custom-made. We price and haggle, price and haggle and decide to sleep on our, her, decision.

Showered and refreshed, we take our list and revisit the shops. Easily accomplished, deals are done! I hire three coolies to carry the goodies home; I don't really - but I should have!

This is our shopping indulgence - an expense outside of our travel budget.

BED LINEN

The fitted sheets in Hanoi seem skimpy, so it is a good idea to measure the mattresses (including depth) before leaving home in order to have fitted sheets made. The fabrics are beautiful but choose the wider ones, otherwise a seam magically appears in the middle of the sheet.

PACKING AND POSTING

Part of our travel plans was to pack only warm climate clothes because we intended to buy suitable clothes when about to tackle the coolest regions on our trip. We found that the young travellers often do this and ship home unwanted clobber. As it transpired, we only encountered really cold weather in Hanoi.

I might add that this original 'shipping home' plan is cunningly devised by Barb. Some very adroit shopping sees the whole household of bed linen bought and packed along with our warm clothes. The packages are addressed to our son and daughter-in-law and the shipping costs are about $50 for 10 kg. To ensure sound packaging, we buy a few sturdy $4 Nike sports bags, which are then packed and in turn put into cardboard boxes supplied by the Hanoi post office and securely sealed with industrial packaging straps. Packing and posting is complete and we have two hours until our train is scheduled to leave. We're due for some summer sunshine and beaches and ready ourselves for the train trip south to Hue.

The post office despatch system worked well in Hanoi, Hoi Ann and Na Trang, with Post Office staff always boxing and strapping our existing parcels. In each case, we completed customs declarations citing the contents of each parcel. Too easy.

SERVICE WITH A SMILE

The four effervescent teenagers who tidy our room in Hanoi will always be remembered. Our mornings kick off with light-hearted laughter tinkling up the stairwell. No need for alarm clocks here. Shining smiles greet us and their infectious enthusiasm for life leaves us set-up for the day - a happy and bubbling injection of goodwill.

When we are leaving Hanoi, these girls take Barb up to their fifth-floor room where they have set out some local 'treats' for a farewell party. Just the four of them and Barb in their bedroom; one small bed for all four, and this under the washing lines because they live in the laundry. Pretty magazine pages brighten up the walls and hardly a personal possession beyond a few items of clothing and hairbrushes. What a funny party - they with no English and Barb with no Vietnamese! The Mad Hatter would have loved it. Never mind, the gesture was just wonderfully touching.

Just as we are about to go to the train, these bubbling girls press some Australian coins into our hands and stand in a row to show us their new-found English. 'WE

LOVE YOU!' I might add that at no stage during our stay had we given any of them a tip. Guilt found Barb frantically running out to buy a tin box of imported biscuits, but it wasn't about money.

OVERNIGHT SLEEPER

Once again, the hotel service turns up trumps. Not only do they handle our bookings for the two 'soft' sleepers (First Class) on the overnight train to Hue, but for a few dollars fee they had organised an extension to our Vietnam visas. All so simple. We are presented with our train tickets and visa extensions and the hotel manager insists on getting us a taxi and sending one of their staff to ensure that we get aboard safely. We are ushered to our cabin and once settled, our helper politely leaves. 'We hope to see you both again.' No money at all changes hands and we aren't even allowed to pay for the taxi.

This service spoils us. How can we ever have anything but warm feelings toward Hanoi?

We settle down in our bunks and we look forward to Hue. Our guidebook must have been written by Hue's publicity agent. We can't possibly bypass it.

Should I be more cautious? Had I not believed everything I read six days ago on the Ha Long Bay brochure? The publicity enthused about sunshine, sparkling sea, islands and a VIP boat trip. Would Hue publicity turn out like Ha.Long Bay?

CHAPTER ELEVEN

The voyage you sail is shorter in sunshine.

HA LONG BAY

Almost 2,000 towering, monolithic, limestone islands capped and cloaked with greenery and magical caves, speckled about in a pristine sunlit shining sea. Ha Long Bay is a worthy World Heritage listed sight.

Small clusters of timber and tin floating huts make up waterborne villages. Holiday kayakers skim under the craggy rock arches, swimmers frolic around romantic overnight party boats. Tourists tramp through magical caves. What a blast. It's all there in the travel brochure!

Our 'must-see' visit to Ha Long Bay is squeezed into our time in Hanoi. This unique collection of islands has long held a curiosity and fascination for both of us. Large teak junks glide across the wide waters, a mass of strikingly tall rocky outcrops sky-scraping out of a tranquil sea, an eagerly anticipated event on our travelling escapade.

'Autumn' has no trouble signing us up for a $50 each overnight VIP side trip from Hanoi. (So what if two of our fellow ship mates paid only $42 each!).

OUTWARD BOUND

Our enthusiasm is dampened a little. The tourist brochure sun-drenched, frolicking trip may not be for us. We leave Hanoi at 8.30 am, the weather is overcast and we get drizzled on when putting our overnight packs on the 12 seat transit bus. The hotel happily looks after our other luggage until we get back. We forgo breakfast and squeezing into the last available seats, set off for a three-hour ride to Ha Long. Should I say 'Too Long'?

The boats, when we arrive, are magnificent teak edifices 20 m long and 7 m wide. A whole flotilla of boats, each something like a cross between Noah's Ark and a Chinese Junk. Fly-away roof lines (like the temples) cover the spacious enclosed top deck where tables are splendidly laid with white linen and bright tableware - a welcoming sight for breakfast-less hungry travellers.

Our trusty teak ark reverses out from the midst of all the other arks. We have hopped and skipped and clambered across two to get to ours. Even with a tin hip, there are ever-helpful hands to assist. It's a great experience to see this walloping large vessel detach itself from the swarm of look-alike clones. All the boats are large, all are weathered teak timber and all glow richly in dark umber tones. Weather-proof windows surround every deck. Underneath are the overnight cabins panelled, once again, in mellow teak tongue-and-groove timber. Wonderful boats.

Our skipper adroitly shimmies our vessel out of the pack and off over the wide blue ocean. Well, it may have been wide and it could have been blue, if we could but see. The weather is at its most disagreeable. Drizzle continues and although there's no wind, the weather has turned cold. Other intrepid travellers who, we find out, live in the Swiss Alps for six months of the year, stand with anoraks zipped up to the chin. The only thing for it is to share a bottle of red, maybe two.

HA LONG BAY

This body of water covers 1,500 square kilometres and has 1,969 limestone islands, each topped with thick jungle vegetation. 989 of these islands have been given names.

Several of the islands are hollow, with enormous caves, and two of the bigger islands have permanent inhabitants along with tourist facilities including hotels and beaches.

Visibility is poor. We see shadowy islands to left and right, and are fortunate to see the unique floating villages. Clusters of small tin-roofed wooden houses, with front and side decks, float happily on the water. Through the mist, we spot two little rowboats moving across the grey water. The boys rowing are sitting back with the handles of the oars in their feet. They row as if pedalling, oars clenched with their toes, while merrily chatting to each other.

CAPTAIN'S TABLE

Lunch is served at around 1 o'clock. Prepared in the ship's galley, it is an acceptable meal, but if we want to drink anything, water, tea or coffee, this is an extra. It's remarkable that our all-found fee doesn't include tea or coffee. I feel annoyed at this, I guess because I feel annoyed at the weather. I'm disappointed at not being able to enjoy the sights I'd looked forward to for so long. I have a pain in my butt from the 3-hour bus trip. I am moderately wet and moderately cold and moderately thirsty. To cap it all off, we don't get access to our cabins until the beds are re-made and the rooms tidied. To say the least, I am moderately discombobulated.

'Calm down Grandad,' my grandson's advice echoes in my ear. I say, 'why don't we seek refuge in another bottle of red?'

Stop! Hold everything! What's this I see? Sunshine breaks through the clouds. The sea sparkles and a balmy breeze now dries up the raindrops. We pull into a shingle beach and skip down the gangplank. Above us yawns a huge cave mouth.

The weather is now warmer and, following the guide, we clamber up the rock steps and enter the vastness of the cave. Enhanced by coloured background lights, imagined shapes of limestone monkeys, elephants and other figures are to be seen on the cavern walls. Most outstanding, yes, definitely outstanding, is the 1.5 metre long penis. Penis and testicles highlighted in the political colour of the country, red. Photographers in the group are active with their digital instruments.

Like a well-trained ship's crew, we crocodile-line our way back down to the boat with our evening meal to look forward to. Dinner is a pleasant local style meal and we entertain ourselves with more red wine, crossword books, cards and patience. We had booked a VIP trip with only 16 people aboard and most were Koreans with no English - in hindsight, we should have booked on a bigger boat with more people. Early night; about 8 o'clock we're into our bunks and snuggled in the comfy doonahs.

Cocooned in silent comfort, I drowsily review our experiences so far. The places, the people, their cheerfulness, their beliefs - and what makes them tick.

RACIAL DIFFERENCES

Reflecting on the racial and religious differences we have come across, I remember the quote, 'Comparisons are odious,' or is it 'odorous'? Cautiously, I venture into a mental measurement of the various racial tendencies within the Asian countries. However, having noted the dangers associated with such ventures (Salman Rushdie springs to mind), I write with a modicum of caution.

I am emboldened by thoughts of how some western nations are categorised. The Irish are described as happy-go-lucky and loquacious (my literary agent has explained that garrulous is more apt). Their close neighbour the Scots are described as dour and careful with monies. In Wales, the men are reputed to be chauvinistic. They collect in 'men only' groups in the valleys and sing in order to get away from their wives. Whereas the English are associated with fair play and stiff upper lip, a nation of self-made people who worship their maker.

And so, with the problem of political correctness put in proportion, I marshal my thoughts. All the Asian nationalities demonstrated an ecumenical acceptance of differing religions and beliefs. Religious tolerance was inherent within all the countries we visited. All varieties seemed to seamlessly co-exist, with each accepting the differences of the other. Most surprising was the extent to which Christianity flourished along with the more traditional religions of the east.

Experiencing Christmas in Vietnam was an eye opener because everything we associate with the traditional season was echoed there. Christmas trees, Christmas lights and Santa Claus. A focal centre of festivities was the Catholic cathedral dressed like an Oxford Street store.

Everyday life sees family shrines tended with fresh offerings and newly lit joss sticks. Universally, joss sticks are the indication of people's prayers, whether in Phnom Penh or Hanoi. South Thailand and Malaysia see the Islamic presence more evident, with mosques and traditional dress styles proclaiming the people's beliefs. In Malaysia, the Islamic majority has more influence in civic affairs, yet it is here that we experience the most obvious demonstration of co-existence. In one guest house, the household has family members with Tao, Hindu, Buddhist and Christian beliefs. The Christmas tree next to the photo of ancestor next to the gold Buddha and the Hindu shrine. Eddies of joss stick smoke drift through the Christmas lights.

I drift into peaceful slumber.

8 BELLS...AND ALL'S WELL

Breakfast at 8 am - crisp bread rolls and of course that wonderful Vietnamese style coffee (which we have been striving to blend ever since). Two hours of sailing back through a watery sky to the jetty where we nudge, push and bounce our way into a gaggle of other boats. We succeed in getting our prow pushed in to the wharf where all can de-boat, and with the skill of gazelles, leap onto the slippery wet pier. We head to our bus and are whisked off to a local restaurant to enjoy a lunchtime sit down meal.

Despite all the wet weather, I am glad to have satisfied my curiosity and achieved my ambition to see Ha Long Bay. Even in the gloom, the scene was romantically stunning. Still, I wish, I wish the sun had shone for a longer period.

NOTE TO BUDGET TRAVELLERS
Check the weather forecast if undertaking a two day trip to Ha Long Bay. The cost of the trip for two was equivalent to four nights' top accommodation and our lack of foresight regarding the weather taught us a lesson. A large slice of budget money was spent on a trip seriously impacted by rain and mist.

The same rule should apply to mountain trekking, particularly with packages in the Sapa area. Bad weather had adversely affected the enjoyment of fellow hotel guests on their three day Sapa expedition and we consequently canned our intended trip.

CHAPTER TWELVE

Curiosity is the seasoning spice for travel.

HUE
Local pronunciation "hway"

A couple of garden gnomes would have loved the train's commodious two metre by three metre first-class Soft Sleeper. We ease ourselves around the space. A bit of a squeeze for Barb and me plus two American men, whose overflow family reside in the flanking cabins.

Barb and I have scored one top and one bottom bunk. Calling upon years of cunning, I flop into the bottom bunk and Barb, being more agile, nimble and lithe, has offered to use the top one.

Our fellow-travellers prove to be good sports and highly competitive card games ensue. Gambling on Patience is introduced; something akin to a blood sport, but my Barb is more than a match for Uncle Sam.

Patience having run out, and scared of turning into pumpkins, we make up our narrow beds with the crisp white sheets provided, fumble for our 'Silent Night' earplugs and snuggle down. Night-time visits to the loo punctuate the 12-hour trip. Returning from any nocturnal visit to the toilet is a bit like Russian roulette, particularly when you blindly open a wrong door or two. We snooze our way south.

After a somewhat fitful night, we are reassured by knowing we will be met by car from our internet pre-booked accommodation in Hue. Attempting to restrict any bus trips to under 5 hours, our plan is to use train or plane for the longer journeys. The storybook appeal of Hue in our guidebook suggests that it would be a logical break point on our travels south.

Big sign, 'Welcome Gettinbys' held up, and we are whisked away to our new dwelling. This is a level of convenience most acceptable to train-tired travellers. A nice welcome to Hue.

Romantic Hue. One-time capital of Vietnam. The forbidden city and Citadel, home to the Emperors. Spacious streets, bridges and boulevards. And, Dragon Boats colourfully, proudly, gaudily gracing the Perfume River.

Our first day in Hue gives us outstanding summer weather; we've left our hats back in our digs, so we top up (so to speak) with new ones at $2 each.

PICK-UP FROM THE STATION

If organising accommodation in advance, it is always worth a try to ask for pick-up at the bus or train station. Often guest house owners are happy to do this, especially if you are staying for a few days.

The Citadel beckons. Two hundred years old, the outer moat and enclosure has a perimeter of 10 kilometres - joggers and walkers frequent the boundary path. Most things in Hue are on a wide and gracious scale. Not so with the entrance to the Citadel. The gateway is narrow and pedestrians and vehicles squeeze to get through the portals. We don't have to pay to enter the Citadel but happily cough up $6 to enter the Forbidden City. American bombing has obliterated most of the site, but we inspect the remaining five percent. Restoration is ongoing.

HUE

Hue is recognised as a World Cultural Heritage Site by UNESCO in 1993 and has become a big and invaluable museum.

This city is an important centre of Buddhism with pagodas built 300 years ago still in existence.

The royal mausoleums of Nguyen kings on the banks of the Perfume River are mighty impressive and are open to visitors.

From 1802 until as recently as 1945, the city of Hue temporarily took over from Hanoi as capital of Vietnam and the Nguyen dynasties of Emperors lived, ruled and subsequently were buried here.

Imperial pavilions, with their many examples of gold and jewel encrusted robes and swords, show how the Emperor, his family and servants lived. Hire a costume, sit on the painted throne with plastic headdress, and pout for the camera. A modern-day emperor. Push the many dressed-up day-glo children out of the way to get your photo taken first. Sip a cold drink, lick an ice cream and wonder how such a philistine act as the destruction of the Forbidden City could have been allowed to happen in the twentieth century.

The surrounding grounds are a sunburned wasteland, and shadowy chequerboard outlines of the original palaces push up through the grass and weeds.

We stroll in a leisurely fashion around the massive buttressed walls of the Citadel and gawk at the 4-metre-long ancient bronze cannon. Being absolutely sunburned and bushed, we each take a bicycle-powered rickshaw, the Vietnamese Cyclo, and head back to the city centre. Have rickshaw seats become smaller or has something happened to our backsides?

We are most impressed to see boatmen collecting floating rubbish from the riverside. This explains why the wide, peaceful Perfume River is so clean. It is a beautiful expansive waterway, well used by the Dragon Boats that ferry tourists for day trips to various emperors' temples and tombs. The boats have big dragon heads on the prow, brilliantly coloured in the Asian way.

We stroll in the park beside the Perfume River. 'Barb, better not walk under that shady tree, the pretty red and yellow snake was there first.' It's wonderful to observe how a girl brought up 'in the bush' can jump so high. We watch the snake harmlessly disappear and stroll on.

My curiosity about competitive accommodation prices sees me calling in to five or six mini-hotel style places along the Hue river front boulevard. With little or no bargaining, we could have had a well appointed room in about four of these with an average price of $15/$16.

HOME TO THE SUBURBS

Our guest house in Hue is outside the city centre, so we decide to walk home. Hence, and alas as luck would have it, we get lost in the boondocks of Hue and walk for many miles around the local suburban roadways. Our meanderings are punctuated with delighted cries of 'Hello' 'Hello.'

Every few metres, 'Hello' Hello.'

The children from three years old call out, 'What is your name?' Their bell-like voices ask, 'Where do you come from? Ahh - Ahh - Kangaloo.' Mothers show us their babies; the smiles are infectious and wonderfully winsome. Their babes in arms, usually with astonished expressions, get their hands pumped up and down 'Bye Bye.' These moments linger fondly in our minds.

HIGH FASHION

During our walk, we see every variety of ladies' fashion. Dress style, with Vietnamese ladies, revolves around colour and pattern and the women express it in their pyjama-like costume. Some of the very old and stooped ladies stick to their little basic black numbers, perhaps in readiness for a cocktail party. The rest of the ladies and girls express themselves in colours and floral patterns of every hue and design, and I'm convinced that my mother had curtains made from similar materials.

Everyone uses the same sewing design, perhaps Butterick Number Two Pyjama Style, and there seems to be little or no variation in the cut. Age seems to bring with it a sense of drabness, but the younger women span the spectrum of colour. The effect is one where you feel that everyone is just getting up from bed or is just about to lie down. In the middle of the day and in the middle of a bustling market, you are confronted by the image of 'Wee Willy Winkies'. Perhaps the pyjama look is sensible because the Vietnamese seem to be working night and day.

The stark contrast is the Ao Dai, the body-hugging tunic that flows over wide trousers and is the Vietnamese women's national costume. Some larger commercial businesses and schools encourage the girls to wear the Ao Dai. Stunningly elegant, this costume contrasts strongly with the pyjama look. One cannot but be in awe of the grace of the Vietnamese woman wearing her national dress. The glimpses of young girls in all-white

Ao Dais cycling along together is part of the stark contrast that is Vietnam.

Bamboo hats are in evidence everywhere, perhaps more common in Vietnam, where the simple conical design could easily become a national symbol, something like the Aussie boomerang. The bicycle riders, the market stall owners and the ladies with the balanced baskets on bamboo poles are all wearing the unique style hat - a very strong image of Asia. Regrettably, it seems that the younger people have a preference for cotton sunhats or baseball caps. Let us hope that the conical bamboo hat can maintain its presence and iconic status.

However, we are still lost and are now fed up with aimlessly walking the suburbs of Hue. As luck would have it, we are guided home by three beautifully mannered teenage boys who are now wheeling their bikes. One of the 'guides' offers Barb a seat on his bike while he pushes her, she laughingly declines - he was a very skinny boy after all. They practise their English on us and deliver us safely back to the bosom of our stylish guest house.

PILLION MOTORBIKE RIDING
It is better to hold on to the driver's waist when riding as a passenger because holding the shoulders puts the driver off balance - not a good thing to have happen.

DRAGON BOATS

Dragon boats and the Perfume River beckon, so we book a trip for the next day. This we accomplish through our ever-helpful host at our Bella Gardens guest house. $3 for the all-day trip with lunch included. Yep! $3 with lunch! And that's not all, transport to and from the boats thrown in.

Often the best way to overcome self-doubts is to be confronted with them. So it is that we come face to face with our doubts about doubling on the back of motorbikes when our transport for the Perfume River trip arrives promptly next morning in the guest house courtyard. Two motorbikes, one ridden by a slip of a girl - maybe only a half slip. Come to think of it, the boy wasn't much bigger. This is our 'moment of truth'. I should rephrase that to our 'do or die' moment - no helmets offered, of course! Stoically and with a fixed glazed look, Barb sits on the pillion seat and I follow her brave lead with my driver.

Five minutes later, and with a joyous feeling at having survived the ruts and potholes, we are safely delivered into the jaws of the dragon boat.

The gangplank whiplashes us onto the deck. Red eyed, green nosed, filigreed and frilly scale-necked, the dragon boat welcomes us. Fifty look-alike boats surround us. We settle in and the 'navigator in chief' pops out of the cabin at the back. Clutched in her weathered hand is a menu that is presented to each passenger in turn. Everyone selects their lunch and pays the listed price. My ever-vigilant Barbara turns back the bottom of the menu where, in small print, the all-inclusive meal is shown. A delicious spread of noodles, rice, meat and vegetables is served at lunchtime. No need to pay extra, the river trip is inclusive of lunch.

Feeling good about picking up on the food-ordering scam, we sit back and are joined on board by a local lady with a big basket. As soon as we take off, the basket opens and a wardrobe of clothes springs out. One has to be strong willed and resolute to resist them. Before the lady jumps off at the first stop, I am sporting a new $5 linen Nehru shirt, still one of my favourites.

For half the trip, we enjoy a repeat of the previous day's warming sunshine. A pagoda and five or six tombs are visited during the river trip. After the first three we skip the rest, suffering severely from temple and tomb overkill. We stay on board and babysit a couple of Aussie kids, the parents seemingly overjoyed to get a break. Our return trip sees the start of light showers. Safely back, courtesy of the motorbikes, we happily shelter in our guest house from the now continuous heavy rain that keeps us housebound. Outlying streets are now literally knee-deep in water. Perversely, we enjoy the rain because we haven't really seen much of it on our trip, certainly not this kind of downpour.

PERFUME RIVER TOUR
The journey takes about 6 hours, from 8 am to 2 pm, and costs only $3 including lunch.

Entrance fees to some of the tombs are extra.

The tours take in the Thien Mu Pagoda and several of the Nguyen Dynasty royal tombs. The extravagant mausoleums were constructed along the Perfume River and are situated from 2 km to 16 km south of Hue.

FLOODED IN

By good fortune, our lodgings offer all the luxuries of home. We are staying in a modern, stylish guest house built in the fashion of French colonial. We enjoy home cooking morning, noon and night, courtesy of the lady of the house who is Vietnamese/French. We catch up with our reading and test our 'patience' with a deck of cards each. We learn new card games from two other house-bound New Zealand guests. The moral is to travel with packs of cards and two Kiwis in the hip pocket!

In Hue, we pay more than usual for our accommodation ($15) but have free internet, free breakfast and free taxis to and from the town centre. For the three-course lunches and dinners, we are charged $2 a head. Interestingly, the guest house proprietor thanks us for babysitting the children while we were on the river trip. How did he find out? Small town this Hue.

Our time in Hue is due to end and slightly dampened but not downhearted, we casually book our bus to Hoi An, the city of suit-makers.

Something tells me that this next stopover could cost us a lot of money. Bed linen purchases in Hanoi could pale into insignificance beside this new threat. I am happy that our day-to-day travelling is roughly within budget and any new clobber will be put down to 'extra-curricula expenses'. Hoi An is where Barb's unfettered personal indulgences could affect our balance of payments back home.

Barb sweetly emphasises to me that any modest purchases are a separate matter to our daily budget target. 'Don't worry, darling. Anything I buy will be swiftly sent home. You don't have to carry them. Now take your backpack down to the car and let's get going to Hoi An.'

CHAPTER THIRTEEN

Let your bargain suit your purpose.

HOI AN

Those who cannot resist a bargain should visit Hoi An under advice. Shirts, slacks, dresses, shoes - you name it, it's here. You want it, they'll make it. There are more Singers here than at La Scala. It must be in this town that the expression 'Stitch you up' was coined. Order it at breakfast and wear it to lunch. Henry Ford would be astounded at these production lines.

Excitement, as usual, on arriving for a new adventure in a new place. With this rush of adrenalin for new things, God only knows how we've managed to stay married to each other for so long.

In Hoi An, the bus conveniently stops outside a likely hotel which is moderately priced and we bargain our way into a smart twin room for $8 a night. It has a pleasant ambience overlooking a walled garden 1 km out of Hoi An central. The next day, however, we sacrifice this for a simple ensuite room close to the markets in the very centre of the Hoi An action where we don't have to walk so far to 'save' money on all the bargains.

HOI AN

Thirty kilometres from Danang - Originally known as Faifo, this antique town is bordered on its southern side by the Thu Bon River. Despite the fact that it is now a tourist haven, the artistic atmosphere and friendly local people make Hoi An special.

Hoi An was an important port, developed in the 17th century, with canals parallel to the streets where merchandise could be loaded straight from the backs of houses onto boats. During the early part of the twentieth century, the river became silted up, forcing the cargo ships to call at Da Nang instead.

You will notice the relative silence in Hoi An because there are few cars and people do not feel the urge to use their horns every two seconds. The streets are filled with the hum of voices and the shuffling of thongs along the ground. The town is small enough to get around on foot.

After we've re-settled into our new guest house, we inspect Hoi An at a more leisurely pace. We steel ourselves for the onslaught of shop owners, who are very persistent. Smiling faces almost drag us into 'my shop'.

Old Chinese saying: 'Beware the smile of the shopkeeper.' Almost all travellers quickly learn of Hoi An's reputation as the city where clothes are made quite inexpensively and the sales people are very pushy.

PURCHASING PASTIME

In Vietnam, buying stuff and posting it home has become part of our holiday agenda. Friends have told us of the cities where we can secure great bargains, and this is Numero Uno. Today we're targeting silk cushion covers and maybe trekking trousers with the zip-off legs. Barb's heart is set on low-cost shoes and mine on rip-off Birkenstocks, shirts and slacks. There is a plethora of purchase possibilities; let's hasten slowly.

Learning in the school of hard knocks, we refine our buying approach. We have to overcome the whimsical need to buy something cute and unique:

1. We have to carry it or spend money to send it home.
2. When back home, we have to dust it.
3. In two years' time, we will donate it to the jumble sale.

By error not trial, we know that the first price asked is obviously not the lowest. Our bargaining is handled with goodwill and neither party feels put upon. We all imagine that we come out winning and there are mostly smiles and good humour. But the business of bargaining can be brutal. Barbara becomes a bit fazed by the process, wanting to give them their profit, whereas I quite enjoy the process of the bartering, the cut and thrust of high commerce.

Adventurers will gauge their own comfort level of balanced, fair barter. A street seller starts at, let's say, $20. I say 'No, too much.' (I don't even want it!)

They say 'OK, $15.'

I say, 'It's quite cute but it's too much.' (I still don't want it.)

'OK. How much you give?'

I say something stupid like '$5'.

'Oh, Oh cannot do.'

I say 'Thanks, see ya', and as I walk off they say, 'OK you give me $8.'

At $7, I am usually suckered into some object I never really wanted to start with - jumble sale stuff.

Desmond: zero points. Street Seller: 10 points.

Shopkeepers have a healthy tourist margin built in and will always aim high, taking full advantage of a good profit from the unsuspecting. I try to say no gently but firmly and laugh with them. An acceptable get-out is 'maybe later'.

My examples of buying trousers in a tailoring shop are:

1. Start price of $24 and an eventual price of $14 for Italian cloth.

2. Start price of $14 and eventual price of $8 (non-crush cloth).

I feel, each time, a need to bargain but also to test the level at which they still make a profit for their efforts.

BARBARA'S VIEWS ON BARGAINING

The business of bargaining is complex, and Barb's bargaining leaves her stressed and fractious. In supportive mode I ask, 'What's wrong?'.

'Don't ask me how I feel! I'm stressed. I'm harried. I'm hassled. I'm having nightmares about "You buy just one more shirt". I don't want another bloody shirt. I've ten bloody shirts already. Just tell them to leave me alone. Nobody pressures me like this in Myers. What's wrong with them? I just want a drink and a sleep. Don't you start to tell me what I should buy, what would you know? You go and buy your own bloody stuff.'

'Oh, Des, that reminds me, I should just check out that little shoe shop on the corner. Will you come with me and help bargain?'

Say no more!

BICYCLE BUILT FOR 'TOW'

Accustomed now to unusual sights, we think that nothing will astound us. Never say never.

While we're enjoying a pleasant coffee beside the Thu Bien river docks in Hoi An, we witness an accomplishment to match the building of the pyramids. We spot a trishaw-style contraption, one bicycle wheel at the rear and two wheels at the front, supporting a tubular-framed cart. The proud owner scuttles between vehicle and boat. We sip our Vietnamese coffee.

The riverboat is unloading an assortment of hardware stuff, sufficient to stock a Bunnings warehouse. In turn, the three-wheeled cart is being stacked with miscellaneous merchandise. Flat boxes are laid on the bottom, parcels stacked on top - front and back. When the cluster of goods gets taller than the owner's head, we know that he must be finished. How else can he see over the top and pedal too?

Not so. The solid mass of hardware gets taller, wider and longer. Ironing boards, plastic buckets, curtain rods and garden hoses all thrown up and tied on. Now he looks finished. No, no. Baskets are strung on the sides, shovels and hoes and rakes come up from the docks and are miraculously applied to the already bulging load.

We finish our coffee, but stay seated, transfixed. Now it's impossible to see or cycle from behind. With a look of accomplishment, our erstwhile owner goes to the front and fetches two more ropes from under his trolley; he puts them over his shoulders and trails his three-wheeled vehicle off into the sunset.

AGE-OLD ACCOMMODATION

Our perambulations in Hoi An take us to an Oriental-style ancient lodging house combining antiquity with Chinese culture. A true piece of old Hoi An is the Minh A guest house on Nguyen Thai Hoc. An experience in sleeping to tell our kids about; romantic and rustic and on the cutting edge of the travel experience - or is it the blunting edge. This is the stuff of storytelling. The teak-timbered stairs and wall panelling ooze with history. We can easily imagine old Mandarins sitting amidst the weathered walls smoking their pipes of opium - if we breathe deeply, we could well get some residual passive effect.

Traditional manners are observed - shoes off as we step through the heavy timbered portals onto the worn terracotta tiles. Grand panelled walls of dark chocolate wood exude the feeling of antiquity. Well-worn blackened stairs lead to the high panelled bedrooms with ornate, heavy fretwork at ceiling height. The major concession to modern-day comfort is the spotlessly clean shared bathrooms. These are tastefully secreted behind teak timbered doors. This old Chinese-style lodging house portrays the grace of a bygone age.

'Sorry, all rooms taken. Maybe later.' We content ourselves with our current accommodation, but next trip we will be sure to book into the Minh A, live a bit of history and soak it all in for a few nights.

TOURIST TICKETS HOI AN
Around $7 buys a ticket at one of the prominent booths to cover admission to any five historic sites.

We didn't bother with this and decided to pay-as-you-go at the particular attractions that interested us. The choice is yours, although wording on some information boards makes it appear that the 'ticket' is compulsory.

TOURIST TYPES

People-watching absorbs me whilst in Hoi An. Here I am doing what I do best, sipping a beer in a local Bia Hoi hostelry while Barb is a few doors away. (Yes, you knew she'd be shopping.) I'm leaning on my elbows watching this wonderful world in front of me, and I notice three distinct types of tourist. First the culture and antiquities buff, then the tourist who dawdles through the market stalls, and finally the 'pushed for time, I've got to get the best bargain' person.

The first type, the classic well-travelled and culture-seeking type, is easily recognisable by the single reflex camera slung around the neck and is often accompanied by partner, also with camera. Our seekers of ethnicity amble slowly, with practiced gaze directed at temple roofs, gates, timber portals and all things relating to antiquity. They pause, peruse the guidebook and tick off the relative historic edifice. They must check their scorecard at the end of each day.

The second and third distinguish themselves by their relative speeds. One lot meander and weave slowly along footpaths, gazing furtively into every shop and every road-side market stall. They have their antennas up like kids on a treasure hunt. They know that somewhere amidst this plethora of merchandise, there is a jewel of a bargain just right for them. These people are practised shoppers and manage to adopt a glazed yet nonchalant look, which is to deter the shopkeeper from detecting any measure of interest, any second glance or any buying signal.

The third group is in a hurry, with a determined look and a lengthened stride. Looking neither right nor left, they power-walk against time. The fitting for their newly ordered suit or shirt was ten minutes ago and they only have half an hour to pick up their new shoes. Plastic bags bulging with Haute Couturier swing at their sides. Will they be able to get back to their rooms and pack their bags and still make their departure time?

It may comfort readers to know that Barb and I cross into all three distinct types with consummate ease.

Maybe my memories of Hoi An are more vivid and more numerous because of the time we languish there. Languish is a word used for the periods of inactivity between getting measured up and going for subsequent fittings. And so it falls, mostly to me, to look around a lot.

NOT PEDDLING - PEDALLING

Pedalling comes in a couple of categories. One, the hum and whirl of the sewing machines' foot pedals, sounding like bees breeding. Every market centre, every clothes shop and in Dickensian back rooms - the sound of hives at work.

The other pedalling is of the bicycle variety. Bicycles to right of you and bicycles to left of you drift and wander. Seemingly every man, woman and child in Hoi An has a bicycle. If they are too young to ride, they cling on somewhere, somehow to someone else. They have perfected the art of tandem-cycling on one bike. It isn't uncommon to see three on a bike, two of whom have their feet on the pedals, pushing in unison. Geriatric octogenarians proceed calmly with stately grace on their ancient iron steeds through the throng.

Traffic here is benevolent, less hectic, less frenetic and with fewer motorbikes. From an early age, every road user is trained to take little notice of anyone else and everyone has right of way. No one has wing mirrors. No one cares what is behind them and they don't seem to care what is in front of them. They just proceed. They drift forward. No one gets bumped and no one gets bruised.

Bicycle and motorbike co-exist in some sedate mystical fluid motion.

TO MARKET, TO MARKET

The Hoi An markets are a special experience, serviced from the local countryside by way of an adjacent river and by the ubiquitous bike loaded with huge bundles of produce. The markets thrive, hum, buzz and bustle. Narrow access ways wind through piles of produce in every shape, size and colour. Market ladies hunker down beside their wares and each successive stall or basket seems to differ little from the one next door.

Everything a housewife or restaurateur needs is here under one roof. Fresh produce literally at your fingertips - or even your toe tips. Fishmongers and butchers' blocks have their allotted zones. Fish, vegetables, meat, dry goods and kitchenware; supermarket planning at its best, and all this colourful collection under one roof, awning, or tarpaulin. Just stop and listen, a warbling of sound, a fluttering of voices, perhaps the sound of a chook yard, but certainly a pleasant and comforting sound of an Oriental market at work.

FAST FOOTWORK

Teenagers in Vietnam just love to play Jianzi. No huge green-grassed oval needed. No timber-floored court. Groups of young men or boys kick a 15-cm-long, woven bamboo shuttlecock device back and forth. They gather indiscriminately, anywhere on footpaths amidst the cut and thrust of daily life.

A circle is formed and the Jianzi shuttle is kicked from one player to another. The shuttle is flighted back and forth from random player to random player. It rarely touches the ground and lithe athletic movements keep it in the air, knees, hips, head, anything but hands. With all the skill of jugglers, these boys entertain themselves and astound those westerners who watch. If these guys decide to enter the soccer World Cup, I hope Australia doesn't come up against them.

CAO LAU

Some things appear to be common to particular towns or districts. In Hoi An, we cotton on to a pork noodle dish called Cao Lau, renowned as a specialty of the city. Particularly good value, we eat it for breakfast most mornings and sometimes for lunch and dinner too.

Nutrition-conscious Barbara seems to be parroting my mother with 'You must eat your greens', an almost daily mantra. Cao Lau provides a well rounded, nutritious and flavoursome meal. Noodles with heaps of various local greens and slices of pork in a meaty broth with crispy won ton and pork crackling on top. All this for $1.

This meal indeed meets a couple of objectives. Barb's fetish about greens. My fetish about budget. Taking my tongue from my cheek, I can say that our choices are influenced by flavour and satisfaction. Four internet screens beside our usual table in our favourite restaurant is just one more reason to enjoy Cao Lau.

OLD TOWN SITES

Hoi An being an old city and a UNESCO world heritage site, we delight in visiting the many aged buildings and enjoy retracing our steps through the ancient Japanese bridge. We soak up history by osmosis. Both of us do the travellers' tango through the guidebook sites plus the various market stalls, and even I end up racing against time to pick up the best-buy trousers Barb said I 'had' to have. My initial order and measurements took place while I was musing to myself 'If you put a silk dress on a goat, he is still a goat.'

Before leaving Hoi An, we visit the local Post Office armed with our $4 sports bag stuffed with loot and it is an easy process to send it all to Oz.

We are ready to leave the cute city of Hoi An and bus it to the dive capital of Vietnam, Nha Trang. Sea, sun and sand beckon.

SUCKED IN

Some people never learn. Well, I didn't. Whilst sitting quietly with Barb at breakfast enjoying our Cao Lau noodles and watching the river boat men unload their wares on the old docks on the Thu Bon River, I was lulled into a warm complacency. The young waitress was in giggles at our attempts at the local language and we happily sipped our treasured mug of Vietnamese coffee. We exchanged travellers' tales with a similarly aged, extensively travelled couple who had wandered for three months through China and now Vietnam. They told of the good deals they had arranged with the friendly local tour guide whose office was in this very same café.

Encouraged and impressed by their obvious travel experience and stated success and frugality, we dealt with their tour mentor. He explained departure times and duration for an overnight bus trip to Nha Trang, our next port of call and yes, he could book the trip for us. We'd be picked up at our hotel at exactly 6.20 pm. Only 35 customers on a 45-seater sleeper bus - plenty of room. Only $8 each, very good deal!

Come in, spinner! We book the deal. Firstly the pick-up time changes from 6.20 to 4 pm, then the transport pick-up changes from minivan to the back of a moto (motorbike). The bus leaves 30 minutes late and we have paid $2 more than our fellow travellers. There is some light at the end of the tunnel though, great leg room and the bus stops three times on the journey, now that's a relief! The comfort stop cafes sell bowls of noodles - great if you've got the mid-trip munchies. We find that stops are regular, maybe because of the baksheesh received from the various rest stop shops.

Ocean breezes, sea-side ambience, fresh lobsters, and all the fruits of the sea beckon us. Nha Trang, here we come.

HOI AN SOUP SPECIALTY

Cao Lau is a Hoi An tradition and is supposedly only authentic when made with water from a special well just outside of town.

RECIPE

300 g pork
2 cups hokkien-style noodles
2 cups bean sprouts
4 cloves garlic
1 teaspoon Chinese five spice
1 tablespoon soy sauce
1 teaspoon sugar
1 teaspoon chicken stock powder
Paprika used for colour
1 cup water
Lettuce and Asian greens
Pepper
Spring onions
Deep fried pork crackling

METHOD

1. Heat oil and paprika
2. Fry pork with smashed garlic, soy, chicken stock powder and spices for 3 minutes
3. Add 1 tablespoon water and fry for a further 2 minutes
4. Remove from heat and set aside
5. Heat rest of water and cook noodles for 2 minutes
6. Put noodles in a bowl on top of lettuce, sprouts and Asian greens. Add pork, chopped spring onions, pepper and pork crackling.

CHAPTER FOURTEEN

May the holes in your net be smaller than the fish in it.

NHA TRANG

Good morning, Vietnam.   Well, good morning, Nha Trang.

The Monaco is our new home.   Comfortably, we settle in.   Bathroom with BATH.   Barb has been suffering serious withdrawal symptoms.   And, wonder of wonders, a shower curtain.   Whilst I am reflecting on the luxury of the self-same shower curtain and no wet floors, I notice that the previous guest has dislodged the bracket holding up the showerhead.   Bugger it!   The shower curtain could end up being useless.   Barb's 'she'll be right' attitude comes to the fore.   Resilient as ever, she announces that she couldn't care less about the showerhead as she intends to permanently wallow in the bath.   And here I am thinking that we are working as a team.   But more of this later.

Our new town, Nha Trang; it's 6.30 in the morning and our comfortable overnight-bus experience is behind us. Following Barb's adventurous lead, we arrive without any advance bookings.   The tour bus stops outside its tour office, a hotel. We price their rooms and inspect three. We pummel the pillows and bash the beds. The place is neat and clean but the $10 room is up the stairs on the fourth floor and as yet I haven't got my oxygen bottles! If push comes to shove, we will at least have a bed; but we decline to book in and tell them we are looking for something cheaper and closer to the ground.

NHA TRANG
This coastal city has 300,000 inhabitants and retains its small town atmosphere.

The town is flanked by 10 km of beautiful beaches and the average temperature is 26 degrees centigrade.

A great place to have a beach break, and offshore islands offer some of the best diving in Vietnam.

SUN, SAND AND SEA

We leave our bags with this guest house (most places are happy to do this) and stroll 200 metres closer to the beach and find a better hotel, again at $10. We try to negotiate $8, unsuccessfully, and go on our way looking for a lower price or better hotel.

After checking the third place, we come to the conclusion that the $10 deal in the second hotel is hard to beat so go back and book in there. We had made the decision to come to Asia faster!

We opt for the first floor balcony-room with views into trees and palms. This 'home-away-from-home' for the next four or five days is 50 m from a well-kept and gardened esplanade fringing the beach and surf.

Remarkable what a beach and a blast of sunshine will do to lift the spirits. Clear skies, blue sea, green headland and islands dotted offshore. We have arrived in the diving Mecca of Vietnam, and the surrounding streets sport numerous businesses devoted to diving trips and tours. Personally, Barb and I revel in the thought of lounging with block-out and book on the beach. We toss up whether or not to buy two beach mats and quickly decide in favour of the hired sun lounges.

After reconnoitring the neighbourhood and a leisurely lunch, we are back at our hotel for an afternoon nap to recover from the fitful night's sleep on the bus.

Scribbling details of our trip, I sit on the spacious balcony flanked by golden cane palms and look out over the coconut and pepperina trees. I feel that I must not resort to clichés; but 'All is not what it seems'; 'You can't judge a book by its cover'; 'All that glisters is not gold'; and 'There's no fool like an old fool' ... At least one of these certainly applies to me.

DIVING OFF NHA TRANG

World renowned for its spectacular swim-through caves and outstanding colours from the unique biodiversity of hard and soft corals.

The majority of the dive sites are within a 1 hour boat ride (15 minutes by speedboat), from Nha Trang to the stunning nearby islands of the Hon Mun Marine Park.

Some of the best diving in the South China Sea is here, with some of the favourite spots being Rainbow Reef, Madonna Rock, Moray Beach and Goat Rock.

ALL WASHED UP

Before I settle for my much-needed afternoon nap, I take a shower. Well, I did organise management to fix the shower holder, so I boldly enter the bathroom. Carefully arranging the shower curtain to protect the floor, I hold the showerhead until the water runs hot, put it into the recently fixed bracket: water spouts upwards towards the ceiling. The wall bracket is upside down! Bugger! Cleverly, I manipulate the showerhead so it'll spray me and let water deflect off the curtain into the bath. Wrong! I get washed OK, but the water goes straight through the non-waterproof shower curtain and onto the floor and the bathroom floor is flooded. Usual status quo retained!

Now it's bath time for Barbara. She preens and parades and fluffs out the towels, she gets her gear ready, she confronts the sought-after comforts of a leisurely lazy soak in the tub, her joyously awaited hot bath. The taps are turned on and the plug put in. Ha! I get a modicum of light relief. The hot water runs out with only 10 cm of water in the tub, and to add insult to injury, the plug leaks. I guess the score is even.

SILENCE IS GOLDEN

'Silence is golden.' What is meant by that? Come to Nha Trang and find out.

Despite the shortcomings of the bathroom, we have a lovely room, spacious and airy, beautifully tiled and decorated. We are mad about the view. At peace with the world. No, no - not so. The stillness is shattered at 5.30 pm by a cacophony of martial music and political doctrine. A brittle mechanical female voice is force-fed at a zillion decibels through a Tannoy system 70 m from our hotel. Honeyed words (my foot!) are ululated across the holiday quarter and beach esplanade. Female and male voices alternate and preach the gospel according to Lenin or Ho. Of course this is for the benefit of the populace, not we weary fagged-out foreigners. We had thought that capitalism was alive and well, a market economy. Perhaps it is, but squeezed in between this is evidence of old-fashioned Bolshevik doctrine.

And it bloody well wakes us up at 6 am the next day too. We ask the hotel what it is all about and it is apologetically explained away as government's or an older person's thinking. There is a clear inference that everyone will be better off without it. Notwithstanding, we will be subjected to it at least twice a day, morning and afternoon for about one and a half hours a session. It certainly is noise pollution of the very worst kind. We had previously tried to pick lodgings away from mosques because of the loudspeaker calls to prayer. Well, I am certainly praying this time that the pole with the Tannoy system will disintegrate and take its music and ministrations with it. We feel sorry for the hotel owner because we have no option but to move.

FRENCH LEAVE

My habit of calling into nearby hotels to check prices has some rewards. Rocking into the lobby of one such hotel, we meet a French couple who are booking out - they have found a place for $8 a night 200 metres up the road. They extol the virtues of the new hotel - twin room with two queen beds, etc, etc. Walking with them, we too are going to check it out. One good turn deserves another so I help with one of their two-tonne backpacks. This couple is on holiday for three weeks and could have supplied an Everest expedition with their gear; three backpacks and two daypacks, with a shoe shop of flippers and boots swinging somewhere underneath. Bon chance.

When they show us their room, we promptly see the merits in making a move ourselves. Trudging back to our sound-blasted digs, we are filled with remorse at the thought of telling the very kind owner that we are leaving. We think of staying just one more night but speedily strengthen our resolve to leave before the start of the evening session of martial marching music. The hotel owner is dignity personified, he smiles and says that he understands and graciously hands over our passports and money belt from his safe. And so, off to our new $8 lodgings at No 36, right on the handsome Tran Phu Boulevard alongside the esplanade.

Nha Trang beach suits us well and is only 100 metres from our hotel. The esplanade is wide and spacious with shade trees, cared-for lawns and neat paths. Coiffured trees, flat topped as if groomed by giraffes; others trimmed in the shape of pyramids with lopped-off tops, interspersed with tropical coconut palms. Altogether a sea frontage any town would be proud of. And all of this parallel to a busy boulevard that whisks traffic somewhat sedately (if this is ever the case in Asia) beside the sea front.

Nha Trang is dominated by its beachscape and by majestic municipal buildings and a few hotels fronting the boulevard. The rest of the town creeps back through streets lined with tour offices, cafes, modest dress shops and small hotels. The nightlife street is parallel and one street back from the front.

SURFEIT OF SEAFOOD

We are enamoured of seafood, and heaven awaits in Nha Trang. Lobsters, crabs, prawns and fish of every type, everything our heart desires, all viewable in the restaurant fish tanks. Lobsters as big as my arm, crabs the size of dinner plates, prawns as big as bananas, shellfish as big as tennis balls and fresh fish waiting to be barbequed.

We arrange to meet Rich, a fellow traveller, for dinner. Rich is the only one who has bought more shirts than Barb on this trip. By his own admission, he gets suckered every place he goes. Just having left Hoi An he had been reeled in by an expert - 17 shirts in one shop (yes, she was gorgeous); but he claims it'll save him a fortune back home in the UK. During our dinner, we attempt to count the number of shirts bought throughout his trip and run out at 36. We think he must be setting up in opposition to Harrods. All the while, of course, we're scoffing into crab and fresh, fresh seafood.

We eat local seafood in the restaurants, we eat it at the kerbside cafes and then we eat it from the mobile beach barbeques. Surely this will finish our appetite for seafood forever. But I'm forgetting, this could never be the case for Barb.

Charcoal-burning barbeques are toted on the beach ladies' shoulders and brought beside our sun lounge ($1 a day with mattress and straw thatched sunshade). We eat our favourite seafood sprinkled with fresh lime juice and wash our fingers in the lapping waves. An idyllic setting, this is a pristine clean time-out zone, a respite centre away from Hoi An entrepreneurs. However, as I'm hovering on the sidelines of some of the best diving opportunities in Vietnam, I should think about catching my own crayfish instead of lolling about as I am.

Lolling about wins.

COFFEE

Vietnam brings coffee-brewing to our notice. Through our travels, we casually put up with whatever brand of coffee that is dished up. Usually some variation of instant and usually the local idea of quality is to increase the number of spoonfuls. Often we gratefully consume, nay, even quaff, these different brews because this means that we don't have to drink the locally brewed tea. Local tea is usually made from something that resembles shreds of khaki combat clothes. It tastes just like one would imagine - just like creosote. Strangely though, at about day 80 on our trip I became quite used to the taste. So much for my palate.

Coffee? All is not lost, Vietnam and Cambodia to the rescue. Coffee at last! Nha Trang is where we first notice the Asian version of the dripolator - French influence no doubt. This is a wonderful device when we have been deprived of short blacks, long blacks or any variety designed by baristas. The gadget is made of a light white metal cup and saucer, both with perforated bottom, which rests on your glass and is filled with coffee grounds; hot water is added. The resulting glass or cup of black coffee is rich in flavour and able to be tuned to your taste from the jug of boiling water that accompanies the whole shebang. I will admit that we wait a little time for our coffee to filter - perhaps this enhances the experience. Drip, drip, drip. Delaying of gratification. We savour this coffee with much the same relish as a fine wine.

Nha Trang, Vietnam's fifth largest city, seems to divide into two sections. When we enter Nha Trang, we wonder if we are ever going to see anything but city urbanisation. Sprawling Asian lifestyle oozes along the roadways. The 'same-same' style of living and footpath family life, in front of the now familiar metal concertina security doors. Houses, shops, workshops and eating places, all operating out of the seemingly mandatory three-metre-wide frontages. A grey and somewhat grimy lifestyle.

Now we enter the streets and roads with the trademark of tourism. Shops are brighter, cleaner and fall into categories that commercial tourism demands. Cafes with displayed chalkboards; these essential menus stand like sentinels beside charcoal barbecues at each restaurant door. Souvenir shops, colourful and brightly lit, dress shops, dive shops (not down-and-out dives, but those that offer the ocean experience) and tour-guide shops. The latter offer bus trips to anywhere, flights to anywhere and sight seeing trips to every local landmark. Go by big bus, middle-sized bus or minibus........Or just laze about.

GIANT SEATED BUDDHA
Long Son Pagoda, which has resident monks, is late 19th century and located 500 metres west of the train station.

At the top of the hill behind the Pagoda is the huge white Buddha seated on a lotus blossom. There are 152 stone steps leading up to the Buddha but the views are worth the effort.

CARD TRICKS

There's a quaint occurrence regularly seen on our walks around the various cities. Scattered and abandoned playing cards lie on the ground. Not a full pack, just a random half-a-dozen cards. Everywhere we go, forsaken playing cards litter the streets. Once again in Nha Trang we spot the orphaned objects dis'carded' on the ground. We can only assume illegal games broken up in a hurry by enterprising police. Do I envisage a new TV show? 'Celebrity Jokers are Wild.'

When the sun shines, as it does when we are here, we find bliss on this sandy foreshore. We secure sun lounges for the day and ignore all beach vendors except lobster sellers and the fruit ladies. We suck up the sun, lose ourselves in the pages of our books, sleep and snooze when we wish. We mentally construct our next email home telling of the hardships of our trip.

We enjoy Nha Trang and take out our dice to make our next destination decision. Barb rigs the dice and the decision is Mui Ne. This time, a truly secluded beachside venue. Not overlooked by the tourists, but really just starting to blossom. Seems only the kite surfers and sail boarders have found out about this gem of a location.

Our turn to find out.

CHAPTER FIFTEEN

No use having a precious gem if you hide it from the light.

MUI NE

MUI NE (sounds like a farmyard, Moo-ee-neigh), proves to be a beach-side rest haven. Tall swaying coconut palms shelter our choice of guest house. Well-trimmed gardens and hedges and paved paths lead between bungalows and thatched cabanas, down to a fluffy sand and shell-strewn beach. The Hai Gia guest house will do us. We've all this to look forward to.

Barb's still not sick of lobster, so for the sake of the budget we have to leave Nha Trang. Mui Ne is a few hours south by bus on the road to Saigon. The bus is comfortable (Greyhound style) with good room for our legs and knees, and not quite full. Our driver, whilst not overly prone to horn blowing, has perfected the art of a sustained note with vibrato undertones. We use earplugs for easy travelling, and apart from narrowly missing a skittish goat, the ride is uneventful.

All the signs are promising, a distant fleeting view of the sea as we travel for some kilometres in the shade of prominent sand dunes. The appearance of scattered small hotels, guest houses and resorts on the beach side of the road signal that we're close to our drop-off point.

Just to be different, Mui Ne passengers stay on the bus and 'through' passengers to Saigon get off at the tour office to have lunch.

We have a novel experience when the tour bus kindly drives to five different accommodation places. The bus waits while we check out the options and if and when asked, unloads our backpacks. In major towns, buses may stop at one or two guesthouses so this 'Cook's Tour' is a nice surprise.

WHAT'S IN A NAME?

It is here in Mui Ne that we discover some different nuances in the hoteliers' nomenclature. A 'guest house' is most often reasonably priced, a 'hotel' can be moderately priced and a 'resort' doubles the money you were first thinking of.

Our choice of beach-side guest house sits next door to a resort, yet we pay one-third of the asking price of the resort. Damn it! We didn't notice that the resort had a pool. We'll just have to swim in the sea. What a bummer.

After inspecting the five locations from the security of our bus, we inspect about five more on foot before making our decision to stay at the Gai Hai. Being tightwads, we opt for a bungalow that starts at $15 and we secure it for $10. Admittedly, rather than having beach front, we choose one 25 metres further back. When negotiating, and thinking it may help, I make a point of talking quietly to reception when no one else is around. Next day, our neighbours tell me that they're paying $8 for a similar bungalow - so much for my self-opiniated bargaining skills.

Sheltering under the thatched beach-side sun shades, we lie back on the sun lounges and suck in the atmosphere. Desert island bliss without the boat trip. In front of us, the calm sea sparkles. Bright coloured glimpses of sailboards flitting and sweeping past. Kite surfers breeze along, skimming the waves, the beach and water is dotted here and there with the circular basket-like coracle boats of the lobster catchers. Other multi-coloured banana-shaped boats are anchored offshore or beached. Sun and surf is enhanced by the option to languish in the shady hammocks slung between the palms.

GAI HAI ANECDOTE

Our beds are neatly made up, a folded blanket and top sheet at the foot of each bed. We don't need the blanket, so we each fit the top sheet on our respective beds.

My sheet has extravagant Pollyanna pink roses and is emblazoned with 'A wonderful life - Make each day a celebration of love.'

Across Barb's lime green and yellow sheet, a large fluffy cartoon style rabbit encourages 'Let's go quick! And at the bottom, 'Happy rabbit babies'.

A BOY'S DREAM

As a boy, I dreamed of foreign lands. I'd never seen clusters of palm trees and sun bleached beaches, so I could only imagine. The mysteries of Marco Polo and the adventures of Aladdin or One thousand and One Nights conjured magical images. Now, having travelled in Asia I can see what inspired these stories. Treasure Island,

Robinson Crusoe and Swiss Family Robinson created exciting images of the castaway.

Castles and knights and swords and longbows were easier to comprehend because I could always walk around an old castle. To this day, show me a castle and I travel back in my mind to dream of the days of yore. Now I can see, touch and feel what used to be my desert-island dreams.

As I hide in my hammock and gently sway to the movement of the trees, my dreams of palm trees and sunny beaches have been truly realised. Our joint venture here in Vietnam has bonded Barb and I even closer. Experiences shared and day-to-day decisions made together.

MUI NE

Famed for its enormous sand dunes, these visits need to be made away from the midday sun. Sledding down on sand boards is a thrill not to be missed.

Home of the famous Nuoc Mam, the fish sauce sold all over Vietnam to add spice to dishes. It ferments in huge terracotta jars along the sides of the road.

Thirty kilometres out of Mui Ne is the longest reclining Buddha in Vietnam, with a height of 11 metres and a length of 49 metres. The Buddha is on a hilltop 100 metres above Mountain Pagoda, and if climbing is too much like hard work, visitors can take a gondola ride through the beautiful rainforest to reach the site.

SLEEPY BACKWATER

Mui Ne is not the place for those who want the high life. It's quiet and is spread along about ten kilometres of beach with short stretches of guest houses, lodgings and resorts interspersed with little cafes and eating places. This is not Action Central. It is the haven for sail boarders and kite surfers or, like us, two silly old dudes sucking up the sunshine. So, the hotel sun lounges get lazed upon and the beach offers the chance to amble alongside the lolloping waves.

For Barb, the big bonus is meeting and gazing upon the lean rippling bronzed body of Fernando, the holidaying Argentinean. Never fear, Des was not ill done-by. Augustina is here. Bronzed, bikini clad and with no inhibitions. Truly, a beach beauty.

Fernando and Augustina - what a fabulous, interesting and considerate pair. Great ambassadors for their country. Argentina here we come. 'Barb, I'm sure I said Augustina, not Argentina.'

Shell collecting seems to be a compulsion. Bronzing bodies dip and stoop, like bower birds, to pick up their prize pieces. Funny how the next beach bum to come along still finds some select little shell to add to his or her bower. We fly with the rest and scan the line of beached shells for our own special treasures, shells of particularly vibrant and varied colours (shaped like the logo of an international oil company). Vivid yellow, amber, violet, red and lime. A beautiful little collection brightens up our sunlounge tables for a day or so and now five of them brighten up the window ledge in our office.

IDLE MINDS

It's remarkable how we can be so busy seeing things that we miss so much more. Our less than hectic time on this beach haven gives us time to look twice at things. It provides time for Barb to become inspired by the thatched beach cabanas. 'We could build these at home', says she - not meaning 'we' at all, but rather 'you'.

Sparkling clear fairylights that garland the branches of a prominently positioned tree 'would look pretty in the back courtyard'. Roofs cleverly woven from the coconut palms: 'Thatch would look good on our spa-pool roof.'

All of these sound observations come about from lolling around. Too much time on our hands. 'The devil makes work for idle hands,' my mother would have said. In this instance, it wasn't the devil making work. For my part, the most I could manage would be to string up a simple hammock. I wouldn't have to knit one - there are plenty being offered by street vendors throughout Asia.

Regardless of how remote our destination or how blissfully peaceful, there is always the motorbike to take us to the local tourist site. Even in remote towns, there is always some place of great significance that has to be observed - or so says the local tour office or moto driver. No different in Mui Ne. 'You want to go to reclining Buddha? Longest Buddha of all! You want to go for 4-wheel drive? You want to go slide on sand dune, big dune?'

'No' to the 4-wheel-drive trip. 'No, no,' not another Buddha. 'Yes, yes,' we'll give sand sledding a go.

SAND SLEDDING

Can't resist the lure of the sand dunes. We succumb to the pleas of the moto drivers and in the cool of the evening head off to the sand sledding. At least I can sit on my ass and enjoy the thrill. I overlook the fact that I'll have to walk up through the soft sand and risk third degree bum burns – change that to belly burns.

Sled selling kids clamour around. 'My sled is the best.' With shoulder shrug and big brown eyes, 'You pay me what you think.' He gets triple the value from me - me, the hard-nosed bargainer.

Climbing through the soft sand is hard work and we gingerly position ourselves on the plastic sleds. Belly down bum up, and to the laughs and cries and whoops of the kids, we zoom off. We don't go fast enough or far enough to disappear into the lake at the bottom, still, what a thrill. A must-do for geriatric adventurers.

With feelings of super accomplishment, we return to dinner at the hotel with a new understanding of what Sir Edmund must have felt.

VEGGING OUT

We've used up all our adrenalin, and balmy beaches win the day for us. Solitude requires us to be prepared, so we bring our books, write a book, loll about, drink our water, play cards or eat lobster at the little bistro.

Vegging out, for us, requires the breaking of habits and a new mindset so we don't shirk it, we embrace it and take time to find ourselves again beneath the palms. Lying on the sunlounge sampling the sun and lolling in the hammocks slung between shady trees, we allow ourselves time to be pampered by the ever present massage girls who stroll the beaches looking for a needy (or is it kneady) body. Top-to-toe massage, foot massage, manicure, pedicure - we indulge ourselves in the shadow of our beach bungalow. We practise indolence at its highest level and indulgence at its best. We find great balance between paid guided tours or our own sightseeing in the busy towns and the relaxation of the remotest beaches.

DO WE HAVE TO MOVE ON?

As our travels are more or less decided by whim, Barbara's whim is to stay here for ever, or at least as long as Fernando stays. Thank God she has a somewhat practical husband, so we decide on six nights and then to catch the last bus out to Ho Chi Min city. Last bus, that is, before they close down for the Vietnam New Year celebrations - Tet. We can be lucky sometimes: we only find out that it's the last bus for five days when we book the trip to Saigon. Still, had we been forced to hole-up for a few days more, what better place to do it.

We leave our own R & R area of Mui Ne and bus our way to Saigon in a relatively low-cost VIP bus with heaps of leg-room and air-conditioning. The three hour trip that takes us four hours has us arriving between 6 and 7 pm.

We don't speak to each other very much during the trip as 'in-flight' entertainment is in the form of a travel documentary or rather, a travel commentary. A Swedish couple behind us talk volubly to a Canadian bloke in the seat adjacent to us. All three swap stories about everywhere they have travelled. East and West coast of South America, North Africa, South Africa, Australia, New Zealand. We hear them relating their travel plans and hear all about their high risk adventure exploits. Snowboarding, kite surfing, windsurfing, snorkelling and diving, white-water rafting, parachuting and bungy jumping. Don't these travellers realise that we are high-risk adventurers too? They obviously didn't see us at the sand sledding. Volumes of enthralling information is exchanged. They discuss their future ports of call and what countries will score the next visit.

The Canadian talks about the effectiveness of Aussie insect repellent with 80% Deet and the Swedish girl explains how absolutely dangerous it is and how Deet content of over twenty percent is banned in Sweden. We eavesdrop on the Swedish couple's plans to visit Australia in the next two weeks and the Canadian's authoritative advice on kite surfing. We overhear all the pros and cons of visiting Fraser Island. Both of us manage to remain silent and don't let on that Fraser

Island is on our own doorstep. All in all, the extended bus trip turns out to be most informative. The time goes fast; we should have passed a vote of thanks to our three interlocutors. We don't embarrass them with any comments but we do end up much better informed on many subjects.

Well rested from Mui Ne and well informed from our bus trip, we excitedly anticipate the sights in Saigon. Night has drawn in, the city lights are bright and we de-bus and confidently stroll away clutching our guidebook map. Our hotel is booked so we're sure of a bed - after all, its Tet.

HOTEL WARNING NOTICE

Rules posted behind the door of the Hai Gia hotel room:
The guests who want to stay in room must have:

1. The national identity card or a passport if a foreigner.
2. In case, a man and woman who want to stay together must have clear relationship documents, if the guests haven't got the relationship certificates, the guests must be responsible to the receptionist and the organism in charge.
3. The guests who take the gun, explosive, inflammable, poison must register and give them to the care of the receptionist, absolutely must not take them room.
4. The guests must not cook in the room.
5. The guests must be responsible to keep clean in the house, must not be drunk and make noise.
6. The guests must not take other guests to the room. You can receive your relative at the drawing room, must not yourself take them to the room without permission of the receptionist.
7. If there is a burn in the room the guests must inform to the receptionist at once in order to stamp out the fire with the direction.

Both of us chuckle over this, yet we remember the time when some very similar rules applied in Australia.

CHAPTER SIXTEEN

An optimist sees the New Year in; the pessimist makes sure the old one leaves.

SAIGON (The centre of HO CHI MIN CITY)

Tumblers in fierce colourful lion costumes gyrate and flounce their two-man torsos around the streets. The lions prance and dance about the 20-metre-long yellow or red dragons as they enact their aerial struggle, all of this to the strident vibrant cymbals, gongs and bass drums resonating between the flanking buildings. Red-coloured dragon fighters flip themselves into the air, jump and jack-knife themselves onto each other's shoulders. Three, five, seven-man clusters materialise before our eyes, with the three-man-high formation barely missing the spider web of overhead power lines.

Did we know of these street entertainments? Not when we left Mui Ne.

On arrival in Saigon our bus terminates in the Pham Ngu Lao area where, courtesy of our city map, we home in like pigeons to our pre-booked hotel. Bright lights and the yellow glow of Tet help guide us from the bus stop. The map takes us down the street, around the corner and up a narrow alley (it would be called a mews if it were in Chelsea) where our hotel awaits. Neat, clean, tidy and modern with 6 floors of rooms. Our $13 room is 401 and after climbing the stairs we don't really settle in to our room, we collapse. Once again the standard of fittings is superb and we have a really good night's sleep.

This hotel doesn't have a vacant first floor room so, mindful of our health and altitude sickness, we go shopping for a new address the next day.

SAIGON
Ho Chi Min city, of which Saigon is the centre, is the largest city in Vietnam and is close to the Mekong River delta.

The large city area is called Ho Chi Min City, but the urban centre is called Saigon. A little bit confusing, but the central train station is marked Saigon and 'Ho Chi Min City' doesn't seem to be used very much at all. Even airport signs show 'Saigon'.

Saigon was a Cambodian town before being annexed by the Vietnamese in the sixteenth century and was renamed Ho Chi Min City in 1975.

Saigon is on the banks of the Saigon River, 60 kilometres from the South China Sea and 1,760 kilometres south of Hanoi.

It's the last week in January and accommodation has been readily available everywhere up until now. However, at the start of Tet New Year we think ourselves fortunate to still find a choice of lodgings. We choose a first floor large room for $10 (including breakfast), which suits us better and reduces the threat of heart attack.

TET - VIETNAMESE NEW YEAR

The Chinese New Year and Tet have many similarities and Tet in Vietnam is held according to the lunar calendar, sometime between January 21 and February 19th. Tet is a huge celebration lasting 3 days and is the major holiday in this country.

Vietnamese people take care to start the New Year right with new clothes and debts paid off, as well as ridding themselves of all bad feelings.

Not only is Tet the beginning of the New Year, it is also everyone's birthday because the Vietnamese don't acknowledge their exact birthdays; babies turn one at Tet no matter when they were born.

Tet is a time for family and friends to catch up and the first visitor to the home is important. Often travellers are invited because if the first visitor is rich or prestigious, the family will have good fortune that year.

TET

'Happy New Year' is the catch-cry from the local kids and everyone we talk to. Every shop, business, hotel or house has colourful Tet decorations at their entrances. Yellows and reds, the colours of good luck and happiness, are displayed everywhere. Every shape and size of yellow flowering plant is to be seen. Flowering trees in heavy glazed clay pots stand at the doorways. Two-metre shrubs are being taken home strapped to the back of motor bikes and cyclos.

Conical-shaped cumquat trees a couple of metres tall and dripping with yellow-tinged fruit and tinsel. Entrance ways welcome us with stands of yellow-blossomed buds. Fierce, red-eyed, 2-metre-tall yellow dragons guard some doorways. The dragons' bodies are constructed with egg-sized yellow fruit that look like cows' udders - all mounted on a frame of chicken wire.

The significance of Tet to the Vietnamese is emblazoned all around. Complete community involvement. Red-clad dragon dancers with tall poles whirl and twirl and twist the huge silk dragons down the streets. Traffic stops to see and hear the spectacle.

As spectators, we are absorbed into their world of acrobatics, colour, and big, big sound. We have deserted our breakfast to watch the spectacle and our day has just begun. What a great portent of the night to come.

SAY IT WITH FLOWERS

'Say it with flowers' - what a memorable catch-cry for Tet. Saigon must have heard it. We stroll out to a veritable blaze of blooms. 600 m by 100 m of central city District One parkland is all swathed in pots and tubs of flowers, blossoms, shrubs and orchids. A nurseryperson's version of Nirvana, a veritable yellow brick road of blossoms. The colour of happiness prevails.

GONE

There is a line from a Lord Byron poem 'The Destruction of Sennacherib': 'That host on the morrow lay withered and strown.' And so it is in Saigon one day later. Where have all the flowers gone? Clean. Deserted. Every one. Withdrawn overnight. An amazing logistical exercise to clear the park. Not a plant remains, and city cleaners are removing the remains of the plant debris. A few flat-bed trucks are carting off the last of the massively potted trees and not another bloom in sight. It was trite of me to include the slogan from Interflora 'Say it with flowers' but even triter now to finish with one from the Pepsodent toothpaste people. 'You'll wonder where the yellow went.'

CITY OF STYLE

Majestic boulevards are flanked by wide pavements sheltering under tall elegant trees. Stamped with a smidge more style, Saigon is more Western than cities in the north. Deference is shown throughout Vietnam, with remarks such as 'Saigon Styled' or 'Designed in Saigon'. Perhaps this is why it is referred to as the Paris of the Orient. The streets are still filled with oriental life; street stalls, and of course, parked motorbikes. Again we see demonstrations of national pride all around. The street lighting poles are bedecked with long, narrow red banners with the yellow star and many of the houses and shops sport the national flag.

When we look down most streets or narrow alleys, every second or third door has a small flag dangling from its pole. It crosses my mind that in Australia it would take an offer of a thirty percent reduction in council rates to motivate us to stick a flag on our letterboxes. (I'll write to Canberra and propose this.)

Saigon's traffic is little different from Hanoi, but the major streets are wider and hence more vehicles can criss-cross around us at any one time. I'm still flabbergasted that we witness no crashes.

I'm a fan of the Edinburgh Tattoo and try to watch it every year. I am always in awe of the military motorbike riders who, starting from the four corners, can intersect with each other at speed, like the cross of St Andrew. However, I have to confess that these guys could be easily replaced by the motorbike riders from Ho Chi Min City.

The Tattoo organisers could take a thousand Vietnamese pedestrians and spread them around the arena, then take 500 motorbikes and spread them around the same arena. When the whistle blows, everyone crosses three times in any direction they want. The piece de resistance is where ten motorbikes each with husband, wife, baby and grandmother all stop to shop in the middle. (I guess this is the entrepreneurial showman coming out in me again.)

CU CHI TUNNELS

The Cu Chi tunnels (I am told to pronounce it Koochy) trip is a half-day sightseeing tour close to the outskirts of Saigon. We know of these tunnels and have read quite enough about them to make them one of our 'have-to-go-there' items. Whisked away by bus at 8.30, we get to Cu Chi at 10.30. The bus diverts, as usual, via some handicraft place reputed to be of great interest. The lacquerware process is interesting but we quickly use the toilets and get under way.

On arrival at Cu Chi, we pay our $6 each and sit down to a 15-minute video introduction and a practical explanation showing cross-sections of the tunnels design, same style as kids' ant farms. The information is fascinating but the video quality is awful. We glean 20% of the video dialogue and 40% more from our enthusiastic tour guide pointing at maps and the cross-section model (still leaving a 40% information gap). Notwithstanding the quality of explanation, the information fills us with awe and induces a very healthy respect for the Viet Kong Cu Chi fighters.

The tunnels themselves once extended over a network of more than 200 kilometres. Built at three different levels, they supported everyday life and provided everything necessary to live and also house their bomb-making activities.

Entrances to the tunnels were cleverly camouflaged and could be as small as 40 by 30 cm. For the benefit of bigger tourists, deliberately enlarged entrances give access to actual tunnels, but no way, Jose! I climb down the specially widened steps, am confronted by a small oval entrance and quickly return to terra firma. The entrance is about the size of a bar fridge and my back and knees just won't bend to fit. However, a number of the sylph-like girls crouch and crawl their way through the 150 m. Amazingly, one Irish guy of more than average size squeezes through the tunnel on his knees - must have been all the practice he gets at church.

I'm intrigued by the ingenious tunnel system and even the vicious spiked and pronged man traps. I refrain from paying to shoot a variety of the original weapons. A visit to the photos in the Saigon War Remnants Museum would deter anyone from ever touching a weapon of war.

HORRORS OF WAR

We're ready to move on, but I guess that my narrative about Saigon is not complete without coming back to the 'War Remnants Museum'. Mentally I am trying to avoid this as it is still confronting in my mind. I am trying not to dwell on it. Ignore it and it will go away. Not so.

We walk for an hour through the city to the Museum and the display of captured American guns, tanks and planes. This is Vietnam's story of the 'American' war.

Most emotionally disturbing are the self-indicting photographs taken by American war correspondents. The series of chilling photos depicts war at its worst. The hackneyed phrase of 'Man's inhumanity to man' is never more aptly depicted than here. No side wins, both sides lose. Future generations take heed.

EXPAT RETURNS

We enjoy Saigon, its busy streets and Bia Hoi cafes with beer at 66c for 2 litres. We revel in the great alfresco restaurant on the corner of 'our' street (Quang Dau), you name it and they serve it. Caesar salads, Italian specialties, hamburgers to die for and great banana crepes. (Caesar salad and chips plus banana pancakes and water for $4 a head.)

One breakfast time in Saigon sees us sitting in this same corner cafe next to two of the locals. Barb's query to me about the meals brings a brief exchange and some helpful advice to us on how to read the menu. Both Barb and I congratulate the man on his excellent English and ask about his American accent. 'Sure,' he says, 'I live in America and come to Vietnam to visit'.

His parents had escaped from Vietnam in 1975, leaving behind a very prosperous lifestyle. He had grown up being influenced by his parents to be as American as he could and to forget about Vietnam and its language. His parents believed that there would never be any chance of lessening oppression under the tight communist regime. They had no hope of ever returning to Vietnam. Today, things have changed. The world has changed. Communism is being courted by capitalism - or is capitalism being courted by communism?

He is in Saigon with his Vietnamese girlfriend investigating the possibility of opening his own business with Vietnamese partners. He knows that it can be achieved and he also knows that any success will be conditional upon the amount of graft he and his partners are prepared to pay. We wish him well and think how lucky we are in our own home country.

We find it impossible not to enjoy Saigon, particularly during TET. The Botanical Gardens offer free concerts and the nearby zoo sees children gazing in awe at the animals. We stroll to the river, see the floating restaurants and enjoy a coffee break at the Rex Hotel. This is the hotel where the wartime journalists gathered and it's here we ride the elevator to take in the roof-top view of Saigon. What wonderful memories we have.

MEKONG DELTA
Day trips can be organised to the Mekong Delta but unless you are really pressed for time, it is better to take more than one day to explore this area. Most people say that the day trip is just too exhausting, with hours of bus travel and river tours taking in various tourist operations.

Consider an overnight trip, or going to Phnom Penh via the Mekong, which usually takes 3 days and 2 nights - book at a local tour operator.

SAYONARA SAIGON

We must take our leave of Vietnam or be chucked out - our visas are used up.

So, Cambodia and Phnom Penh, visions of Angkor Wat and forays into the silk shops - here we come.

EMAIL FROM JACKIE AFTER WE GOT HOME

Saigon is an interesting place. Locals seem to be misery personified (but I'm still prepared to be proven wrong.) I've taken to grinning like an inane cat just to annoy everyone or, heaven forbid, provoke a similar response.

My only saving grace is Mr Dat. Mr Dat is my scooter driver and together we take on the world and its scooter population. Mr Dat may well be nearing 60 and may wobble the bike dangerously about the town, but give him the super highway and it's a different story. He hits the turbo button and we belt on into the fast lane.

Mr Dat does not believe in usual road rules. Red lights are green lights. One way can be either way, and designated scooter lanes are for wimps. Why thrash it out with your fellow scooters when you can rough it with the big boys? Namely, trucks/buses/cars and me and Mr Dat. Failing that, we just ride on the pavement. Anything goes.

Tomorrow my new pal and I are heading off into the sunset again. This time to the Mekong Delta. We are liable to break land-speed records en-route.

Watch this space. Jx

CHAPTER SEVENTEEN

When the dust is washed away, the jewel shines

PHNOM PENH

Our room brings its own challenges, the wall-mounted fan rattles like a stick on a fence and the satellite TV remote has run off into a dark corner with the air-con remote, never to be seen again. The toilet cistern takes rostered time off and only fills up again on a whim. But let's be fair - the bar fridge works. The pillows are soft and cuddly, just our choice. To sleep, perchance to dream, the mattresses are great, crisp top and bottom sheets with the bedspread comfortable and warm. (We need the warm bedspread because the air-con on the wall is set, permanently, to 'Ice-maker'.)

We don't know if a warm welcome or a cool one best describes our arrival in Phnom Penh.

But now we are heading towards the Cambodian border and Phnom Penh. Only a hop, skip and a jump away from Angkor Wat. Personally, I'm keeping fingers crossed that Tomb Raider II is being made and I'll be cast as an extra beside Angelina Jolie. I quietly fantasise from the comfort of our VIP bus.

I've opened my carefully guarded coffers and have splashed out on the up-market bus, paying $2 more than for the rattler. I spare no expense in cosseting my wife and this is a good decision because both of us are looked after by the on-board hostess. The main benefit of this slightly more expensive trip is that we stay on the same bus through to Phnom Penh - no change of bus at the border and to boot, someone to hold our hands through the immigration centre.

Tootling through the Vietnamese countryside, it is clear that we're well and truly in the dry season. Dust is everywhere. The roads are dry and dusty, the villages dry and dusty, even the cows and the cowherd are dry and dusty. The only indication of anything wet is the muddy splash marks on the stumps of houses. Brown blotches reach a metre high to remind the locals that the monsoon rains do eventually come.

The houses themselves look like cute little prototypes for old Queensland homes. Huge Ali Baba style jars are beside the houses to store water. The jars are so big that if the house was washed away (some chance), three kids could live in a jar.

Just to make Australians homesick, the locals grow eucalyptus trees, palms, bananas and pandanus along the roadside. The ever-present plastic bags bobble around the verges.

Barb and I know less about Cambodia than about any other country. Our limited knowledge stretches sketchily around the Pol Pot era and we know quite a bit about Angkor Wat and its history. Our knowledge and interest in local silk was sparked by our friend Karen, who imports silk products. Whilst I am musing on Angelina Jolie, Barb is mentally arranging and redecorating every room in our house with silk. As it transpires, Barb accomplishes all her dreams; as for me, I'll just have to watch the video.

BORDER CROSSING

Through the bus window and a dusty cloud, we see the sparkle and gleam of a group of handsome buildings. Our crisply-dressed hostess collects everybody's passports, visas and immigration forms. Willingly I foist my documents on her, delighted that someone experienced in these matters is in control.

The border post is newly built, clean and impressive, our bags are conveyored through, we trail along and the Vietnamese guard points us to the adjacent flash and imposing building. Now it is our turn to be welcomed by the Cambodian officers who, with matching fluency, streamline us through to our waiting bus. Voila, there we have it, another border safely crossed. Thanks to the bus hostess - worth the higher bus fare.

As we scramble into our seats, we notice a low-cost rattler bus dumping its passengers to deal with their own bags and paperwork. We've been told that when some visa difficulties arise, palms have to be greased at this border post. The rattler turns round and heads back to Saigon.

Phnom Penh, here we come. The usual excitement about new cities grips us once again.

Our first impression of the city is like a Christmas pudding, a bit of a mixture. Similar to many of the villages with dust and unpaved streets, yet interspersed with splendid, bright clean-lined buildings and wide boulevards and roundabouts to match Piccadilly Circus. Side streets with patches of grey dusty cobbled-together houses and shanty-like markets.

TUK TUK CHAOS

With uncertain thoughts, we arrive at the central city bus terminus. Elton John must be one of the passengers because thousands of bodies flock around the bus. Well, hardly thousands, but maybe forty or fifty. We push our way to get our bags. Attempting to hand one to Barb, I see it disappear into the arms of one of these Tuk-Tuk-owning bodies. Three people fight for it before someone clutches at mine. What a welcome, what a drama and distress as a Tuk Tuk driver tries to pull Barb towards his buggy. A veritable Babel, or is it Bedlam?

'Hoi! Hoi!' yells I in my best strong Belfast accent. I rescue Barb and send a search party for our bags. My thunderous yell has cleared a modest spot around us and spying a likely, clean-cut driver, we whisk our packs to his Tuk Tuk.

I produce our guidebook city map in which I have highlighted three possible guest houses at $6 to $8 a night. Our cheerful, wide-smiling driver snakes his Tuk Tuk through people and traffic and we hedge hop from one guest house to another (all this for the quoted price of $1). When we return to the first, we find that our original choice of room has been snaffled up by someone more adroit than me, so we settle for another room in this same hotel with twin beds and costing $8.

Curious and impatient, we dump our gear, clean our teeth and head off into the wide dusty yonder. Armed with water bottles and shoulder bags, we deposit passports and spare credit cards in the hotel safe and scurry hand in hand towards the river.

INTERNET PHONE

'Never mind lollygagging around the shops, we've got a grandson in New Zealand whose birthday it is, and he would expect to hear from his grandfather.' No mention that it is she who wants to catch up on all the hot goss from our daughter Kelly. I look at my watch and, taking a reading from the sun, work out on my fingers that the boy won't be asleep.

'Let's go.' A friendly neighbourhood internet café is nearby of course and we pop in and book a low-cost internet call to New Zealand. In fewer minutes that it took me to work out the time difference, the call is placed.

'Hello Jack, how are you? Is the birthday boy there? Hello Sam, this is your granddad.' Clear as a bell, as if we were next door.

From Barb, 'Here, let me speak to Kelly.' Fifteen minutes later, the phone is put down. We pay our few dollars and I get an instant replay. 'Kelly said to me … etc, etc.' How is it that the women can communicate so much in such a short time? That has always baffled me.

RIPE FRUIT

The local markets near our hotel are busy, bustling and bristling with a wide selection of fruit & veg and the usual Asian produce. The stalls spill across the street, we step over the cabbage leaves and plastic bags and scuttle through those sections with the over-ripe smells. Flies and more flies. Other markets in other cities had been fly-less. Not here. I think there must have been windsocks to guide them in to land.

Pre-trip feelings of caution emerge. 'Make sure you wash any fruit in bottled water. We have avoided the dreaded trots so far so let's not spoil it now.'

I say, 'Yes, dear.'

'We have to be careful only to eat what's cooked before our eyes.'

'Yes, dear.'

We're reaching the end of our trip, I can count on one hand the times when we have experienced flies or mozzies, and this is a source of astonishment. We had heard lots about malaria but preventative tablets weren't an option we had taken up. We were right, as our period of travel must have been the mosquitoes 'off' season. By day 95, we've seen very few of the critters. This really surprises us because there are plenty of places where dirty water lies about in puddles and ditches. Same-same goes for flies, very few of them.

BLACKOUT

Both Barb and I are talented in the area of knife and fork and have added further skills with chopsticks and spoon. Here in Phnom Penh, we're anticipating our first night's meal. Showered, shaved and all spruced up, we skip along the street to find a suitable café.

The bright city lights have an eclipse! Or is it a haemorrhage? We become shrouded in darkness. Often a nightly occurrence. Blackout.

However, a stunning miracle happens. Lamps, candles and torches magically appear and it's as if we're at a night vigil at Lourdes. Discretion being the better part of valour, we retreat to our brightly lit hotel complete with generator.

FREE ADVICE

We dine in, and this has its compensations as we meet sisters Johanna and Freda who give us lots of low-down on Siem Reip, our next port of call. The girls are top travellers from Sweden and work hard to get the money to travel for 6 weeks each year. They have been to lots of places through Asia, South America and Africa. Apart from their charm and good looks, their English is superb. We often remark on the quality of English spoken by every Swede we meet. The girls tell us of their horrendous border-crossing bus trip from Thailand to Cambodia at Poipet. Same route that Stewart (in Phuket) told us NOT to take.

They had a 'Fangio' driver in a half-crippled bus, with brakes that needed regular fixing by the driver crawling about under the vehicle. Screaming to a halt 1.5 metres from the edge of a gorge could have been a bowel-loosening experience for them. They wore red dust, they ate red dust and their back teeth rattled over the bumps. Their comments were 'Never again! Don't enter or leave Cambodia via Poipet on a ramshackle bus.' The same advice was to be repeated to us on quite a few occasions.

CAMBODIA

Cambodia has a population of 14 million, principally Buddhist.

The Khmer revolution saw millions slaughtered, and the country is still recovering from Pol Pot's purges of 1975/79.

46% of Cambodia's population is under 15 years of age and poverty is at distressing levels; life expectancy is 54 years. However, this country receives an enormous amount of aid from international governments and the future looks bright.

NOT ANOTHER MARKET!

Our new day, a brave new world and sunshine beating down. We're off to explore the town and to enquire about various tours and markets and department stores in preparation for our last spending spree (presents for home).

Breakfast is a quick rice dish and coffee at a kerb-side café - about $1.50 for both of us. So, fuelled up for our fact-finding mission, we head off.

On leaving the riverfront area, the streets become cleaner, broader and with less traffic. The buildings seem larger and newer and higgledy-piggledy shops turn into fresh-fronted stores with trendy gear. We find the covered Central Markets under a huge domed roof, with displays of the spectrum of goods we've become accustomed to seeing. Designer shirts, watches, shoes, cosmetics and perfumes, CD's and DVD's - all rip-offs of course. Everything we need to buy as gifts to impress our friends. We suspect that the low-cost cameras (no instruction books) were probably being used the previous day by some unsuspecting traveller.

Close to the covered markets is the modern department store, coming to our rescue with KFC. Truth to tell, KFC is a rip-off too and called something else. Probably CFK, the Cambodian Food Kitchen. Still, the day injects some positive feelings about Phnom Penh. We scoot through the very clean, modern supermarket, buy beer, meat pies, custard pies, fresh fruit and French bread and then scuttle off home. Voila, miracle of miracles, there is an Italy/Ireland rugby match on the satellite TV. I ensconce myself, like Norm with beer and pies, and settle in for a quiet evening in front of the box. (I have been suffering rugby withdrawals and at last I get my fix.)

Our extended roam around the city of Phnom Penh shows a city of contradictions. On one hand, there are wide boulevards and shady spreading trees and green parks, but under the trees, the footpaths are disappointingly cracked and rutted with big sections of broken pavers. Our mission is to track down a charity organisation selling silk. An hour and a half later we find the workshop, but their silk prices are three times the price of local shops. On our way, the spectacular gold and shining temples, palaces and universities contrast strongly with the occasional blot of hovels, slums, tattered markets and unsealed streets.

BIRTHDAY SURPRISE

Early morning, Barb is seen talking to a cute, neatly dressed local five-year-old in the hotel lobby. 'Hello. Your ...dress...is...very...pretty. How...old...are...you?'

'I'm five and it's my birthday today and this dress is my present.'

'Goodness, your English is very good, did you learn it at school?'

'No, I've been living in Sydney and I've just come here last week.'

Turns out her mother, whom we have met, is the hotel manager and she has just returned to work in Phnom Penh.

CHILDREN

Memories of Cambodia are filled with the smiles of children. Less fortunate than those in other places; more disadvantaged, dustier and with older clothes. The eight-year-old sister is to be seen carrying the baby on her hip and grasping the smiling four-year-old by the hand. Their clothes are less clean and sandals more worn, their poverty invades your heart, but the timid smiles break across their faces and white teeth gleam.

You can't give to all of them, but all induce great depths of emotion. We are told that the general rule is not to give money - buy their postcards and trinkets. Still, there are occasions when we break the rule. The wide variety of needy cases of children, mothers, babies and cripples leaves me trying to look the other way. If I don't see, I'm not as emotionally affected. Coward. No escape, I can't run away from it. The pathos of the underprivileged invades my senses. So, two kids score 25c; I turn around and there are about 10 kids. It costs me $3 to pacify them. What a ridiculously small amount of money it is to us. Something's very wrong here.

Cambodian people carry on the tolerance and patience seen elsewhere on our travels. Their lot in life is harder, their quality of living less and the dust on the roads more. The negative effect of the Khmer Rouge is still being felt. City and town infrastructure is less modernised, with temples and religion less in evidence. We feel that to date we have handled the disadvantaged and beggars quite well, but not in Cambodia. Our emotions are tugged, our eyes water and our pockets are emptied. Heartstrings will rarely be as continually plucked as by a trip through Cambodia. Very, very few 'haves' and multitudes of 'have nots' - maybe that should read 'have absolutely nothing at all'.

It is comforting to see the extreme cases of poverty or disability being helped by the local bar, cafe and shop owners. The shopkeepers quickly and quietly press money into a needy hand and retreat. Cafes will give food to those with begging bowls.

LOCAL HIGH SPOT

The nearest thing to Singapore's Raffles hotel (well, vaguely similar) is the Foreign Correspondents' Club. On advice from our silk importing friends, we freshen up and stroll a few hundred yards to enjoy refreshments and drinks in the lounge overlooking the river. Clearly the refuge of the foreign business people and the odd itinerant. Expats from anywhere gather here like moths to a light.

ICONS

Each country has its distinguishing icons, the Tuk Tuk in Thailand, the conical hat in Vietnam, the head scarves and minarets in Malaysia and the Cambodian checked head gear. To emulate the latter, take a long, checked kitchen tea towel, crush it into a bundle, throw it in the air and catch it on your head. There you have it. A genuine Cambodian hat.

Ingenuity comes into play with the Cambodian version of the Tuk Tuk. A pivot point is mounted on the back seat of a motorbike and a two-person covered trailer/trap/buggy is hitched behind - simple, effective and comfortable. A longer version is regularly seen transporting local village people, merchandise or farm goods. Same motorbike, 4 metre-long narrow trailer with demountable planks for seats. Cambodians must have high-tensile bottoms to ride any distance on these vehicles.

SNIPPET

Barb trundles her backpack to the front pavement of the hotel preparing to go to Siem Reip. She is pacing about waiting for our bus transport when advice is offered by the friendly taxi man.

'Don't leave your bag unattended like that.'

'Don't worry,' says Barb, 'I've only got a few shirts and stuff in there.'

'Oh,' says the taxi driver, 'I only own one shirt.'

POL POT

Pol Pot's Khmer Rouge captured Phnom Penh in 1975 and for a time, the name of the country was changed to Democratic Kampuchea.

In a city of about 8 million, Pol Pot's regime exterminated almost 2 million and the entire population of Phnom Penh was driven out into the surrounding countryside.

The people were told that the evacuation was due to the threat of American bombing and that it would last only a few days.

Apart from those executed, a large number of the Cambodian population starved to death.

KILLING FIELDS

I feel compelled to visit the Killing Fields but Barbara is definite. 'I've seen enough of the results of wars and genocide. 'No, I won't go.' She is adamant.

The horrors seen in the museum of the 'American' war in Vietnam had left her horrified and numb. The Killing Fields dredge the depths of barbarism and Pol Pot's acts of genocide defy comprehension. I know that the Killing Fields is something I must confront, but it leaves me in a sombre mood.

The ever-ready moto driver outside our hotel agrees to take me. I clamber on the back and he and I scoot off through the city streets and out into the country.

In Europe, the stark remains of Hitler's gas chambers still physically confront. In Cambodia, only the holes and depressions of mass graves are left as reminders of the atrocities in the Killing Fields. The grim evidence is in their tall temple of remembrance, a huge collection of skulls - a tiered arrangement of shelf upon shelf of skulls sorted by age, from babies to grandparents. I walk from one information board to the next and I circumnavigate the big craters of mass graves. If I were to do it again, I'd book a tour with a tour guide to explain everything in order to understand the history and political background. Whilst my mood is sombre and contemplative, it does not compare with the sheer frontal attack of the Saigon War Remnants Museum.

RUNNING REPAIRS

Our travels so far have been rather conventional in a backpacker sort of way. It is time now for me to breathe some gut-wrenching, nail-biting and hair-raising excitement into the daily humdrum.

With nothing particular in mind, I decide to fix the still rattling wall fan. Moving the moulded plastic chair close to the solid dresser, I climb up and eliminate all evidence of the click, clack, clicking. I turn and, rather too quickly, step down firmly on the plastic seat. Well, not actually down on the seat, through the seat. Shards of broken plastic fly left and right and the remaining edges rip up the front of my leg. I flip over, flailing at the end of the bed.

Copious blood cascades from my leg (I'm going for the sympathy vote here.) Barb springs to my aid and, not sure whether to run the shower water on the wound or not, she wraps a towel round the gash. Wanting to see the extent of the damage, I run the shower and wash the nasty-looking scrape.

'Hotel lobby, we've had an accident, can you get a doctor or ambulance to room 106, please?'

'Sorry Maam, that doesn't happen here.'

'What does happen then?'

'You get a taxi to the medical centre and they get a doctor.'

So, with my leg wrapped in a towel (now red), we arrive at the American Medical Centre at 7.30 pm. Pay up front, $100 US. A doctor is summoned and meanwhile a nurse cleans the wound. The doctor appears in her evening dress, tut-tuts, inspects the damage, oversees the repair job and presents antibiotics and spare dressings along with a warning not to get ANY local water near the wound.

Another $26 and into the cab and back to the hotel. $10 for the trip to and from, including an hour's wait. We ask the driver for a receipt but he returns a glazed look and the receptionist writes the taxi details on the back of a hotel card. Amazingly, this is honoured as part of the medical expense when claiming on our travel insurance back in Oz. I make up my mind that the trip should be less hair-raising from now on.

Phnom Penh, for us, is to be the springboard for both Siem Reip in the north-west and Sihanoukville in the south, then finally Bangkok.

It's time to use the springboard and bounce (or limp) off to Siem Reip, a targeted highlight on our trip. Employing my knowledge of Asian buses, I book our trip for early the next day.

Ankhor Wat - we wait to be wowed by the wonder of the Wats.

CHAPTER EIGHTEEN

The magnificence of the temple pales beside God.

SIEM REIP

Our wonderful, friendly welcome to Siem Reip stops at the rear garden wall of our guest house. Looking through the gate, we see ten 3-metre-long crocodiles in a backyard wallow. They languish, thresh, snap or just stare. Unusual house pets - cats, dogs I understand. The sign in the cafe explains all, 'Croc Burgers $1'. Different!

What a breath of fresh air. Siem Reip. We had been told to expect a dust-blown, untidy town. Dust? Yes. Crocodiles? No. Untidy? We don't think so.

Not by comparison to Phnom Penh. The unsurfaced roads have been watered down, the streets are wide, admittedly some unsurfaced, but there is far less obvious litter. An interesting introduction for us, following the knee-crushing trip from Phnom Penh, which was of course an organisational masterpiece. Once again we have stuffed up the important issue of VIP seating space. It really is so simple to ask 'How many seats on this bus, and how big is the bus?'.

The bus station, we agree, is a dust bowl. However, arriving buses are surrounded by cute little Tuk Tuks ready to whisk us to a hotel or guest house.

Are we losing our adventurous spirit? Our cavalier bravado? Or are we becoming content in the knowledge that satisfactory accommodation is quickly and easily sorted? We had forward booked by recommendation from our Phnom Penh Hotel and are met by our personal 'chauffeur' with an airport-style name card held on high. Very sophisticated. The bus station reminds us of those in Turkey where any bus is met by guest house operators displaying colour pictures of their rooms, cafe and gardens. Here, 'same-same', and disembarking passengers get a free ride to lodgings of their choice.

We enjoy the Tuk Tuk tour through town to our guest house. We drive into a garden courtyard, fresh and clean, and are given our choice of rooms from $10 to $15. A twin room with satellite TV, air-con and hot water for $11 wins the day. Rustic bamboo garden cafe, games room with billiard table - it suits us just fine. Both of us feel warmed by the friendly people at the Tokyo Guesthouse. No need to find a substitute guest house here. I can rest my skinned shin bone in comfort.

Angkor Wat beckons. At the guest house, we eagerly negotiate the hire of the local version of a Tuk Tuk to see the afternoon sun set on the walls of the Wat. The ticket, if bought after 4 pm, allows entry all next day. $20 for one day, $40 for three days.

Our driver takes us along leafy tree-lined tarmac roads and out to Angkor Wat.

Luxuriant trees and grass verges evoke a feeling of serenity. A green relaxed country scene and then, in front of us and spread out along the lowland, is the ancient vista of old stone-carved temples with light from the lowering sun playing off the crests of the ancient Wats. The temple complex is as awe-inspiring as the pyramids. Tall pillars, thick walls, prolifically and prodigiously carved and sculptured.

ANGKOR WAT

According to Guinness World Records, Angkor Wat is the largest religious structure in the world.

Built in the 12th century as King Suryavarman's state temple and capital city, this site attracts more than half a million tourists a year.

Sadly, only 28% of the ticket revenue is spent on restoring the temples. Most of the restoration work is carried out by foreign sponsored teams rather than the Cambodian government.

We wander through the Wat and wonder at the scope and scale, the height and width of each intricately carved and hewn stone block and pillar. As the red-gold sun drops behind the trees, it perfectly lights up, with rose tones, the splendour of the Wat. We head home for a coffee and a meal. Seems mundane after the glories we've seen.

Refreshed and ready, the next morning we head out for a full day's conducted tour of the closest and most popular Wats. The currently known complex of Wats covers an area of 300 square kilometres and as yet, much of the area remains unexcavated and uncovered. It is difficult to relate to the temples as a spiritual or religious testament to a God King, but I continue to marvel at the huge ornamental and architectural achievement. There is no evidence of the huge conglomeration of domestic houses that would have surrounded the many temples. It is hard to imagine that this was, at its zenith, the largest city in the world.

Yellow, red and blue stripes flash in the sky and a large hot air balloon is seen hovering over the tree line. Neither Barb nor I have ever been ballooning before. An instant decision from Barb, 'Let's put some of your hot air to good use and go ballooning over the Wats.'

HOT AIR BALLOONING

It is with pent-up anticipation of adventure that we Tuk Tuk over to the ballooning centre. It's the same balloon we had seen high above the trees and we know that, from an aerial perspective, we'll get a full view drifting across the vastness of the original city and multiple temples.

Up in the air? Not quite, more like up in smoke.

We find that the $15 balloon 'trip' is tethered to go straight up, twirl around and then straight down with only 10 minutes in the air. We don't buy the trip. The basket travels over 150 m up to the sky and the view would be fantastic, but our disappointment is all related to our own false expectations. My imagination has taken me floating across the spread of temples, but reality has put me on my backside, or at least on shank's pony. As a UNESCO site, ballooning over it is prohibited. This was one of the trips that we hadn't checked on the internet and I've since been told that we made a serious boo-boo and that the experience is amazing. Still, our exploration by Tuk Tuk of the many temples of Angkor Wat leaves us with an abiding sense of awe.

AMPLE ACCOMMODATION

We find Siem Reip to be hospitable. The people are kindly and gentle, and less forward and pushy during our usual night-time perambulation around shops and cafes.

Here we see some splendid state-of-the-art hotels with rooms up to $2,000 a night. Well-tended gardens and resplendent porticos and entrances. Hotels and guest houses abound, so it's easy to spend as much as one wants or to select from rooms as low as $7 a night. Certainly $12 to $20 will secure rooms of equal or better quality than most Aussie motels.

No need to book, for a couple of dollars a Tuk Tuk driver will show 3 or 4 different guest houses and the most suitable can then be selected. This is a 20 to 30 minute exercise and will give a general idea of the layout of the town. There are many new hotels being built, so I can't imagine there will ever be a shortage of lodgings in Siem Reip.

The contradiction in Siem Reip is the road surfaces. In the town centre there isn't any bitumen, yet the road to Angkor Wat has a perfect tarmac surface and is well tended, with extensive grass areas around the temple area, tidily mown and free from litter. It is here that tourists can go for a trundle on the back of an elephant. No grey elephants here, they are as black as boot polish. In the town centre, the roads are reminiscent of outback towns of 50-odd years ago. However, there is an active network of drains and kerbing under construction - maybe a sign of improvements in the near future.

MEDICAL RELAPSE

We've travelled now for 100 days with 20 to go. Just to prove that I'm not fireproof, I suffer from a reaction to the Phnom Penh antibiotics and spend a day in bed. It is apparent now that the antibiotics are not quite right and I have to stop taking them, either that or I had tried to walk too far. Never mind, no infection appears to have set in and we are being very careful with dressing and ointment.

One of the lessons we learned early in our trip was that we had to listen to our bodies and self-diagnose. Miraculously, apart from a sore throat or two, neither Barb nor I have had any sickness during the whole four months we've been away and this little bout comes as quite a surprise. Never mind, 24 hours clears it all away and our minds turn to the wind-up of our trip and the journey home. However, the lure of Cambodian silk sees Barb buy a dozen or so cushion covers and throws.

'Don't worry; I'll carry them in my back pack,' she assures me. Funny though that the loot is immediately distributed across two packs.

PRESCRIPTION DRUGS
Before leaving home, you may wish to copy down the names and dosages of any particular drugs you use - antihistamines, pain killers, etc - because prescriptions aren't needed, medicines are very inexpensive in Cambodia and the pharmacist will recognise the drugs by name.

MISSING THE MEKONG

The gash in my leg, treatment and bandaging makes it inadvisable to undertake any style of river trip due to the risk of infection from the water. The doctor had been quite clear on this danger. Our intention to travel into the Mekong Delta is abandoned and three more days will be taken up on the beaches of southern Cambodia.

To return to Phnom Penh and our pivot point, we dutifully book the bus through our guest house. We learn from our knee-crushing trip to Siem Reip that we must ask more probing questions about the buses. We have a much more comfortable trip back to Phnom Penh in a bigger bus with fewer seats and for the same price.

ROAD USERS

Bus trip travelling allows us to experience some sights not normally to be seen at home. Barb points out the motorbike rider travelling with hand over his shoulder holding on to the blue strapping of a cardboard box, a big cardboard box with the logo 'Samsung Refrigerator'. We just don't get that kind of dedicated personal delivery service in Oz any more. Additionally we see, coming from the other direction, a bicycle complete with a haystack and defying all the laws of physics. Little surprise when some time later a bicycle comes into view with a tree strapped on the back pannier. The tree could have filled the inside of our bus. The single mitigating factor of aerodynamics is that it is only in bud and not fully leafed.

Still on the subject of bus travel, or rather other road users, we are astounded at the volume of road traffic. Outside the cities, we see more than one bus a minute pass by. These local buses have everything but the kitchen sink strapped to their roof and I bet that if they stopped, we could even find that sink. Inside, the buses are jam-packed with people and kids. It looks as if a mass exodus is taking place. Suitcases, boxes and bicycles all up top. Something like a remake of Moses' flight out of Egypt. All in all, an interesting trip back to the capital. We'll spend a few days then head off south, via Kampot, in search of new beaches.

Back to our hotel and the friendly cry: 'They're back. Your same room is ready.' Bit of a pity that, as we are hoping for a room where the fan is fixed and everything works.

CHAPTER NINETEEN

Great disappointments come from extravagant dreams.

KAMPOT and POINTS SOUTH

Before spring-boarding off again to the South Coast from Phnom Penh, we take advantage of the central markets and of the big flash department store.

COSMETIC HIGHLIGHT

As every husband knows, hours can be spent at sweet-smelling cosmetic counters. Every fragrance is smelled, sniffed, patted onto wrists and wafted around. Every shade and tone of makeup is smeared and blended onto any uncovered skin surface. Every tone of red lipstick is produced and poutingly plastered on the back of a hand between the smears of foundation.

It is here amidst the glass counter tops with shiny brass edges, elegant girls in stylish suits and classic coiffured hair that disaster strikes. Jurassic Park revisited. A rat scuttles into the Lancome counter.

Cries, yells, screams. Shoppers scatter, sales girls jump on stools and cans of hair spray are flung at the poor frightened rodent. Barb palpitates with 'Oh oh ohs' as she clutches my arm and climbs up my leg. Clearly, this is the proverbial rat with the gold tooth shopping in a manner to which it has become accustomed.

The collected male shoppers laugh and smile. When order is resumed, one guy sneaks up behind Barb and says 'Boo!' The wet spot on the floor could well be spilt perfume. Normal programme will be resumed as soon as possible.

Stoically we resume our shopping. This is to be our last spend-up before going home to Oz. We purchase DVD's, a camera, toys and shirts, and arrange to leave this luggage in our hotel's security room whilst we spend our next few days in Sihanoukville.

Both of us have enjoyed the change to glass and glitter shopping in the large western-style centre. It is here I pay twice as much for the same camera we saw in the markets, only now the camera has a box and instruction book. I see a battery-operated dog that jumps, barks and backflips onto his backside. Memories of a similar purchase 25 years ago force me to relive my youth and buy it. Our Noosa grandson James will enjoy this, just as his dad did all those years ago.

Another big hit in the shopping centre is shoes. Not for me, but for grandson James. Not so much for grandson as for his mother Nessie. I have visions of the resulting chaos and cries of 'I could kill that bloody grandfather of yours.' The shoes in question are dubious-quality bright-yellow plastic with goggle eyes in front and super squeaky soles. Baby walks, shoes squeak. $1 later, I smile to myself and wrap up my purchase. Squeak, squeak, squeak.

After a few days of eating, drinking and shopping we again leave Phnom Penh for the village of Kampot, which the tourist info tells us is the home of marvellous pepper plantations. From Kampot to Sihanoukville on the south coast of Cambodia. To the sea, the surf and the sunshine.

Everyone must understand of course that when arriving back in Australia it's obligatory to be bronzed and suntanned so as to make our friends jealous. Coastal Sihanoukville is the place to be in order to rest up for the direct and quick route home.

Our final leg will be back up to Phnom Penh, fly to Bangkok and connect to our Brisbane flight. At this stage, we are fit and have lost quite a bit of weight. The Asian food seems to agree with us, Barb's asthma is gone and my heart arrhythmia has all but vanished too. We must have touched the hem of Buddha's sarong or maybe his bare belly. What an amazing and unexpected outcome from the trip.

KAMPOT/KEP

Escaping Phnom Penh, we head south for the Kampot/Kep region. Our research tells that Kep is an older established beach area close to Kampot, which in turn has a wide river and all surrounded by protective hills and pepper plantations. Sounds idyllic.

We had more than usual difficulty in booking our bus as not many companies seemed to go there. We should have been suspicious. Our 3-hour bus ride takes 5 hours; we must have caught the local milk run. Milk-run buses have their advantages because we get to stop every half hour for someone to get off, or to be waved down by a roadside passenger, or to have men run to the trees on one side and women to the other following the call of nature.

PORCUPINE PEOPLE

The road tests out our inner springs and we switch-back our merry way over every bump on the road. We pass all styles of local transport from bullock carts to goat carts. Most hair-raising of all is seeing the oncoming minivans - not one, but dozens. In themselves, the minivans are innocuous, but these vans have people stuck to them like porcupine quills. People inside, people outside. The normal complement of 14 people inside swells to 26 plus a dog, and on the outside and roof another dozen or so cling on by fair means or foul. Nerve-wracking for us driving towards this mass of sticking-out humanity. How they cling on beggars belief when one considers the bumps and lurches we are experiencing.

Still, some of the road is quite good, at least until we take a left turn into the orange dust road through the paddy fields. This proves to be a detour to Kep. Kep sur Mer turns out to be a long stretch of connecting beaches with once-splendid buildings left to decay. Clearly ready for an entrepreneurial developer. So, we decide to stay on the bus. No stopover for us. On, on to Kampot.

A BRIDGE TOO FAR

Surprise, surprise, just out of Kep the orange road stops at a huge bridge works, one of many, only this time there is no bridge and the bus is 8 km short of Kampot. We de-bus, put on our little backpacks and follow the leader down dirt embankments and over the plank bridge – our leader obviously inspires confidence. Planks are laid end-to-end over sticks and light poles stuck into the riverbed. Somewhat rickety, but the locals are riding motorbikes across. One minor blessing is that we have crossed on the 'big' bridge. Alongside is the 2-metre-wide slatted pontoon mounted on floating oil barrels, obviously reserved for locals who don't weigh 90 kg.

Into another bus and on to Kampot. At the bus station, there is the usual gaggle of motorbike and taxi drivers begging us to stay at their establishment. We choose a likely lad who extols the virtues of the 'Riverview Guesthouse' and loads our gear into his taxi boot.

He is such a successful salesman that he has too many people for the taxi. Barb and I each hop on a 'cousin's' motorbike and 'follow that cab' to the guest house. Very trusting, I must say, with our luggage in the fast disappearing cab.

KAMPOT

The provincial capital of Kampot Province, located near the base of the Elephant Mountains on the Prek Kampong River.

Quiet streets, few tourists and with smatterings of French Colonial and Chinese architecture.

Bokor Hill Station is perhaps the most popular day trip – a mountaintop collection of buildings constructed by the French in the early 1920's. Once used to allow foreign visitors to escape the tropical heat, Bokor is now a ghostly ruin often shrouded in cloud.

Bokor Mountain is heavily jungled and trekking can be arranged where wild elephants and other jungle animals can occasionally be seen.

RE-THINK AND RE-GROUP

Our guest house is indeed overlooking the river. The backdrop of blue mountains shelter from a distance. The

225

river is broad and full, with pleasant cooling breezes. But the beer is warm. We stroll around the town and can't find the famous historic pepper centre - in fact we can't even find a shop that sells the amazing pepper.

My research was clearly inadequate, flawed to say the least. The article we read about Kampot pepper being sought after by the Great Chefs of Europe may have been true. For us, no sign of pepper, white, black or ground. Kampot seems pepper-less. We could have done with the help of Peter Piper to pick a peck.

There is no life emanating from any sector of the town except two big fat white pigs cutely and contentedly wallowing in puddles at the side of the road. On our thorough inspection of the village, we don't even find a tour office to book the next bus out of town. We'll have to re-group and re-think. Our plan was to spend two or three days here. On our way home, we've seen nobody to talk to, so we say 'Hello Mr and Mrs Pig, and how are you today?' It's okay, this kind of behaviour is expected in the over-fifties.

TRANQUILITY

Back at 'Riverview', I settle myself on the clean veranda and ease out the reclining sun lounges. I grab a drink for each of us, making sure it's cold, and sit back. My mood is changed. The river is wide and peaceful. The banks are treed and scattered with tall palms fringing the skyline. The red-gold sun is dropping behind the surrounding blue hills. The water shimmers with the slice of orange flame from the setting sun. Perfectly peaceful. A flock of silver-white birds swoops the length of the river bisecting the reflections on the water. My best mate, Barb, a cool drink and complete tranquillity.

It's at this point on our adventure that we do some serious navel-gazing and ponder the big question. Why? Why are we doing this?

We have a perfectly comfortable home back in the land of milk and honey, we have loving kids and grandkids just around the corner, and good friends waiting. Why are we wandering about in Asia and loving every minute of it?

Our already healthy relationship has certainly strengthened since we undertook this journey. We are continually surprised that there has been no friction and no 'I hate you' moments. One of the reasons surely has to be about the 'you and me against the world' feeling. It's a case of looking out for each other and appreciating having someone to share with.

The placid tranquil river setting dispels all negative feelings, another little memorable moment on our trip. Memories of the old song:

'Hello, Mother, Hello, Father, Gee that's better, Kindly disregard this Kampot letter.'

We eat at the guest house restaurant that is built out over the river and have a wonderful meal with some Scottish guests as fun companions. We are aghast, however, when the wait staff clear the tables by throwing the empty bottles into the river ...

A CAB TO OURSELVES

The next morning, we pump the guest house people for information on how to get to Sihanoukville. One choice from the guidebook is to catch the train, but, 'Sorry,' the receptionist says, 'the government stopped the train from taking passengers 12 months ago and it only runs every other day at that.'

So, let's look at a bus trip then. 'Sorry, there isn't a bus to Sihanoukville - only back to Phnom Penh!'

I don't think so! But they're right. It appears that the only alternative is to hire a taxi for the 2- hour trip. $25 for our own car or $4 a head to share with 6 people.

Extravagance is not my long suit but, throwing caution to the wind, we book a cab for ourselves alone. Sihanoukville beckons.

We have no regrets about leaving Kampot. We put the experience down to another stitch in the great Tapestry of Travels.

So, off over the wide river in air-conditioned comfort, eagerly looking forward to the seaside at Serendipity Beach. We liked the name 'Serendipity': 'A happy gift for making fortuitous discoveries.' The definition may not be precise but the location lived up to our expectations.

CHAPTER TWENTY

A truly great man never puts away the simplicity of a child.

SIHANOUKVILLE

Serendipitously, all the Asian beach services are on offer as we prepare to sit out the last days of our Odyssey at Serendipity Beach. Oops, did I mention the Happy Pizzas, Happy Pancakes, Happy Smoothies and Happy Everything?

Read 'Marijuana' for 'Happy'. No dis-jointed prose here! Are we prepared for this?

We affectionately wave at the wallowing pigs and gratefully leave dusty and dull Kampot, over the river bridge and head south on good roads. Our taxi driver knows a top guest house at Serendipity Beach in Sihanoukville and we agree to inspect that first. Our decision to stay at Serendipity Beach is eagerly supported by the backpacker grapevine.

On arrival and ever cautious, we check the rooms on offer and delay our decision until I spend 10 minutes and visit three more hotels. Our driver was right. We check in with the surly, sulky bloke at the front desk at the GST guest house - $11 a cabin a night (no negotiation). Large, airy twin room with an enclosed patio and comfy chairs, Satellite TV and cold water ensuite. For four dollars more we can have air-conditioning. This will do us to hide out for the next two weeks. Our single night in Kampot and missing out on the Mekong trip has left us with spare time. By now my leg is almost healed and I'm sure some sun and salt water will help the process.

Serendipity beach, what a fortunate choice of destination, good luck we say. The GST guest house has lots of cabins. In sight of the beach, we drift our way onto the sandy foreshore. We look along a 2 km stretch of clean sea lapping the clean sand. Locals with exuberant kids splash in the gentle surf. Inner tubes from trucks are the order of the day for the kids.

HAPPY, HAPPY TALK

Curiosity drives us along the extent of the beach. We pass nearly 1 km of restaurants and bars with coloured umbrellas and sun lounges. The deck chairs beckon better than Blackpool. Every 50 metres, a new variation of bamboo and thatch bar tempts us to quench our thirst or feed our faces. We eat fresh pineapple from the beach vendor and large yabbie-like barbequed crustaceans - 10 for $2.

We are warned. Indulgence in the 'happy' mixtures can lead to a couple of days of total wipe-out. Our new best friends Greg and Lachlan from Melbourne suggest avoidance of the Happy Pizzas and Happy Shakes and if people do want a quick hit, they try the free joints so at least the intake can be judged. This is sound advice as we can see one poor fellow who is certainly away with the pixies. Well into his second day of oblivion we're told. With wise heads on old shoulders, we give the happy stuff a big miss.

SIHANOUKVILLE

Sihanoukville, on the Gulf of Thailand, was founded in 1964 to be the only deep-water port in Cambodia and its beaches are popular as tourist destinations.

This place is the Mecca for the young. Accommodation can be had for free when one drinks or eats at the attached bar. Very tempting to the young backpacker, and parties on the beach to dawn are often of the 'drink till you drop' variety.

The city of 175,000 inhabitants is named after King Norodom Sihanouk.

However, it is remarkable that in this new-age 'flower power' haven there is very little obvious over-use of the dreaded weed. Little trace of the tell-tale perfume. Nobody with a paper clip on a roach. Nobody with an obvious Munchies craving.

Certainly plenty of beers and buckets of margaritas. These kids may be smarter than we think, and of course we are in bed pretty early, so who can tell what the small hours bring.

Beach vendors all display a pleasant and congenial demeanour. Although we are regularly asked to buy in a somewhat gentle way, there is no continual hustling. Evocative woody-smoke zephyrs waft along the beach. Barb can't help herself. Charcoal-barbecued small lobster hits a particular soft spot with her. Peeled, salted and lime-juiced - what a feast. This, combined with cold beer from a beach bar, translates to absolute bliss.

It is here that we enjoy the company of Andrew, the likely lad from Liverpool, quietly reserved until one mentions English soccer; we drink a beer or two with him. We are to meet up again in Phnom Penh airport and indeed he proves to be the first of the backpackers from our Asian adventure who takes up our offer of hospitality when back in Australia - Maria and Jackie quickly follow.

As we lie back in our deck chair or sun lounge, the beach vendors dance attendance. Massage, manicure, mangoes, miscellaneous bracelets, books or beer all brought to our side by smiling locals.

SHOE REPAIRS

And here a one-off and novel service is offered, a travelling shoemaker. His shoulder bag proudly displays 'Expert shoe repairs'. Asking to look at Barb's sandals and a hefty tug later, he indicates very loose stitching. Turning over my sandals, he points out how down at heel I am. He will repair both for $6. Off he goes for 5 minutes and returns with crudely 'noughts and crosses' stitched footwear and a wedge of car tyre stuck onto my sandal heel. Knowing we've been taken, we have a chuckle to ourselves as we part with the $6. Truly stitched up.

We feel at home on this beach and consider ourselves to be fortunate in finding such a suitable spot for our holding pattern prior to starting the trip home. We had, throughout our trip, decided our destinations pretty much on the run. Our key internet-researched sites of interest created a kind of join the dots plan. How long we would stay in any one place was decided by whim. If the action was there we stayed, and if not we moved on. We had always known that we would take up any time leeway in Sihanoukville.

HANS AND GRETEL

It is at a cosy coffee bar here that we make friends with Gretel and Hans, the German couple who give us a few good travellers' tips. On a couple of nights we enjoy their company at dinner.

I know - I know the story of the kids and the breadcrumbs being lost in the woods, but this Hans and Gretel are not lost. They are very modest about their travels and speak English better than Michael Caine. They have come to South East Asia from China with intentions of continuing south into Indonesia. Hans is older than me at 70 whilst Gretel a smidgen younger than Barb at 60. They exude health and vitality. They admit to having had great fears initially about how things were going to pan out.

Apprehension had dogged them for the first month. Could they get a bus? Could they get lodgings? Could they make themselves understood? Would transport be on time? Would they eat cat or dog and not know it? They both agree that their actual experiences have put all their fears behind them. They have adopted the oriental attitude of 'no worry, no hurry - it will all be the same in the morning'.

Whilst we get the impression that monies are not a problem for them, both seemed anxious to stick to a daily budget. For them, like us, it has become a challenge to travel to a tight budget. Amazingly, both our budgets are much the same. Our budget is $50 Australian and theirs is $50 American. OK, so they get an extra beer with every six-pack. Internet is their link with their families and they have experienced no hitches. They travel with a level of insurance cover that will see them medi-vacced out of any serious trouble and they are prepared to fly home immediately at any juncture for whatever reason.

They are already talking about backpacking through Argentina and have gained a few contact addresses whilst on this trip, as have we. On top of all this, we have an open invitation to stay in their unit in Heidelberg - reciprocated of course. We look forward to playing host to them in Oz and providing them with a base from which to practise their Waltzing Matilda act.

PLIGHT OF POVERTY

The most poignant memories are of the kids who sell their small pieces of merchandise. We find out that Dor, 10 years old, goes to school twice a day. He sells trinkets, bracelets and necklaces in the afternoon to pay for his education. The English School costs $8 a month and he has to sell enough each day to pay for his education. No money, no school. Dor is emphatic that he has to go to the English school so that he can learn to read and write in English.

He tells us that he makes about $40 or so a month and when Barb asks him if he saves the spare money, he just looks at her.

'I have to pay for the house and there are 8 kids in my house.' How to make Barb feel stupid! Does it make Barb feel bad? Yes. Do we reflect on how many Christmas presents our grandchildren got last year? Yes.

Every afternoon, Dor sneaks up to get a cuddle from Barb and every afternoon he sells her something else. Before we leave, Dor gives me a silk bracelet that he has made. 'For you, a special gift.' He told me of his ambition to own a guest house. 'You and Barb can stay for free.'

Clearly it is children like Dor and his friends who will make a difference for Cambodia.

Contrasts confront on every side whether we sit surfside sipping on our morning coffee or in the bar with our afternoon beer. The needy kids, ragged, unwashed and clinging to a tiny sibling tug at your sleeve and heart. The smudged faces beam a heart-breaking message, with eyes as big as Bambi's and smiles as wide as Julia Roberts'. We can't give to them all and yet we can't refuse them all. Mothers with babies in their arms push forward for food in their begging bowl. Blind invalids are guided along the beachside bars and sun lounges by the youngest of children. Hungry, unwashed and often unwell, they have limited means of support. No medical system. The extended family system is all they have. That, and whatever they beg and scrounge.

POST-TRIP SNIPPET
Through the principal at the Regent school, arrangements have been made to pay Dor's fees. Friends have rallied to pay for other deserving children on an annual basis. It is a good feeling to know that some of Cambodia's children will benefit, for less than $2.50 a week.

WESTERN INFLUENCE

The influence of Western backpackers and travellers on Serendipity Beach is most evident in the places where we eat. Our guest house restaurant is splendidly rustic with dressed timber steps leading up to a large open-spaced dining area. The timber influence continues with the roof trusses, joists and wide floor boards. The roof is tightly-stitched thatch and the waist-high bamboo walls let us look across to the beach and allow the balmy warm breezes to waft through. Fairy lights and woven bamboo light shades add a glow at night on our table. The menu offers a wide range of foods, blending a choice of western style meals along with traditional Asian fare. Meal prices range from $1.50 to $7 for the most extravagant.

As usual, the hotel has an internet room splendidly equipped with 16 screens, no shortage of internet access in Asia. Because of the regularity of our frequenting of the internet cafes, I become aware of a peculiar phenomenon.

Girls on their own sit down at a screen and merrily plough through their emails with the speed of a scalded cat. They devour the keyboard with consummate skill. The boys access their correspondence less speedily, doggedly. Internet plays a key role for the young travellers. It seems that they will spend half an hour every day connecting with everyone they have previously met on their travels, their friends at home and even their mum and dad. But the major difference lies with the couples, who sit down at a screen and pull up two chairs. Invariably and almost without exception, the female takes the lead. No matter what age group, the ladies control the keyboard. Just the same as in our family! The pen is still mightier than the sword.

I've noticed a similar trend in fast food outlets. The man gets the difficult role of finding and defending the table. The woman invariably has the easy role of taking the kids to the queue, deciding what they will or will not eat, dealing with the changing of minds, paying the money and answering 'Do you want fries with that' before balancing the tray and escorting assorted kids to the obscure table in the back corner.

MAGICAL MOMENT

Our big splurge in Sihanoukville is at the Treasure Island restaurant, out on a headland. Seasoned pillion passengers that we now are, we ride out before sunset. We trust in the first-hand advice of our neighbouring adventurers. Greg and Lachlan, with various girlfriends, have enjoyed lobsters as large as a Thermos flask and prawns par excellence! Good advice. We certainly are there to find out. The crescent-shaped sandy beach nestles between a rock outcrop at one end and a cluster of tall coconut palms at the other. The rays of the setting sun bisect our view of the sea. A spectacular view. Great meal with attentive wait staff. A memorable night. So who cares if we spend $12!

THE TOWN

Sihanoukville town seems to sprawl. Much of a muchness with any other Cambodian town, but straggled out. The same dusty streets, the same disregard of litter and the same multi-product central market bazaar where everything has its allocated area. Hardware, household goods, hats, dresses, rice, fresh greens, poultry, meat and fish all squeeze into their proper places. No doubt designed by decades of tradition.

The popular beaches are divided on each side of the town centre headland, with commercial life straggling between them all. Every beach has its style and character and it could be worthwhile to rent a motorbike for $5 a day, or as I did, take a $2 moto tour just to see all the beaches. The busy port is at the extreme edge of the town.

SIHANOUKVILLE PORT

A bigger port than that of Phnom Penh, Sihanoukville is Cambodia's only deep water, commercial and international port.

This port has undergone continual development since the 1960's. Current capacity is estimated at 1,000,000 tonnes per year, with the ability to move 200 containers in an hour.

Warships, cruise ships and container ships - all to be seen creating a hive of activity in this busy port.

Searching to find an improvement on our current hotel close to the beach proved to be unsuccessful, and indeed unnecessary. If we have time up our sleeves, we sometimes change our guest house location - same town, different beach. Good fun and a feeling of travel without the usual hours on a bus. But after my grand moto tour, I see no advantage in moving.

ATM/BANK

At the time of our visit there were no operational ATM's in Sihanoukville, so we each hopped on the back of a moto and were zoomed into the bank in town. We simply handed over our debit card, signed the form, and voila! there was our money. Too easy. Barb having put money on these cards before we left home was a good idea. It may have been just as easy to withdraw money from a credit card, but we didn't have occasion to try that option.

This was only the second time in 110 days that we hadn't had easy access to an ATM. We did, on another occasion in Saigon, have to use a Money Exchange with our debit card, due to a 3-day Tet bank holiday. (All of the nearby ATM's seemed to be locked up inside the bank buildings.)

On both of these occasions a traveller's cheque would have been readily accepted, but we hadn't bothered with these as they are increasingly difficult to cash now in some parts of Asia.

For Australians, Serendipity offers the halfway between Byron Bay and Fraser Island: throw in the romance of the local people, colour and friendliness and you have a perfect place for a travellers rest.

Our last night and what a pleasure! The gorgeous Jackie bounces in to Sihanoukville from Thailand just to wish us Bon Voyage, of course over a meal and a few drinks, after all, it is beer o'clock.

The trip home looms ahead. We've paid our final guest house bill and to our surprise are each presented with a checked Cambodian head scarf - plus a wide smile from the normally sulky manager.

In our minds, the trip is finished and we've closed the door on 4 months of adventure. It only remains to join the last dots. Phnom Penh, Bangkok, Sydney, Brisbane and Noosa.

Off to the bus on the back of a moto and so to Phnom Penh, again. The last ditch shopping - those cheap DVD's, that blue shirt, those Birkenstocks.

CHAPTER TWENTY-ONE

'Tis afterwards that everything is understood.

PHNOM PENH AND HOME

We're happy to see Sydney and delighted to be back in Brisbane. Like every traveller, there is something comforting about being back home. Familiar welcoming features and familiar faces. Our friends, Neil and Jennifer, unexpectedly meet us and whisk us off to their Brisbane city unit to the enticing aroma of a roast lamb dinner. Roast lamb, mint sauce, roast potatoes and gravy.

In a somewhat mechanical frame of mind, we had enjoyed a smooth bus trip from Sihanoukville back to Phnom Penh and the usual kerfuffle with Tuk Tuk drivers to our hotel. An afternoon nap and then off to grab last minute 'too good to miss' bargains.

After a final night's sleep, we collect our stored luggage and take the $13 taxi to the airport. Duly processed by check-in and immigration people, we board our free - yep, free - Air Asia trip to Bangkok. We had booked it from Hanoi at Christmas time when these amazing offers were the talk of the backpacker grapevine.

241

Our travel tactic this time is to stay in the central transit lounge in Bangkok; we will save $40 departure tax each by not leaving and re-entering immigration during our 5-hour stop-over. Good plan. Old traveller's trick.

INEXPENSIVE PHARMACEUTICALS
Tablets such as antihistamine and ibuprofen are inexpensive here in comparison with Australia.

There is a wide variety of vitamins and cosmetics available at a fraction of the prices we are used to paying. Antibiotic ointments can be obtained too, but take in your existing tube because explaining what you want can be difficult.

A good chance to stock up.

LAST MINUTE MAYHEM

On our arrival in Bangkok, a fatal flaw emerges. We had assumed our bags would be transferred to British Airways in Bangkok, our big mistake. Air Asia has no agreement in place to forward baggage to the British Airways connecting flight and our bags are in limbo at Air Asia baggage collection. They won't deliver them to British Airways. British Airways won't collect them from Air Asia. Stuff it, our careful plans to stay in transit blow up in our faces. Malcolm Fraser must have travelled this way. 'Life wasn't meant to be easy.'

This transit time turns out to be an absolute nightmare. Barb ends up going out through immigration, paying her departure tax and booking in again at British Airways with both sets of luggage. This is, of course, an oversimplification of the events. Even recounting the story brings back the feeling of frustration. The lesson to be learned is to ensure that baggage can be booked through to the eventual destination point. If not, the only alternative is to cop the immigration process and departure tax.

For her efforts that day, Barb earned herself the 'St Christopher's Blue Ribbon award for Troubled Travellers'.

So it transpires that our free promotional flight ends up causing unaccountable angst, but even had we paid for the flight, the outcome would have been the same. Our worst travelling experience is kept to last. Recovering from the sheer emotional pressure, Barb collapses into her seat prepared to wake up in Sydney.

God, it's good to be home.

CHAPTER TWENTY-TWO

One pair of good soles is better that two pairs of good uppers.

GETTING KITTED OUT

Friends returning from a 3-week trip through Vietnam delivered the telling blow! 'Boots? boots? What, in the Asian climate? Don't take heavy walking boots, they're too hot. The only things we wore anyplace anytime were good sandals.'

Well in advance of our trip, we had both set out to acquire our 'pre-travel requisites' and purchased sound new hiking boots. We loved them. We put on our walking socks and our new heavy-duty shoes every morning and set off on our usual walk of an hour or so. We did this conscientiously for 6 weeks and the boots were well worn in, or at least, well-loved.

Every cloud has a silver lining. The 'Op-shop' scored some good walking shoes and we were able to go on a second shopping spree for suitable serviceable sandals. We drove to the big smoke and spent an hour or so sampling sandals. Not being convinced of style or model, we upped and off to another shopping complex. This only served to convince us of the suitability of the original pairs we had seen in the very first shoe store. Do not throw a six, go back to go. Happily shod, we retreated.

PACK FOR THE CLIMATE
Not taking cold weather gear reduced the weight of our backpacks amazingly. Only one pair of sandals, no shoes - buy cold weather gear if needed. It is relatively inexpensive to post back home or give away when gear is no longer needed.

Next day, next challenge, two new travel packs! Our old, very expensive aluminium-framed and strengthened Macpacks, one with swivel hip support for ladies, had been donated to our original trekking tutors. Kiwis are good at trekking and tramping, so our offspring and grandchildren are making the most of them. Our Turkey and Greece escapade had taught us that, for us, they were too big and heavy.

The new challenge was to sort out what luggage options we had. Let's invade the camping shops, we love looking at all things camping. This will be easy, we thought. Firstly, we knew we were not going to burden ourselves with 15-kilo packs again. Secondly, we knew that we'd only take a minimum of clothes and buy replacements if and when needed. Also, on this trip, we were avoiding locations with very cold temperatures and hence only light clothes would go with us.

We scampered with great fortitude, in our newly acquired sandals, all through the multitude of camping stores in, you've guessed it, Brisbane's Fortitude Valley. This was after a quick cursory sortie in the city centre.

Déjâ vous. Once again, it was back to the city to the first store we'd been to. We were greatly enamoured with these particular flash travel packs, featuring retractable handle, wheels, plus concealed shoulder straps. We could carry them, use the shoulder straps or trail along by the extendable handle. A breakthrough. In fact, more than a breakthrough, a break off. When the shop assistant tried to demonstrate, the handle jammed, stuck then came off, and two of the zips broke. All in all, not a good day for that salesman. He had, however, sold us on the style we wanted.

BACKPACKS
Select from the range of small packs. The bigger the pack, the more you will carry - it's human nature!

Widely-spaced wheels, wide two-bar handle, inside pocket, good shoulder padding, flap to protect your shirt from dirty wheels and half the size you think you will need.

We quickly located a popular franchised bag store and were delighted to find two or three sizes of our chosen style of backpack. The trail-along extending handles were sufficiently long to allow me to trundle without bending up like a paperclip. Short extendables can be a pain in the - yes, back. We make sure, too, that the handle and wheels are wide so that the bag doesn't flip as readily as with some single-handled or narrow-gauge models.

The fact that we could wheel or shoulder our luggage was invaluable and the size meant that we could 'carry-on' to buses, trains or planes. Our packs weren't much bigger than a kid's school bag. We even scaled down from our original choice to the smaller version.

When we were buying the pack, we checked that the padding on our shoulder straps was adequate. Too late to do that when we are three days into our trip.

As it turned out, Barb's zip toggles tugged off after 3 weeks' travelling and we had to fit key rings on her main zips. (Nurturing my pack, I had no trouble). No wonder Barb's mother always described her as 'Rip, tear and bust'.

Inside the pack lining was a large pocket in which we could secrete copies of our critical papers. Our itinerary, contacts back home, e-tickets, etc. Safely home, we attended to the gear we had to pack. Previous experience of overloaded packs conditioned our selection.

What we packed worked for us, but I doubt if any two people will agree on the exact same list of items. Our principal concerns were related to health issues, with 4 months away from the security and ministering of our protective doctor. We researched our needs. I had enough concerns with existing ailments before I started on fighting off Festering Feet, Bird Flu or Amoebic Dysentery. So, a medical kit was cobbled together. Four months' worth of this and four months' worth of that, precautionary stuff for this and pre-cautionary stuff for that. And so it was that I carried a medical kit the size of a brick.

MEMORY STICK

For added security, some people like to carry a computer memory stick in addition to paperwork hard copy, with all personal information and scanned copies of documentation.

Other items in the armoury included a money belt and super-light plastic raincoat. Once we landed we acquired a folding knife, a sunhat worthy of the Crocodile Man and a shoulder bag each, big enough to hold a water bottle, for day-to-day tramping around. The old saying 'buy cheap, buy twice' proved to be the case. My first Asian shoulder bag ended up frayed, frazzled and in the bin and I found myself paying again for a better quality number.

After meeting with many travellers during our trip, we were repeatedly complimented on our foresight in the selection and style of luggage. Everyone agreed that they had packed too much and could have cut back on 'comforts', could even have left their hairdryers behind! We made a decision not to take any electrical equipment, including cameras, phones, chargers and adaptors, all of which are regularly lost or stolen. In fairness, all of the backpacking kids had phones and we didn't hear of them being stolen very often. More commonly we heard reports of stolen cameras.

Nobody ever told us that they should have taken more. All agreed that books were the heaviest. Luckily one is able to buy or swap inexpensive reading material whenever the need arises. Everyone travelled with their guidebook of choice.

Our selection of the small backpack would be a good starting point, or choose the next size up as a safety net. At times we would have enjoyed another shoebox or two of space but always knew that space equalled weight so put up with our restricted wardrobe. Full marks must go to Barb, who forsook some claims to her usual elegance and left her Versace gear at home. It must be said though, that there was never an occasion when she wasn't appropriately dressed. Juggling a limited but well balanced choice of shirts, shorts and slacks (roll-up-able and crease resistant), she was a proper princess.

BOOKS ARE HEAVY

English language books can be readily obtained almost everywhere in Asia.

Second hand novels, photocopied masterpieces and new books are all there for the asking - swap with fellow travellers, browse the many bookshops or buy from the hawkers.

Don't take up precious space with too many books. One guidebook, and one or two novels each was adequate.

CHAPTER TWENTY-THREE

A kindly message needs someone to carry it.

KEEPING IN CONTACT

Before we left Australia, we made a tough decision to leave our phones behind and to use the internet and internet phones on a regular basis. As it was, we would have had to buy new phones because ours are CDMA and won't work overseas. Each new country requires a new SIM card and different power plug adaptors, so we thought it was just another thing to look after and all too hard. We could always purchase second-hand local phones and local SIM cards for very little money when in Asia. In fact, we didn't buy a phone because we found public phones, especially those at the internet cafes, easily available at low cost.

TEXTING

I will admit that when you are over 60, the technology gap can be quite a challenge. For me, texting is an exceedingly mind (or thumb) bending task - digital RSI.

Youngsters sit with their fifth digit flitting over a miniscule keypad happily communicating in nano-seconds around the globe, or indeed across a room. I am somewhat envious of this highly developed and practical skill. I comfort myself; perhaps delude myself, with the knowledge that I can barely read the numerals on the phone pad, never mind the alpha characters.

Can I cope with starting to compose a text message? Not when technology takes over and finishes my words for me. Next year the phone will be able to send my whole message, without my help.

Yes, I can hear you. The cry rings out, 'I couldn't possibly NOT be available for the children. I must be contactable at all times. Our daughter could be giving birth while we're away!'

Yes! Yes! Yes!

At this stage, you may choose to take your phone, but don't forget that you will have to carry the phone at all times because leaving it in the room makes it easy pickings for the light-fingered - hence the abundant supply of phones without instruction books available in local markets. Additionally, you'll need a charger and adaptor.

One Canadian couple travelling without a phone remarked that their 21 and 23-year-old kids left at home had grown up and become much more self-sufficient in their parents' absence. They had found that the internet was available absolutely everywhere and provided all the security of contact they needed.

EMAIL ADDRESS

Our broadband address at home was lost when we disconnected the phone, but some broadband providers will offer a dial-up link for a nominal monthly cost so that you can keep your same email address and access it via Internet Explorer.

Hotmail offers free internet addresses, so if you don't have internet at home just join up to Hotmail. It's a good idea to go into your Hotmail before you leave and key in all your friends' addresses. We organised one 'group' to cover family and close friends so that, with one message, we could bombard them with emails to let them know where we were and how things were going. Made us feel safer somehow.

INTERNET
Throughout Asia, internet is readily accessible in guest houses, hotels or internet cafes for very moderate charges and phone links are offered at low cost. Every street in a popular area will have a number of internet cafes.

PHONE

Your home phone can be left on if friends are house-minding, otherwise consider suspending the number with a redirect to family or friends. House sitters or tenants can then put the phone on in their name with a different number and yours is easy enough to re-connect when you return.

CHAPTER TWENTY-FOUR

Men grow old, pearls grow yellow, there is no cure for it.

HEALTH ISSUES

Mark Twain once said to be careful of reading health books; one may die of a misprint.

A major priority overseas is health. Rightly, it should assume a position near the top of the list. Tee up a session with a doctor who will explain and reassure regarding travel in Asia. Alternatively, in most Australian capital cities there are medical centres that specialise in travel health, but keep in mind that this option can be expensive. Have the required injections, fill the scripts and keep these medicines in original packing. On request, a yellow Health Card detailing the shots you have received and a letter confirming your drugs and medical history will be supplied by your doctor.

MEDICAL PRECAUTIONS

Medical precautions can assume a larger than life position. Imagination, helped by friends who are too scared to go walk-about themselves, conjures up every tropical illness and aliment found in a healthcare almanac. The stay-at-homes will relay every gory tale about rabies, scabies, foot rot and galloping gangrene.

> **TRAVEL VACCINATION CERTIFICATE BOOK**
> Mainly for your own information. We carried the booklet but weren't asked to produce it at any stage. It may be helpful, in the case of illness, to know which particular vaccinations are up-to-date.
>
> In Yellow Fever countries such as Africa, some parts of South and Central America and the Caribbean, the official proof of vaccination for yellow fever will be required.

Whilst I believe the extreme comments are excessive, let's balance things and adopt a practical approach. It goes without saying that prescribed medicines go in your kit along with some sort of treatment for the dreaded trots. We carried tablets for mild doses of the trots plus an emergency quick-cure 2-tablet treatment for extreme diarrhoea. We had these with us, but didn't need to use any of them.

We opted not to take malaria tablets. They need to be taken regularly and can induce feelings of nausea. The decision on malaria tablets is really an individual option. We listened to advice on the mosquito risk and took mozzie repellent.

You will need some type of antiseptic for scratches and cuts and an antibiotic cream is a good idea, but these products are readily available throughout Asia. In our case, there was one occasion when we needed a prickly-heat powder for my back. Barb remembered her mother using it when they lived in the bush. Easy-peasy, the first pharmacy we checked had it, and two minutes later we saw it on the supermarket shelf for half the price!

We had a mind-set to wash and shower even more regularly than usual and to ensure that we paid particular attention to washing our hands at every opportunity. (There is antiseptic gel available that doesn't require water.) We took to showering and washing with a disinfectant soap, Dettol, which was readily available in the supermarkets. We had no sickness and no need for our medical kits for the whole 4 months of our trip.

BASIC MEDICAL KIT
Anti-diarrhoea tablets
Anti-vomiting tablets
Antibiotic cream
Antiseptic cream
Antiseptic gel for waterless hand cleaning
Germicidal soap
Headache tablets
Prescription drugs
Band-Aids

All these treatments are readily available in Asia, but having some basics on hand can help if stricken in out-of-the-way places.

WATER

Drink the local water and die - well, at least die-arrhoea. Tap water should simply not pass your lips.

Aqua Vita. The water of life. Water will be your ever-present companion throughout your Asian adventure. Little bottles, big bottles or giant bottles - you will end up buying each at some stage throughout your trip. Everywhere you go, the mineral water bottle is tucked into a bag of some sort. The giant bottle, bought at a proportionally lower price, can stay in your room and allow you to top up the smaller bottle.

Many stories are told about the dreaded trots setting in after drinking the local water or having ice cubes in a drink. We were careful not to take any chances and even cleaned our teeth with bottled water. I did however clean my toothbrush under the tap and lived to tell the tale.

A cafe owner informed us that the people who supply the restaurants and cafes with bottled water also provide the clean ice each day. We did have ice on a few occasions with no ill effect.

CHAPTER TWENTY-FIVE

The beginning of wisdom is to call things by their right names.

TOILETS IN ASIA

There is little more daunting than the spectre of some overseas toilets.

While travelling in Turkey, we visited the Roman ruins at Ephesus, where of great interest was the Lavatorium. A generous-sized communal room and along three sides, bench seats graced the wall. Holes the size of dinner plates perforated the bench seats at 2-ft intervals, and below all of this ran an enclosed channel of water to whisk away the business of the moment, or should that be movement. Apparently sponges on sticks were used as a finale.

Seemingly, these were the precursors of the go-it-alone pedestals we use today - so what if we miss out on talking about the weather with the bloke next door.

In Asia, the peoples' choice award goes to the two-footed flat toilet, the squat toilet, known amongst the backpackers as the 'starting block'. It is these toilets that strike fear into we Westerners. And rightly so. After all, we're used to the high-rise variety. Crouching and balancing over a circular hole with each foot on a ceramic footprint can be a death-defying act. The toilet toll (or should that be roll?) of westerners who are never seen again is not published.

However, the Asians are scrupulous in the personal-hygiene stakes. There is always a tank or basin or bucket full of clean water under a tap. The hand is used to scoop water to wash, a dipper is provided to scoop water and flush. Fair to say that Kleenex won't go out of business because the convenient toilet roll is used to dry off and is discarded in the disposal bin in the corner. (The underground sewer system is prone to blockage if paper is flushed.) Whilst personal hygiene is strict, most of the public lavatories themselves could benefit from a good, extremely good, sluicing and disinfecting. The exception is public toilets in major business and shopping centres.

WORLD TOILET ORGANISATION

A non-profit organisation established in Singapore in 2001 and dedicated to improving toilets and sanitation globally. Delegates from all over the world attend conferences, seminars, toilet exhibitions and go on amazing toilet tours.

World Toilet Day is November 19th.

The ultimate in our western style bathroom suites is the matching toilet and bidet. Asians have employed the bottom-washing, water-cleansing system for aeons, and we westerners were slow to catch on. Nowadays, Asians have brilliantly combined our conventional pedestal toilet with a hand-held water-cleansing bidet device that is in many ways like a hand-held garden-watering gun. Neatly plumbed by the side of the pedestal toilet, the silverchromed trigger-operated water rose is brought into play to complete your toilet hygiene, a wonderful addition to any western closet. (OK, tell me I'm eccentric, but I loved them.)

In all our travels, we never once had accommodation without pedestal toilets. All the guest house toilets were clean, but on one occasion the plastic toilet seat had been cracked and was mended with a short metal strip and pop rivets. I expected a nip on the bottom but survived, un-nipped and un-pinched.

To slay the dragon of toilet phobia, I must restate that ALL the hotels and guest houses we stayed in had pedestal toilets, and we only confronted the 'starting block' style at public places such as bus stations and cafes. When you are out and about and need a toilet, just ask at the nearest eating or drinking place, shopping complex or department store. Fast food outlets come in really handy, Golden Arches can be a blessing.

CHAPTER TWENTY-SIX

A dry roof and a good bed make long nights short.

FINDING ACCOMMODATION

Can we do it? Yes we can!
Place all fears about accommodation behind you.
Simple Simon could find a place to sleep even without
Little Boy Blue. From your guidebook map, go to the
central area that has the most guest houses listed and
start there. This is often the 'Old Quarter' in the large
towns, often a highlighted zone.

We consider ourselves lucky to have enjoyed some
great accommodation. Oft times, Barb made
spontaneous decisions like 'This is a cute little guest
house, let's stay for a few days.' Alas, alack, at five
o'clock in the morning, reveille sounds from the mosque
five metres from our bedroom window. The quality of
their Tannoy system outclasses anything to be heard on
Piccadilly Railway Station or a Live Aid concert. Perhaps
some gods need contact five times daily whereas others
only need to be wakened by bells on Sundays.

ROOM FOR THE NIGHT - EASY PEASY

Notwithstanding all of these attempts at reassurance, guest house hunting can initially fill one with some apprehension. Will we find one clean enough? Close enough? Cheap enough? Will we find one before nightfall? Will there be a 'House Full' sign? Never fear, not once did we have a problem finding a suitable guest house, even if, sometimes, one night was enough.

ACCOMMODATION QUICK TIPS
♦ Use your guidebook.
♦ Look first in a town's 'Old Quarter'.
♦ Look for a cluster of recommended guest houses.
♦ For every mentioned guest house, you'll find twice the number when you get there.
♦ Book one night and re-locate if you find a better option.
♦ Inspect the room - it's standard practice.
♦ Ask if breakfast and internet is included.
♦ Always offer a lower price.
♦ Ask fellow travellers about accommodation in your next port of call.

The default position is always on hand - book into a regular small hotel. There are plenty of these close at hand ($20/$25) and although you may pay up to double the guest house price, you will have a guaranteed place to sleep, a good bed, shining clean bathroom and toilet, soft fluffy towels, air-conditioning, TV and bar fridge. You don't often get all of these in your guest house. Still, there was only one occasion when we didn't have our own ensuite bathroom, and that because of choice, not necessity.

DON'T PANIC! DON'T PANIC!

I am a bit of a panic merchant when it comes to getting accommodation and like to be sure of lodgings being arranged and sorted. I tell myself to slow down, calm down, there will always be a place to sleep - and there always was! After two weeks, I no longer panicked over accommodation.

WHEN PRICING ACCOMMODATION, CHECK FOR 'INCLUSIONS'

♦ Breakfast is worth around $3 for two people.
♦ Internet is about $2 per session.
♦ Air-conditioning costs around $4.
♦ Hot water can sometimes be an extra bonus.
♦ It is worth a little extra to secure a room on a lower floor if you find stairs difficult

---

Internet booking ensures accommodation, but it reduces the ability to touch and feel and choose a better deal. The inclusion of such things as free internet, satellite TV and breakfast can be overlooked in the cut and thrust of the pre-bookings. You can readily put a value on your daily internet and breakfast costs (about $3 for two breakfasts and $2 internet charge) and the accommodation at $14 may be better value than the one at $10, not to mention the luxury of up-to-date TV news and sports programmes to fill in the odd spare recreational moment.

The only exception to taking a chance on digs is if you are arriving late at night, when it is best to book ahead. Your current guest house will often do this for you, but remember to specify the price you want to pay. For daylight arrivals, give yourselves a little time to seek out the best deal - this never took us longer than 20 minutes.

When canvassing hotels, ask for all details then inspect the rooms, mattresses, pillows and bathrooms. They expect this and invite you to look at their rooms.

INSPECTING ROOMS

♦ Check the mattresses and pillows for comfort.
♦ Make sure that the sheets are clean and that a top sheet is supplied.
♦ Turn on the taps in bathrooms.
♦ Flush the toilet.
♦ Check air-conditioning and fans for noisiness.
♦ Try for a room with cross ventilation, with windows that open.
♦ Check to see that there isn't a nightclub next door.
♦ Check the towels.
♦ Inspect the door locks.

We were always able to quickly find a bed for the night, but as we were working to a tight budget, we sometimes compromised on the facilities.

'Come into my parlour', said the spider to the fly. Initially, some rooms look inviting, but after booking in, you may discover that the toilet doesn't flush, taps drip and the fan suffers from St Vitus's Dance. It's only one night and having booked into a close and convenient guest house allows you to search around for a better one next day.

Somehow, best bargain became my charter, my personal challenge, my raison d'etre. To my delight and great joy, rooms were readily available at $12 to $15 a night. Twin beds, clean sheets, soft pillows and most of the time back-friendly mattresses. Neat ensuite with clean shower and pedestal toilet. Hot water is not always on tap in the low-cost rooms, but all have electric fans.

The compromises we made were based on several factors - size of room, size of beds, number of stairs to climb, good airflow with windows, fan or air-conditioning, fridge and cable TV, breakfast inclusion. If most of the factors were right, we negotiated a price according to what we were prepared to forfeit. This was most often the air-con because we didn't feel we needed it and this saved us $3 to $4. Free breakfast and internet proved to be a worthwhile inclusion.

BED LINEN
Some guest houses have the quaint custom of not supplying a top sheet. A blanket - yes. Top sheet - no. Either ask for a top sheet, use your sarong or carry a silk sleeping-bag liner (readily available in Asia).

A day-to-day pastime was comparative guest house costing. My habit was to call into the nearby mini-hotels and ask about room charges. Certainly there was no problem in getting two-star plus quality at any of the nearby small hotels. Invariably, $25 or less would secure you an absolutely first-class and acceptable room, spacious, clean and well serviced with all the comforts of home. We didn't need swimming pools, saunas, gyms, nightclubs and cocktail bars, so the basic mini-hotel served well. This change in level of accommodation could well allow an indulgence, some minor decadence, as a change from guest houses.

The trick, in the small hotels, was to persist in asking for the cheapest twin room - the words 'lowest cost' didn't seem to be understood. Perhaps negotiate with some humour and also put on your best impoverished look. Twin rooms, often with two queen-sized beds, always afforded more space and hence we always asked for these.

If I asked for the cheapest room, the $25 room often came down to $15, and if I really hemmed and hawed, came down to $12. The cheaper offering was usually without air-conditioning and maybe up one flight of stairs. Again, in these matters, your own needs dictate the price, but do try to push for the cheapest as it is often the same style room that was initially offered for $25, but at the rear of the hotel.

Many backpackers stay only one night, so you can offer the carrot of staying for 4 or 5 nights; later you can always change lodgings if not happy - music is too loud, road is too noisy, walls are too thin; you'll think of some reason to move.

Given that your start point is your guidebook, you'll have a very good knowledge of where you want to stay and the names and addresses of some guest houses. A note to remember: some of the bigger hotels that are less central can be charging 4 to 5 times the price for a similar room to your $12/$14 one. My feeling is that these hotels are used by the major tour companies and take block bookings from their captive, or is it unsuspecting, audience. There again, these people could be the 10-day/2-week tourist (T'weekers) who don't have the time or the inclination to shop around - indeed, their bookings would have been made before they left home.

NEGOTIATING PRICE

Price can be negotiated easily if humour and good manners are used.

Forfeiting some of the more common facilities can give cause for a price reduction.

Often rooms at the back or on the higher floors come at a cheaper price.

If you are staying for a few nights, a better deal can often be struck, as one or two nights is the norm for young backpackers.

TO BOOK OR NOT TO BOOK

Whether or not to pre-book guest houses was a well-discussed point between us. Barb's sense of adventure (foolhardy, I say) left her opting to arrive unannounced and prepared to walk the streets searching for suitable lodgings. Her aim was to find something equal in quality to the Ritz at the price of a rundown doss house. Perhaps if her lineage is checked we will find an Ebenezer Scrooge.

I was constantly amazed at the casual nonchalance with which the young backpackers arrived with no guest house booked. They would arrive at say, midday, sit down and have a beer, a meal, a beer or two more and then they would stroll through the backpacker area (selected from the guidebook maps) and check out various guest houses at random. Pot luck seems to work well. Still, I always remained more confident when I knew that any late night arrival saw sleeping arrangements in place. After all, this still gave us the chance next day to shop around for a better-value alternative.

Some towns seem to have a 'Guest House Union'. The rooms roughly the same, the facilities roughly the same and the price roughly the same, with any variation price-linked to additional features. The more ramshackle or paint deprived, the lower the cost; the more polished and prim, the higher. Cleanliness is next to godliness, they say, and godliness comes at a few dollars more - who says it's more difficult for a rich man to enter the kingdom of heaven?

SHARED BATHROOMS

For rooms with shared bathroom facilities, the price of a room can be reduced by about 30%. We made a point of trying these to see what they were like. The shared bathrooms were great: clean, tidy and convenient. We had no trouble with the concept except that we had to leave our room to go to the loo at night. If you have ever stayed at an Australian outback pub, you will find these Asian shared bathrooms a big improvement.

Budget accommodation can become easier to find as you talk to fellow travellers. Each of the young ones has covered, it seems, half the continent and is able to supply a fund of information

The young travellers are inspirational. One feels like writing to their folks back home, complimenting them on the courage and behaviour of their offspring. Travelling alone through China, Laos, Vietnam, Myanmar, Cambodia, Thailand etc, etc, they all seem to be fit and vibrant. They carry backpacks the size of a small car and tell of experiences their parents won't want to know about.

BATHROOMS

PEDESTAL TOILETS Every room for our complete 4-month trip had a pedestal toilet. We didn't even SEE a guest house room without this western facility.

BIDETS Personal hand-held systems were installed everywhere.

SHOWERS Bathrooms can sometimes be too cramped, with the shower actually wetting the whole room, toilet and all. Check this out before turning the shower on and soaking towels and toilet paper.

HAND BASINS Often without plugs

TOWELS Ask for fresh ones if they are too thin. Check the towel quality and quantity first and ask straight away if extras are needed.

In 30 years time, they may not be so lucky when they are the age of today's baby boomers, they may not be able to find a deserted beach with only a handful of visitors. Ko Samui, Phi Phi and Langkawi islands, the dream deserted locations of 20 years ago, are now nearly out of the range of budget travellers. The price gap is ever widening, with the onslaught of major hotels buying up the once pristine playground of hippie adventurers.

LAUNDRY

Chinese influence seems well established. Laundry services abound, and for a few dollars you can wash the complete contents of your pack - you'll have to stay in bed until it is all returned, of course! We each usually wash our own clothes and find that shirts, shorts and knickers will dry in quick smart time when flung over the wall fans. My fellow male readers will understand the difficulty I face when writing up daily expenses with chaffed and red-raw fingers.

NOISY NEIGHBOURS

If some of these words of wisdom are falling on deaf ears, this could be a blessing. Someone has to warn you that guest houses, by their very nature, have a wide variety of patrons. Some need to play loud music and some wear hob-nailed boots, but this is only noticeable after 10 or 11 o'clock when you have retired for the night. Usually the hob-nailed booters are in a party of four and have, by arrangement, elected to arrive back to the guest house at hourly intervals. Deaf ears are a nice attribute to have, so arm yourselves with some good industrial ear plugs, just in case!

COUNTING THE COST

I had allocated myself the nightly task of counting our money-in-hand, checking against yesterday's balance and trying to reconcile the difference. Of course, every day there was some minor shortfall, which necessitated a feat of mental gymnastics to track where the offending monies were spent. Funny how there was never an excess of funds at day end. The one aspect I constantly got right was the accommodation cost, probably because it was burned into my brain from bargaining!

Finding accommodation: Did we do it? Yes, we did!

HOW NECESSARY ARE THE 'EXTRAS'?

TV If the hotel has cable, most programmes are in English. We found TV useful for catching up on sport and were surprised at the excellent coverage of international news and events.

AIR-CONDITIONING Most people say that this is not really necessary unless the weather is particularly hot - or cold. Fans and cross ventilation worked best for us.

HOT WATER Again, depending on the weather. Not really a must when the weather is very hot, but of course, an individual choice. In some towns, all lower-cost guest houses only offer cold showers.

FRIDGE Depends on whether you need cold food and drinks in your room. Sometimes it is good to have a cold drink waiting in your room at the end of a long hot day. Bars and restaurants are so inexpensive, though, that a fridge isn't really a must.

FANS Always provided, and for extra comfort you can often add air-conditioning. Fans are great for drying clothes in a hurry too - just fling your damp shirt over the wall fan (wipe the fan first.

BEDS Twin rooms often have two queen beds. Even if you only sleep in one, the other is handy to give extra room for spreading out.

IN-ROOM PHONES Rarely found in lower cost guest houses. These calls are very expensive anyway, so better to use low-cost internet cafes or Post Offices.

IN-ROOM SAFES Never in cheaper guest houses. Use the front-desk safe.

MOSQUITO NETS November to March is not the mozzie season. Nets may be helpful when the critters are bad.

MINIBARS Not found in the cheaper guest houses.

LAUNDRY SERVICE Available on request at every guest house.

CHAPTER TWENTY-SEVEN

The journey is the reward.

BOOKING TOURS AND TRANSPORT

Throughout our trip, we are confronted with making travel arrangements for tours or for the next stage of the journey by plane, bus or train. Here feelings of uncertainty emerge.

Do we use a tour office? Do we book at our guest house or do we find the rail or bus station ourselves? Will we get 'ripped off'? If we go to the local rail office, will they speak English? Do we need to get a visa or renew one?

Have we enough local money? Where is the nearest ATM to pay for our trip? Will we trust the Money Changers? (Money changers! I vaguely remember Shylock from my limited study of Shakespeare and immediately perceive each Foreign Exchange office to be staffed by his offspring - not so of course.) Drawing money from ATM's, banks and money changers presents no problem and travel offices are quick to give directions to the nearest money source.

Money aside, one is still confronted with making all the arrangements for travel. We found little or no difficulty booking buses, trains or tours - all too easy.

We think we want to see everything ... well, at least we want to pick and choose. Where to go? When to go? How to go? How much? When overseas, the simple answer is to head for the nearby tour office; there's one on almost every street. If you need travel bookings ... bus, train, plane, boat - even new visas - you've guessed it, call into the next-door tour office! Even ask your hotel or guest house. Personal, custom-built tours are easily chosen and options for length of tour (hours or days) are smoothly accommodated.

HUGE SAVINGS: PACKAGED TOURS VS DIY
Travellers win out with stunning cost savings when they do-it themselves rather than book a package tour from home.

Sparing everyone a litany of examples, only one is used here. Know that huge savings will be made if you shop around when you are overseas.

HANOI TO HA LONG BAY 2-day/1-night VIP trip. Bear in mind that this example is for the same trip on the same boat.

Australian-booked tour price $300 to $600
Local tour office price $40 to $55

My abacus tells me that around 90% is saved - give or take a few beads.

BUS TRANSPORT

Buses can be booked at each town's central bus station either the day you need to travel or in advance by any tour operator, or even at the front desk at your accommodation.

A rough estimate of cost is about $1 per hour of travel time, with a 4-hour bus trip costing about $4 per person. It's useful to get several prices before making a booking. Adequate English is spoken everywhere. Ask about the number of seats and whether it is a VIP bus, as legroom can be an issue.

Our approach to getting the best deals is to ask advice of young travelling Cavalieros in cafés and accommodation lounging areas. They are a fund of information and are very willing to tell of their touring triumphs. The best deal, the quickest travel and the most helpful tour operator. The 'cons' are also exposed, like which routes and which transport NEVER to take. Most are ready to tell of their near-death experience and with what fortitude and resourcefulness they saved themselves and their fellow travellers.

MOTOS

Everywhere in Asia, the motorbike is used as a 'taxi' service. One doesn't walk far without being solicited by the moto driver. This is a low-cost and quick method of transport. Hop on the back, hang onto the driver's waist or the luggage rack behind - no helmets offered - a great leap of faith.

TRAIN BOOKINGS

Our train trips were reserved for the longer hauls. Having used the bus for one long overnight trip, we resolved to pamper ourselves with sleeper berths on the train for long hauls. Over twice the cost of a bus seat but ten times more comfortable.

In Thailand, the corridor runs through the centre of the carriage and is flanked on either side by conventional double seats facing each other. These double seats fold down to a broad bed on each side of the aisle, with the top bunks folding down from the wall. A steward arranges the bed and makes it up with sheets. Each very comfortable sleeping space has its own light and curtain for privacy.

Despite our initial nervous cautiousness, train bookings are easily accomplished. Our first booking experience is in Hat Yai, Thailand where we follow signs to the station booking office and wait for a few minutes on comfortable seats for the booking clerk to be free - pick a ticket and wait till your number is called, just like at a deli counter. We ask questions about departure times, on-board facilities and cost options for top or bottom sleepers. From Hat Yai to Hua Hin it is to be an overnight 12-hour trip so we book the slightly more expensive $25 bottom bunks for easy access and comfort. Good English is spoken and the staff couldn't be more helpful.

The Vietnamese-style sleeper (soft sleeper) is a cabin for four with the bunks one up and one down on each side of a fixed table. The bunks, about 750 mm wide, have 100 mm mattresses with what appears to be a carpet runner on top. Sheets, pillow and blankets are stacked ready for the bed to be made up. Surprisingly, the carpet-topped bed is quite comfortable. From Hanoi to Hue, Barb and I, with two strange men, sleep happily through the night. Unlike the Thai trains, there are no privacy curtains in the four-berth cabin and there is a toss-up as to whether you or they snore more - we have our ear plugs ready.

During the night, when going to the loo, make sure you take note of the compartment number; Barb didn't. Hence, like Wee Willie Winke, she was running through the train 'rapping at the windows, crying at the locks'. She had to open quite a few doors before she found the right sleeping buddies.

TRAIN TRAVEL - VIETNAM
Comfortable, safe and inexpensive.
There are two types of trains in Vietnam. The best trains are SE1 to SE6. Trains TN3 to TN10 are slower and older.

Soft-class sleeper
1750 km $30 to $55
700 km $14 to $16
500 km $10 to $11

Train options
Soft-class sleepers 4 berth
Hard-class sleepers 6 berth

Seats Soft class, hard class, air-con or open air.

Price range Sleeper cabins are twice the price of ordinary seats.

Style and sophistication of the train affect the price. Read all about it. www.seat61.com/Vietnam.htm

---

TRAIN TRAVEL – THAILAND

Comfortable, safe, cheap with three classes. 1st class cabin. 2-berth air-conditioned sleeper cabins with washbasin. Single travellers can pay for sole use or share. Shower and toilet at end of carriage. Approximately 30% more expensive than a 2nd class sleeper, and only available on some trains.

2nd class sleeper Sleeper beds flank the aisle. Double seats convert to beds. Top bunks are narrower and cheaper. Crisp sheets and mattresses are made up by steward. Curtained for privacy. Book early to secure bottom bunks.

2nd class air-conditioned seats Comfortable recliner seats in an air-conditioned carriage.

2nd class ordinary seat Recliner seats with ability to open windows for great air flow.

3rd class Padded or wooden bench seats.

Relative scale of cost per person for journey approximately 1000 km:
1st class cabin $40
2nd class sleeper $25
2nd class air-con seat $20
2nd class ordinary seat $14
3rd class ordinary seat $10

HINT With second-class sleepers, booking the more sought-after bottom bunks early often results in the top bunks being left unoccupied.
Read all about it: www.seat61.com/Thailand.htm

MINIVANS

In Thailand, we enjoy the relative comfort and ease of travel provided by the local minivan. Our local contact, Bangkok Bill, has told us of the minivan southbound staging point near Victory Monument, easily accessible by sky train.

From Bangkok to Hua Hin, we pay $4.50 each for a two-and-a-half-hour trip in the 12-seater minivan - this compared to red-bus public transport at half the price, trip twice as long, open windows and blaring music. These minivan stations seem to be harder to locate than the big bus central station. Ask at your guest house if there is a minivan available and about the location of the terminus. One tourist shop quoted us around $50 in a minivan for the same trip that we paid $9 for, but the dearer minivan would have been for our personal use (door to door). Probably a good idea if there are a few in your group.

On our initial arrival into Bangkok, we had pre-booked a taxi due to the late hour of our arrival and paid $58. On our second visit to Bangkok, we booked a shared minivan back to the airport and this time we paid $3 each. Something wrong here! Next time around, we'll ask more questions of our travel agent or better still, do it ourselves and check the guidebook for alternative travel options into each major city.

TUK TUKS

Tuk Tuk taxi travel is an institution unto itself. These magnificent little vehicles are built onto the top of a motorbike. The name is clearly onomatopoeic. Tuk Tuk.

The little buggies cough and splutter, belch and hiccough when starting up. About the size of a vitamin-enriched rider mower or small golf cart, they sport anything colourful, paintwork, seats or tailgate. The beak-like roof protects both passengers and driver. The double seat in the back is open to all fumes but protected on each side and back by low stainless steel metalwork, obviously there to keep inebriated tourists from flipping out into the Asian traffic.

Waiting drivers call out 'Tuk Tuk' and often have a minder or procurer who spruiks the economy and desirability of these denizens of driving. The catch cry 'Where you go?' is heard from every street corner. These clever fellows usually ask 'where you from?' An open-ended question inviting some positive answer. 'Australia,' say I. 'Melbourne, Sydney?' says he. 'Brisbane,' say I, and so the interlocutory starts.

He's sucked me in and now the list of local sites and places of interest are recited. 'Yes, I'd like to see the Golden Buddha.' Only 50c to go there and 50c back. Once you have declared your destination, the smooth-talking procurer passes you on to a nearby Tuk Tuk driver. Their charge is miniscule (negotiate a price first) and they often wait for the return fare. Well, I was looking for something to do anyway.

TOUR/TRAVEL AGENTS

Every town and every busy street has its travel agent or tour operator. One gets the spiel that the best tour in the best bus at the best price is from the company owned by their brother or cousin, hence you'll get the very best treatment on your tour. Nevertheless, to a person, they are all your best friends within seconds of greeting you.

Once again, the line that always gets me in is 'Where are you from?' I say 'Australia', they say 'Melbourne, Sydney, kangaloo?'

Haven't I heard this somewhere before? Didn't I extend the hand of friendship to someone else?

Shouldn't I have become more wary? Nevertheless, when they ask 'What is your name?' politeness makes me answer 'Desmond' and so an intimate friendship is immediately born.

Getting out of this situation is difficult. A strategic retreat is called for. The art is to extricate yourself by saying 'maybe tomorrow, maybe later' or some such whopping fib. Before you go, ask their price for a bus or minivan to your next port of call or for the package tour you have selected. This can then become your bargaining position in shopping for the cheapest fare.

Being collected from your guest house is a nice-to-have inclusion in any price. Often accommodation houses act as tour agents, with photographs and tour details displayed on walls. Knowing the going rate is useful when your guest-house owner wants you to book tickets through them, which often ensures pick-up from your doorstep.

These guest house owners can be a fund of information about the local scene. Make inquiries regarding local sights or cheap minivan buses (used by the locals) to your next destination although it's best to check tour prices from more than one source. A day trip can vary by quite a few dollars depending on which tour office you pick.

We find ourselves asking the cost of onward travel almost as soon as we arrive, no doubt preparing ourselves for a quick escape if deemed desirable. Often prices vary by about 20% between adjacent tour offices.

ASIA - INTERNAL FLIGHTS

Whilst in Malaysia, we make the on-the-run decision, or is it on-the-fly, to get to Hanoi before Christmas. We'll book our flights, allowing time to sort out the Vietnamese

30-day visas on our way through Bangkok (allow 3 to 4 days). From there, straight to Hanoi.

> **CARRY PERSONAL INFORMATION**
> It is useful to have all personal, insurance, credit card, passport and visa details listed on paper, coded where necessary, and small enough to slip into your wallet. Don't forget to add the expiry date of your passport.

ONLINE BOOKINGS

The backpacker grapevine has let us know that Air Asia has some amazing specials, so off to the local internet cafe where we carefully search through the Air Asia website, checking prices for several different dates. Finally we break through the mysteries of on-line pricing and obtain four varying prices on four different dates.

In our enthusiasm, we decide on a date and load our details in (after being thrown out five times because of server problems). Hooray we think - we've decided the date, we've OK'd the price, we've entered both names with absolute care and now we progress to confirm our bookings. Oops - oops - we haven't brought our passports with us and cannot complete confirmation for an international flight without passport numbers and expiry dates. Damn! Damn! Damn! After eventually completing all the boxes, we now have to start all over again, tomorrow. The lesson we learn here is to carry a note of our passport numbers AND expiry dates in our wallets.

Well, there's a bright side to everything! Newly refreshed, we sign on again bright and early, we judiciously re-check the price and departure date and lo and behold, the price at which we would have agreed yesterday had dropped by $15 a ticket. With a spring in our step, we leave the internet cafe confident of having nailed down our exit strategy from Thailand to Vietnam. We include in our forward planning a 4-night stay in Khao San Road, Bangkok, to provide the 3-day time lag to get the Vietnam visas issued. Had we checked that our time lag didn't include a weekend? Nope! But again, the luck of the Irish took over and we were happily positioned with sufficient days to get the visas and make our flight.

It's during this process in Bangkok, and again in Vietnam, we find out that to get a visa you quite simply ask at a tour office. They'll arrange it, charging a few dollars for their efforts.

AIRPORTS

At one time, airports held a mystique and promise of new horizons and indeed a promise of in-flight pampering. Not now; despite being an integral part of adventuring, one has to borrow some patience and prepare to be processed and X-rayed.

Relating one experience may serve to prepare travellers.

On leaving Bangkok with the internet printout confirming our booking to Hanoi clutched in hand, we queue, as the printout instructs, at the Air Asia counter. We wait while the people in front of us (other Aussie Baby Boomers) attempt to fathom how their flight booking just happens to be cancelled and they are neither re-booked nor informed.

Eventually we are looked after, only to be told that we didn't need to be at this booking counter - the printout really meant 'check in' counter. We should go directly to the Departure Tax area and then to check in.

Off now to the Departure Tax machine, which only takes cash and only in the local currency. Fine. And so we duly arrive at the check-in counter clutching e-tickets, passports, departure tax and immigration paperwork. Do not pass go! No, try again! We should have had all luggage security-checked at a different counter. One of us takes the bags to the x-ray machine and gets blue security stickers placed over the zips. We weigh in our bags, now with warm weather gear making them 1 kg heavier, at 8 kg each. What a relief, we've got our boarding pass, seat and gate number.

Off we trot. Hanoi, here we come. We saunter our way arm in arm through to the departure terminal and are confronted with the usual festival of light, glass and glitter of terminals everywhere, with the familiar looking concourse full of duty-free stores. We don't want any goodies, we just want to get coffees and toast.

Having remembered to keep a modicum of local money, we inspect the food counter. Our remaining local money allows us to buy, at exorbitant prices, coffees and chicken sandwiches without the chicken. (This might be the cafe's pre-emptive protection against bird flu.) We don't know whether to be mollified or miffed.

We walk what seemed like 41 miles to our gate 41; we scrape together all our remaining loose shrapnel and feel better by giving it to a pink-clad cleaner - big smile.

And so, to the gate 41 departure lounge. Here we watch our fellow travellers. They, to a person, arrive with carry-on luggage the size of a 65 cm TV. We make a mental note to wait until the mayhem of packing overhead lockers is finished before we board, only to discover that the allocated seat numbers mean nothing, just sit anywhere!

Call us romantics. Despite all of the hassles with air travel, unabashed enthusiasm emanates from both of us at the thought of the 'pot of gold' at the end of each flight.

CAN THE TWO WEEK TOURIST FOLLOW THE DIY TRAVELLERS TRAIL?

Lets look at both sides. The first premise is that if you're reading a book relating to Budget Travel you have some interest in minimising cost outlays.

The ball-park cost of Australian 15 day travel packages to Vietnam is $3600 for two, or $240 per day (Airfares not included)

The author and his wife travelled at less than $50 per day for two.

Daily cost difference $190.

Tour Operator

You read the colourful travel brochure and select your trip costing $240 per day (for two).
Your trip is finely tuned, pre booked hotels, rooms, shuttle transport, day tours, all at fixed times in your itinerary. You travel with the same group for most outings, with some free time allocated to roam as you please. A tour guide is included in the package.

DIY Budget Travel

This allows you to choose your hotel, your tours, your choice of transport, your times of coming and going, it gives flexibility and freedom. Stay a bit longer, leave a bit earlier. Local Tour Offices are friendly, helpful and can be found easily in all holiday spots. Your choice of itinerary can be from a Guide Book or copied from the Tour Operator's brochure.

CHAPTER TWENTY-EIGHT

*There is not a tree in heaven that is higher
than the tree of patience.*

FILLING IN TIME - BOOKS AND CARDS

Two types of patience were required on our trip. The first variety was of an unsolicited nature. This was the one we needed when waiting half an hour after the scheduled departure for any mode of transport. Time can hasten slowly.

The second variety of patience is the one my great aunt Minnie taught me whilst sitting, straight-backed, at the walnut table dealing and dispensing playing cards. For us, this second variety was a pleasant revival of old-fashioned time wasting. Patience helped one or other, or indeed both of us, to amuse ourselves during the less busy times.

We carried a pack of cards each and these were employed on the lay days when there was no crushing requirement on our time, no buses to catch or tours or trips. We would settle ourselves at an umbrella'd table in the sunshine, drink at hand and the cards for company. This sounds all very well and decadent except when your table happens to be on the guest house pier with the waves gently lapping underneath. The cooling breeze skittishly whisks your two of spades from the table, off the pier and into the lapping briny beneath - retrieved with difficulty. Is this a Royal Flush?

And so it is that my pack of cards to this day has an easily distinguishable water damaged deuce.

The cards proved invaluable in filling in the leisure time. On occasions, we were joined by other travellers, or otherwise we played cards between ourselves. This is not something we do often back home, and we enjoyed the experience of being taught new games. Thank you, Maria. Blackjack, your version, will always remind us of you.

Books, too, became a very necessary evil. Evil, you say? Evil, because they are so heavy. Necessary, to while away those spare evening hours or when lolling on the beach. Books are a personal choice for entertainment and so much a part of life at home. We had to juggle the extent of book weight we could carry, a bit like the horseracing 'weight for age' conundrum - their weight, my age! Apart from the essential guidebook, the most we could find space for was two books each. Purchase of English language books was always easy, with bookstores or street vendors ever at hand.

Most towns and districts where backpackers hang out have second-hand shops or swap shops. Some hotels and guest houses have a swap system, leave your book and take another on the honour system. Regrettably, the rate of default means that often these swaps now have a small charge.

Then again, there are the rip-off books. Allegedly, these are photocopied from the original and reprinted with an identical cover. Sold by street hawkers and shrink-wrapped so you can't check the quality of the reproduction, which we found to be surprisingly accurate anyway. Hawkers either proposition you in the street or have a roadside rack. The usual business of bargaining still applies. You may be asked for $10 and end up paying $3. Truth is, you'll pay anything if you're desperate. These rip-off books were readily available in Asia but more prominent in Vietnam. Other travellers tell me that some must have been retyped as mistakes have been found with paragraphs, pages or chapters missing.

One of the most popular books offered is the Lonely Planet, but when the page with all the guest house accommodation is missing, I'd rather stick to the genuine home-grown variety and be confident that all the pages of information are accurate.

The trap that we sometimes fell into was running out of reading material in one of the towns where books were expensive or more difficult to find. Bouts of deprivation will fall upon you. You've sequestered yourself on some remote balmy beach for a number of days and wham-o, you have 10 pages to finish in your last book. Distraught, deprived and de-booked.

This is where you are prepared to sift through your partner's choice of books. I always questioned Barb as to what was wrong with my books of blood, battle, bombs and espionage, couldn't she broaden her mind? As for her choice of romantic, historical, autobiographical and educational books, well, I suppose it was her holiday too! Funny thing, when your own book is finished, you'll read anything. I must say we compromised and we now meet in the middle in our choice of books. I pick 'Jack the Ripper, who was he?' and Barb picks 'Galileo versus the Catholic Church'.

Sometimes, when we found good-value second-hand books at $3, we each bought two and then had to carry four new books between us. A curious selection criteria set in with big, thick and fat books becoming much more highly valued and the first to be inspected on the book shelves.

Some shops or road-side stalls sell books in 'as-is' condition, but some vendors re-work the books. Holding the spines tightly, they use fine sandpaper to freshen and clean the edges. Others iron the covers and then shrink-wrap them. Bundled in groups of 3 or 4 is another method of selling less-known authors or older books. In all cases, the search for reading material took on the proportions of the search for the Holy Grail, and yes, Dan Brown's book did appear regularly in the areas where book sellers thrived.

Choose from the histories of each country, 'Thoughts of Chairman Mao' or 'Night time stories by Ho Chi Min', latest best sellers and the ever-present travel observations of Bill Bryson. They're all there.

CHAPTER TWENTY-NINE

*He who could foresee affairs three days in advance would
be rich for a thousand years.*

THE THINGS WE DID RIGHT

ATTITUDE

Top of our list was mental preparedness. ATTITUDE.
We were undertaking an adventure and we were
swapping the comforts of home, or indeed five-star
hotels, for less flamboyant accommodation. We were
pushing our limits and we understood that we would be
apprehensive.

We were excited about seeing Asia at a grass-roots
level, and not from the glass and glitter aspect of the
two-week tourist. Our 'Give it a Go' attitude towards an
adventure holiday was right and we made a deal not to
say 'Oh, I could never do that'. Our budget
accommodation surprised us with the good facilities in
low cost guest houses and hotels.

FOOTWEAR

We chose comfortable sandals and wore them in. We found no requirement for any other footwear.

SHIRTS

I took three shirts, all Bisley seersucker double pocket ones bought at a menswear store. Barb bought a couple as well and with some adroit tailoring (darts in the back and some shaping of the sides), was well equipped. They proved to be easily hand washed, dried in minutes when draped over the wall fans, and showed no signs of needing to be ironed. We didn't need to compete in any fashion stakes and were certainly well dressed amongst the other travellers.

LUGGAGE

We picked suitable-sized dual-purpose luggage with shoulder straps and wheels.

Severely limiting our baggage to under 8 kg, our philosophy was 'buy as you go and send home surplus.' We did this and it worked well.

WHEN TO GO

The best time of the year was selected (November through February) and this time frame minimised the effects of the monsoons and mozzies.

We took advice from all quarters and filtered it to suit ourselves.

PAPERWORK

We updated all paperwork - e.g. power of attorney and wills.

We thought ahead as to the worst disasters, planned our reactions and gathered emergency phone numbers for embassies and medical insurance help lines.

TRIAL RUN

We packed our gear and booked onto a train to Brisbane and a local backpackers' motel for a night's trial run.

SPARE BASIN PLUG

My Boy Scout preparedness made me take my one-size-fits-all hand basin stopper cut out of an inner tube. It's very difficult to do hand washing if there is no basin plug. Take four, each the size of a beer coaster. I gave away two along the way.

SPARE PASSPORT PHOTOS

We took extra passport photos and they are needed for some visas - take at least four.

ELECTRICAL

We excluded all gear that was power-dependent and so avoided taking the various power plugs, leads, chargers, etc.

THINGS WE DID WRONG

ROUTE PLANNING

We flew, return fare, into Bangkok and 4 months later we flew home from Bangkok. Perhaps we should have gone one-way to Hanoi and home one-way from Kuala Lumpur. Although the flights would have cost more, it would have eliminated back-tracking.

USE OF INTERNAL FLIGHTS

We learned that flights within Asia were inexpensive and maybe we could have made better use of them. Still, we did travel to Hanoi from Bangkok by plane and indeed got a free Air Asia flight from Phnom Penh back to Bangkok.

PRE BOOKING

Bottom line lesson is to use the internet more fully to research and book online.

Our comfort feeling of having pre-booked hotel and taxi for the first few nights was not necessary. It would have been simple and easy to get a taxi at the airport for ourselves, or a bus or train into town, and much less expensive. Internet booking would have given us a most acceptable hotel at a much better price in the district of our preference.   There was sufficient advice in the guidebook to allow us to choose an area and hotel.

WEATHER WATCHING

Our intention of visiting Ko Samui and the other east coast islands of Thailand was shelved because of monsoon rains. Two weeks either side would have been OK. Next time, we would check out the weather patterns.

CHECK THE INTERNET GOSSIP

We should have visited, via a Google search, the Lonely Planet 'Thorn Tree' internet chat site each day prior to leaving to get the feel for current gossip, top bargains and places to avoid at all costs.

PILLOWS

We didn't start out with a travel pillow and we should have. We are accustomed at home to light fluffy numbers and even then we only sleep on the corners. Next time we would do some testing at home and check out the inflatable varieties. Hotel pillows varied a lot and sometimes impacted on a good night's sleep, so carry a baby's pillow or make one up using crumbed foam. We now carry a loaf-sized pillow stuffed with foam and it squeezes easily into our packs, especially if flattened into a clip-lock plastic bag.

REPAIR KIT

We didn't put enough cotton into our tiny sewing kit and found that running repairs seemed to be needed more often than we imagined.

ALARM CLOCK

We had to buy an easy-to-set small analogue alarm clock with a light in the dial, as this allowed peace of mind when catching early morning transport or conducted tours. Our flash digital one was hard to set, it didn't have a light and we didn't feel that we could trust it. Better to be able to see the alarm clock hands - we're not getting old!

CHAPTER THIRTY

A hundred men may make an encampment, but it takes a woman to make a home.

HOUSE MINDING

Most likely the house will need someone to mind it. If the plan is to have house sitters or short-term tenants, some actions will need to be taken. Should you rent your house out, your daily overseas travel and living costs will be covered. If you have house sitters, you won't receive extra monies but the normal costs of living in Australia will serve to cover daily Asian expenses. You may be lucky enough to have family or friends nearby to keep an eye on things and there may be no need to do too much except pack up and run off.

HOUSE PREPARATION

If you are getting house sitters or tenants, the cupboards need to be sorted and the wardrobes emptied. Clothes can be put into heavy-duty plastic bags and stored in the roof space (scatter pest repellent and rodent baits). Choose a big cupboard or spare room wardrobe and fit a suitable lock.

Store all personal paperwork, family silver and crystal plus the best of the wine cellar. Your house sitters will not want to be concerned about damage to treasured ornaments. The house needs to look like a fully-equipped holiday rental.

Complete an inventory for each room - this would be required by any rental agency. Check that all house fixtures are working. Write clear instructions for things like the automatic watering system or sound system, home theatre and satellite TV.

TRADESPEOPLE

Murphy's Law will of course come into play at some stage of your trip. You'll be away one week when the drainpipe falls off or a tap leaks. It is wise to leave the names and phone numbers of trusted tradespeople who can come to the rescue. Alert them before you leave.

CHAPTER THIRTY-ONE

The palest ink is better than the best memory.

LEAVING PAPERWORK IN ORDER

Discuss your decisions with your family. A 'no surprises' policy is wise.

For example, our children seemed to be concerned with what would happen if one of us died overseas. We made a decision on cremation, with ashes to be returned to Australia (even though our medical insurance covered the return of a body). Family will worry when oldies pack up and run off overseas, so it's probably a good policy to keep them fully informed.

SHARES AND ANNUITIES

Share portfolios may require instructions regarding dividends, so put actions in place before you depart. Remember too, that yearly annuities require proof that you or your partner is not deceased, so be aware of the timing of this kind of document.

BANK

Alert your local bank branch to the fact that you are travelling. Arrange a signatory on your cheque account to allow whoever is minding your affairs to pay any bills.

GOVERNMENT OVERSEAS REGISTRATION

The Australian government holds a voluntary register of people travelling overseas and you can register a time frame and countries you intend to visit. Register at www.smarttravel.gov.au and you will continually receive, via email, information and warnings relating to travel to your part of the world.

VISAS

Some countries do not require a visa in advance. For example, Thailand visas are issued at the airport or border crossings. Other visas are easily obtained through a tour operator overseas, given a few days' notice.

Take some extra passport photos with you. Visa conditions change, so check on the internet, or at tour offices, for latest conditions.

SECURITY

Purchase a money belt to wear under your clothes. Keep duplicate copies of all paperwork in each backpack. Use hotel lockers or safes for passport, spare money and credit cards. Perhaps scan and download a record of all relevant paperwork and keep it all with you on a memory stick or in a folder in an email account such as Hotmail. Keeping copies in cyberspace makes all documents such as Birth Certificates, Drivers Licences, Marriage Certificates, Passports, tickets, travel insurance etc available wherever you have access to a computer.

You will sometimes use a small combination lock on a security locker, and sometimes you may even lock your backpacks to discourage pilfering.

Warning: The small brass 'keyed' variety of lock can be easily picked.

Exercise good sense: Often guidebooks alert to particular areas of danger, late night dodgy areas or areas of danger for women alone at night. We felt absolutely safe travelling Asia and at no stage did we ever feel threatened.

CREDIT CARDS

You will need one each and perhaps one spare to be left with valuables in the hotel safety box. Remember that if you lose one credit card and a second card has been linked to it, both will be cancelled. ATM's are almost everywhere except in less developed countries such as Cambodia (your guidebook will give you all the latest details). Take different styles of card, eg. Visa and MasterCard, as sometimes one company's computers will be down and the other card will work just fine.

Lodge sufficient funds to add debit facility to existing credit cards because this makes it easier to draw money at a bank if you can't find an ATM. If you don't have telephone or internet banking, now is the time to set it up. This enables you to move money around easily when on the road.

MAIL

Organise through your local post office to have all mail redirected to your 'minder' of choice and of course, ask them to open it and let you know, by internet, if something is noteworthy.   We make this person a signatory on our chequebook.

INSURANCE

Your peace of mind often relates to insurance. Contact your home and contents insurer to check the conditions relating to a house sitter or renter and adjust the policy to suit.

Ninety days of travel insurance is offered free of charge by some credit card providers when part of your travel is paid for on the primary card holders card.   Additional coverage needs to be organised if your trip exceeds 90 days.

Some private medical benefit funds allow you to suspend your Australian membership for the time you are away (remember that your Australian fund doesn't cover you overseas) and a simple phone call will re-instate it when you return.   Check this out because some funds need to see a stamp in your passport and these stamps aren't issued now unless you ask for them when you pass through the immigration counter.

WILLS

It seems morbid to plan for the worst, but make sure that your wills are updated and that your family knows which law firm they are lodged with.

POWER OF ATTORNEY

You must give someone the authority to sign on your behalf and make decisions should you end up temporarily incapacitated and unable to make decisions for yourself. Talk with your solicitor to make sure that you get this right. Ask about an 'Advance Health Directive' because this takes care of your health-related wishes if you are in a coma or can't speak for yourself.

An itemised checklist is attached just to ensure that all the things which need taking care of have been attended to.

QUICK CHECK LIST

☐ Book flights
☐ Organise house minding/rental
☐ Prepare house for minders/tenants
☐ Empty cupboards and wardrobes
☐ Locked cupboard
☐ Inventory
☐ Instruction sheet
☐ List of Tradespeople for minders/tenant
☐ Check all fixtures are in working order
☐ Shares and Annuities
☐ Advise bank of your travels
☐ Government overseas registration
☐ Visas
☐ Medical certificates including immunizations
☐ Combination padlocks
☐ Copies of all documents
☐ Credit cards
☐ Passports
☐ Internet
☐ Phone
☐ Car
☐ Mail
☐ House Insurance
☐ Travel insurance
☐ Wills
☐ Power of attorney

BEST BARGAIN EXAMPLES

KRABI Harry's B & B and guest house in the centre of Krabi. 075- 632315. $6: first floor, twin queen beds, wide windows, two fans, shared bathrooms with hot water. Sixteen rooms. Good English. Coffee bar, drinks and snacks available. Centrally located.

NHA TRANG 36 Tran Phu Boulevard, Nha Trang. $8: second floor, twin queen beds, balcony, two fans, ensuite with hot water, Vietnamese tea on call. One hundred rooms. Opposite main beach. Little English spoken.

HANOI Vinh Quang Hotel. 24 Hang Quat, Hanoi. $13: first floor, twin single beds, two fans, air-conditioning, cable TV, ensuite with hot water, daily room tidy and clean, internet and continental breakfast included. Twenty rooms. Good English. Located in the centre of the Old Quarter. Water Puppet theatre at the end of the street.

SAIGON Cu Chi Tunnels tour at $6 each

HOTEL	GUEST HOUSE
Restaurant	Café style meals
Room service	Rarely offered
Swimming pool	Sometimes available
Security safe	Usually a front-desk service
Travel desk	Usually only local tours, trains and buses
Gym	Never available
Lounge bar	bar Common area for guests
Entertainment	Sometimes videos or TV in lounge area

TEN TOP TIPS FOR BUDGET TRAVEL

1. Buy a good quality Guide Book. Everything you need to know in one compact book. Find a bed, a feed, a train, plane or bus – it's all there. Local conditions, local customs.

2. Be brave. Book your flights and go. Budget travelling can be easily achieved. Apart from your return air ticket, all tour bookings, sightseeing, accommodation and ongoing transport can be easily and less expensively organised when you arrive at your destination.

3. Travel lightly. Buy an airline carry-on sized backpack – this will stop you from packing the kitchen sink.

4. Dress comfortably in lightweight, wrinkle-free, quick dry fabrics. Buy more clothes if needed and continually post home extra purchases and unwanted gear.

5. Shoes? What shoes? One pair of top quality comfortable sandals will take you everywhere.

6. Bargaining – apart from the savings, it becomes a fun pastime. Almost every purchase can be bargained down and can drop by 20% or more (including accommodation).

7. Money. Use ATM's to draw money in local currency. Available almost everywhere except in remote villages. Best to have two credit cards – not linked. For emergencies, carry some US dollars.

8. Security. It's smart to leave all valuables at home and wear a next-to-skin money belt for passport and big money. Theft happens mostly because of carelessness – if you value it, carry it with you and don't leave it unattended anywhere. Most accommodation provides security lockers – use them.

9. Precautions. Scan all documents into an email and send to yourself (we use Hotmail). If ever needed, simply login to your email account and you will have passports, visas, home contacts, tickets, insurances, vaccination details, drivers' licences etc all available to be printed out.

10. Traps. Don't run up accommodation tabs. Pay as you go or at least every day - this way you stand some chance of checking the amounts.

PRE TRIP ASSESSMENT

RELATIONSHIP:
Barb and Des enjoy a sound personal interaction - both have a happy and carefree outlook. Barb enjoys her own time and space writing and publishing cryptic crosswords (finneganscrosswords.com). Des uses his time to indulge a love of art, undertaking commissioned paintings (large naïve-art street scenes).

HEALTH:
Des - sixty-nine years of age with a tin hip and affected by Atrial Fibrillation (Heart Arrhythmia), high cholesterol, overweight at 98kg and with threatened diabetes. Other associated problems such as wobbly knees, sore back, ankles etc. (Just a few of the issues confronting any silly old codger). Barb - sixty-two year of age and allergy prone. Asthmatic (sometimes hospitalized), subject to the first twinges of back problems, a dickey shoulder and overweight at 76kg. (Obviously striding enthusiastically towards her Golden Years).

POST TRIP ASSESSMENT

RELATIONSHIP:
Better than ever bonding, having been forged in fire.

HEALTH:
Des - Ceased to experience heart arrhythmia, his cholesterol has dropped as has his weight - to 87kg - and his blood sugar is well within good health guidelines.
Barb - has experienced no asthma or allergies, both back and shoulder problems are considerably reduced and her weight has dropped to 67kg.

EPILOGUE

Wisdom is good in the beginning - even wiser at the end.

In looking back over our trip, it's the memories of people we met that predominate over the tourist attractions. We are imbued with a great feeling of fulfilment. We have been touched by a collection of encounters that leave us with warmth towards Asia and its people and towards numerous fellow travellers. We have challenged ourselves and succeeded.

Our four months of adventure started with some apprehensions. There were doubts, there were a few moments of hesitation and we were confronting unknowns.

It was all worthwhile.

THE JOURNEY

You've shared our literary walkabout.
You've read of our pleasure and woe.
Don't just sit back and talk about it:
'Get off your ass and go!'

Your body is approaching the time
When things are starting to slow.
Don't wait for the steady decline:
'Get off your ass and go!'

'I couldn't do that,' said my partner,
Self-doubt, as ever, her foe.
'It's better done now than done later,
'Get off your ass and go!'

You've now read of our overseas travel,
Been told of both high spots and low.
It remains for the armchair reader to
'Get off your ass and go!'

Too young to go caravanning,
That journey is ponderous and slow.
Postpone your all-Aussie adventure:
'Get off your ass and go!'

With Asia now as your plan,
Don't wait till airfares are low.
Act quickly now while you can:
'Get off your ass and go!'

www.budgettravelsecrets.com.au

LaVergne, TN USA
15 February 2010
173128LV00009B/15/P